In this work the events actually happened. The characters existed
although some of the names are changed.

Many thanks to my friends Nick Tucker and Keven McNulty, and to
my wife Gladys and son Adam for so much help and patience. Thank
you also to my friend Mark O'Leary for the superb cover and interior
artwork.

Dedication

I dedicate this book to those police officers who were both friends and colleagues and who lost their lives during my own service as a result of criminal acts, misadventure or accident. I hope some of my tales make them smile.

PC John David Taylor

PC Graham Whitehurst

PC Robert David Owen

PC Steven Mack

PC Dennis Tunnicliffe

PC John Hunt

PC John Cornes

PC 'Jock' Smart

PC Daniel Burnside

PC Robert Michael Potts

The Nick of Time

By

John Pye

ONE

Quiet Please! Examination in Progress.

The notice was fastened to the door with four brass drawing pins. The fountain-penned signature in the bottom right hand corner bore an air of authority: *'A. Green'*. The added title of *'Sergeant'* compounded the instruction. Silence reigned.

Sergeant Green was the pleasant-sounding man I'd spoken to on the telephone inviting me along for my cadet's entrance exam. Now here I was, actually inside a police station, sitting and nervously tapping my shoes (silently) against the thick khaki-coloured lino.

Most of my friends at school were amazed that I hadn't been to a police station before this. The end of term riot I'd helped to arrange and that prank that put the cleaner in hospital should have been a bar to my becoming a police officer. The memory of that letter of apology I was forced to write sent a cold chill down my spine.

Dear Mrs Huxley

Following your recent stay in hospital, I wish to apologise for what happened and hope that your head is now better.

If Sergeant Green had been tipped off about my previous life I hadn't a chance of getting in.

There was something else written on the notice, underneath Sergeant Green's signature – tiny spidery letters, blue biro: *'BALLS,'* it said: *'BALLS'*.

'Quiet Please! Examination in Progress. A Green (Sergeant) – BALLS.'

It must have been a criminal, someone who'd been arrested. No policeman would write such a thing. But how did a criminal come to be up here in a corridor on the second floor of Newcastle Police Station? It was only offices up here.

"Hello, young man, what are you waiting for?"

I sprang out of my seat to answer the policeman with the bold silver stripes on his sleeves.

"Er… Sergeant Green, Sir… Sergeant… Is that you, Sergeant… Sir?"

"Sarge'll do nicely, son," he laughed, "sit you down. No, I'm Sergeant Haywood. You're after Sergeant Green, are you?" He smirked as he said the words. "Still, it's not *your* fault."

Sergeant Haywood was a short, plump man who hardly seemed tall enough to be a policeman, let alone a sergeant; still I don't suppose you have to be any taller to be a sergeant, otherwise a superintendent would be enormous. I had to stop thinking stupid things, I *must* be serious. Policemen *were* serious. Sergeant Haywood seemed to find everything funny though, so he wasn't being serious. He was wearing a wide grin and in turn was showing off a mouth packed with brown teeth. Under his arm was a large bundle of documents and, clipped between the fingers of his right hand, was a minute cigarette. Many years of smoking had turned two of his fingers a similar shade of dark brown to that of his teeth. A line of coloured military ribbons adorned his left breast pocket, including the blue and white of the Police Long Service Medal. This handy little tip was something my dad had found out for me.

"You'll have to wait a few minutes for Sergeant Green, son, he's downstairs practising his limbo dancing… You're here for the cadets, are you?"

"Yes, Sir… er… Sarge."

Limbo dancing! Why would a police sergeant be practising limbo dancing, and at ten thirty in the morning?

"How old are you, son?" Sergeant Haywood asked, tilting his head to one side and smiling.

"Sixteen Sergeant," I responded in semi-military fashion.

"Hmm," he murmured, crinkling up around the eyes as if about to laugh again.

I knew what he was thinking… I looked about twelve.

On top of the bundle of papers under his arm I could see a handwritten note held securely with a rubber band – tiny spidery letters in blue biro. The word 'balls' immediately sprang to mind. The note was signed. I craned my neck slightly to one side, trying not to be too obvious, as I read the signature – *H Haywood (Sergeant)*.

"Oh, he's here now, son… Alwyn, a young man to see you for the cadet exam."

Sergeant Green appeared from the stairway, fresh-faced and not at all as I imagined him. He didn't seem very old. He wore the same stripes as Sergeant Haywood, but no military ribbons, no long service medal, no cigarette, no documents and no brown teeth. He was wearing his full uniform, complete with peaked cap, and wasn't even sweating. How could he have been limbo dancing?

Sergeant Green bounded forwards, right hand outstretched, "Ah, Mr Hibbs is it?" he said.

I sprang up from my chair again and shook his hand, trying to appear serious and grown up.

"No, Sir, er... Sergeant, John Pye... that is, Mr John Pye not Sergeant John Pye…"

'Shut up, you fool', a voice inside my head shouted.

"Oh, Mr Pye, nice to meet you." He added a smile as he determined the level of my nervousness.

The Sergeant's attempts to ease the tension were immediately followed by a loud farting sound which was accompanied by raucous laughter. It came from the office where Sergeant Haywood had gone. Sergeant Green grimaced as though he had a horrible taste in his mouth. It took every last bit of self-control for me to keep a straight face.

"Right then, Mr Pye, come through and we'll get on with this exam," he said, placing his hand on the doorknob.

As the door swung open I imagined a large room with rows of desks each with a pad of paper and a pencil. But no – two tables and two chairs. A figure was seated at one of the tables with his back to the door. He turned in his seat as we entered.

"Oh reight?" the young man bellowed, in a broad Potteries' accent.

My God, I thought, *it's Hibbo from my school.*

"Hey up, Pye," Hibbo said, "are you joining up too?"

Hibbo was almost shouting. I felt embarrassed by his stupidity; it was as though Sergeant Green wasn't even there.

"Mr. Hibbs, I presume?" Sergeant Green said with a frown.

"Yes, mate. Another bloke showned me in," Hibbo explained, stretching the accent to its fullest.

"Right. I gather you two know each other." The Sergeant's frown was now even sterner.

"Yes, Sergeant, we live around the corner from each other," I stated in my most precise attempt at a non-Potteries accent. *Had my dad paid Hibbo to come and make a fool of himself?*

"Anyway, gentlemen," Sergeant Green said, ushering me into a chair, "Let's make a start. This is an English test, turn the question papers over and begin. You've got thirty minutes."

No rows of desks, no queues of applicants, just Hibbo and me. We both turned over the papers and a brief scan made me think it wasn't too difficult, but I was still nervous. That was until Hibbo coughed, paused and with more of that accent – "Er… Sarge. Does spellin' caint?" (Does spelling count?)

How much had my dad paid him?

"Well, young man," the reply was accompanied with a slight shake of the head. "It is an English exam, so do your best…"

Hibbo didn't make it.

TWO

MONDAY, 2ND JANUARY 1967 was a wet, dark, cold winter's morning. My seventeenth birthday was still nearly five months away and I felt a little out of my depth as I looked up at the big round clock which hung out over Platform One of Stoke-on-Trent's Victorian railway station. It was half past seven and I was off into the unknown – a train to Stafford and then a bus up to police headquarters. These were new experiences to me. At least, having to do them on my own was. Would the train be late? Would I get off at the wrong station? I nervously picked up my suitcase at the sound of an approaching locomotive only to replace it as a goods train rumbled through.

"Hi, John, where are you off to?" the familiar voice came from behind.

I turned to see Ian Bruckshaw, an old schoolmate, also complete with suitcase.

"Police cadets, a course at Stafford,"

"Me too," said Ian.

Great! I had an ally – we could get lost together. We exchanged interview and exam stories throughout the half-hour journey, both puzzling about limbo-dancing police officers. We giggled about the graffiti-writing, brown-toothed, farting sergeant, and tried to imagine Hibbo's English paper. We were still daft schoolboys.

A short bus ride from the town centre took us up to the headquarters of the Staffordshire County Police. The HQ was a large and imposing complex. A one-way tarmac road encircled a neatly trimmed grassed area in front of the main building.

To the left lay another big turfed space and on this stood several white painted wooden structures, including ramps, ladders and fence-type arrangements with large circular holes. The Headquarters was the home of a regional police dog training school and this was all part of a semi-permanent dogs' assault course. Constables from Staffordshire who had opted become dog handlers would be joined in their intensive initial training by other officers, not just from different parts of Britain, but occasionally by colleagues from other countries. They would spend thirteen weeks training their police dogs and learning all the skills that went along with this branch of the service.

Cadet's Hostel. Photo courtesy of Bill Wrench.

A policeman directed us to the Cadets' hostel, which would be our home for the next sixteen weeks. Within ten minutes Ian and I were ushered back outside where we met the other youngsters who had also made the life-changing decision to join the Police Cadets.

Left… left… left right left – twenty-one of us – fifteen boys, six girls. We'd only been here an hour and now we were marching. What a sight! No uniforms, but suits, jackets, overcoats – tall, short, plump, thin, but all with spots. Was it possible for everybody to be out of step? Yes, and Rita, who had more spots than anyone, couldn't get her arms and legs going properly; it was as if her left wrist was connected to her left leg and her right wrist to her right leg. Every time she raised an arm up shot the leg beneath it.

"Left, right, left, right, get those arms higher, they should be in line with the shoulder," bawled the inspector.

Rita was now beginning to take on the appearance of a drunken Nazi soldier.

The cadets' hostel, which was for the boys, was a dark old building with the same thick khaki-coloured lino that I'd first come across at Newcastle Police Station. There was a TV room downstairs with a black and white set in the corner. No one was allowed to stand by the window because it made the picture go all fuzzy. Several tatty armchairs stood about and a small threadbare rug lay on the floor. There was a kitchen with a kettle and, in the front room, a table-tennis table.

The bedrooms upstairs were all different sizes; some had as many as four beds, but there was only one which was a single room. There was a communal bathroom with four basins and a bath. If you wanted a bath you'd have to share the room with others who were having a wash. As there were only two toilets it wasn't long before people started peeing in the basins.

The rooms had already been allocated and by chance I was awarded the only single room. This wouldn't have been so bad, but for the fact that it was universally known as 'The Wankers' Room'. We were all soon enlightened to the niceties of apple-pie beds, beds thrown out of the window, drinking and being sick into washbasins.

During the first week we made several visits to the Headquarters' Stores where we met the manager, Mr Ryan, who would be fitting us out with our uniforms. Mr Ryan, a civilian, was a slim, middle aged man with a slick of Brylcreemed black hair, a grey lab-type coat and a permanently-around-the-neck tailor's tape measure. He judged our sizes by eye and almost everything came off the peg. The tape measure never moved from its place around his neck.

Our two uniforms included: one peaked cap with a bright blue band, a raincoat and gloves. The three light blue shirts which were handed out were all of the collarless, 'grandad' style with just three buttons down from below the neck. Half a dozen separate collars accompanied these and the only things we had to buy were our boots and collar studs.

Pressing trousers and ironing shirts took up a lot of our time, but boot bulling consumed every waking moment, both on and off duty. If those boots were not polished to a mirror finish then watch out! If, however, you could see your face in them then you might even get a commendation.

The age-old accepted method of bulling boots was, of course, 'spit and polish'. No doubt this was from where the expression came. The method of the day though, was to wrap one of those soft orange dusters around the first two fingers of your right hand. The remainder of the duster was clutched into a ball in your palm and an opened tin of black shoe polish was strategically placed nearby. With the tin's lid filled with water you were ready to go.

A smear of polish onto your duster-covered fingertips was followed by the monotonous rubbing in tiny circles onto the toecaps. The occasional dip into the water of the polishing fingers would be followed by more rubbing. The 'spit' had been superseded by simple water over the years and was now universally considered to produce the best result.

After many hours of this mind-numbing pastime, and as long as nothing had gone wrong, the result would be superbly gleaming boots. A downside would be that the black polish soon leaked through the weave of the duster and you could expect two deeply stained and sore fingertips. My weekends at home were spent on more pressing and bulling and then posing for various people my mum and dad had invited around to see – *'our John in uniform'*.

We had to make our sheets and blankets into a neat box shape every morning in readiness for the shout of: *'Stand by your beds'*. The bawled command was given by Inspector Gladstone or 'Gladys' as he was better known. The inspection that followed would usually result in Gladys probing several of the neat piles to destruction with his inspector's stick. It didn't take long before everyone was using sleeping bags and retrieving beautifully constructed *blanket boxes* from their wardrobes, pristine and ready for inspection.

We were regularly woken from our sleep by the trainee police dogs whose kennels were not far from the hostel. Once one started then all the others would join in.

Cadets on parade

Our course was sixteen weeks of square-bashing, sport, law lectures and bollockings, but not necessarily in that order. At least an hour of every morning would be taken up with drill. The parade ground at the back of Mr Ryan's stores was the setting for this exhausting and initially confusing duty. Our first efforts exhibited an unruly bunch of disjointed gangling idiots dodging about in an uncoordinated pack. But by the end of the first month we actually started to enjoy it and began to look so good that passers-by would spend several minutes watching us.

Around this time, one of the dog handlers, on a training course, was a young black policeman from the Seychelles. The poor chap had a badly deformed head with a big dent in his forehead. Arrangements had been made for him to overlap his course whilst he had surgery in London to correct the dent. I saw him after the operation and he looked great. I often thought what an experience it must have been for him to come over to Britain. Eventually he would go back to his island town with all these new skills, a wonderfully obedient police dog and a brand new head.

Back in the classroom we were all filling our brains with endless lists of police procedures and powers. Criminal law lectures would often take up a whole morning, whilst road traffic regulations could fill a heavy-eyed afternoon. Other sessions would be taken up with general police duties, police rank structure, Coroner's duties, first aid and self-defence – too many new things for a sixteen year old to remember.

The chairs in the classroom were made from a red metal frame with a moulded black plastic seat fitted to it. One afternoon, as I concentrated on WHY it was an offence to shake a mat outside before eight o'clock in the morning, I found myself involuntarily twitching both my arms into the air. My strange behaviour was accompanied by a muffled grunt. The rest of the class all turned in their seats to see what the hell I was up to. The visiting lecturer glared at me. He was no doubt thinking that I was either a troublemaker or that the doctor had let someone with a serious medical condition slip through the net. The truth of the matter, which even I at this stage hadn't realised, was that I had received a hefty electric shock generated by a build-up of static in the plastic and metal chair.

At the end of the lecture the speaker left, no doubt heading for Inspector Gladstone's office to express concerns about 'the young man in the back row'. I was quizzed by my laughing colleagues as to what the devil I was playing at. It turned out that several other people had also had similar shocks from the chairs. Later experiments revealed that the more you shuffled about then touched the metal legs, the bigger shock you'd get. In between electric shocks and all the other things that we had to cram into our heads, most of our time was spent on learning and being tested on 'definitions'.

Definitions were the legally worded interpretation of a particular offence or piece of law that someone had decided we must all know. Each definition had to be learned absolutely word-perfectly. We were frequently called upon to stand up in class and recite verbatim the definition of the criminal offence or piece of law that was being discussed. If you got it wrong you would have to do press-ups at the front of the class (the girls would be punished with half measures).

I was amazed that my brain could hold so much stuff. We had each been given a little beige booklet, which contained all eighty-nine definitions. By the end of the course most of us knew nearly all of them off by heart.

It was annoying when, after spending many evenings on the course learning the extremely long and complicated definition of 'larceny', I was told that the law was to be changed. The new Theft Act was about to come into force and this meant another list of brand new definitions would also be added to our list. How I wished that I could have pasted it all into my brain over the top of the old Larceny Act and not have to use up any more memory space.

The day of our passing out parade came. It was Saturday, 22nd of April 1967. I was seventeen years and three days old, and much wiser, fitter and stronger than I had been sixteen weeks before. All that work on the parade square had done the trick. We looked terrific – perfect, well, nearly perfect; Rita still hadn't quite mastered it, but her spots had nearly all gone.

My mum and dad came along with all the other proud parents and we stood to attention as Councillor Ash inspected us. We carried out our drill display and knew that we'd pulled it off handsomely. We did a march-past and a salute, which was taken by the Chief Constable, Arthur Morgan Rees, before finishing off with a physical training exhibition in the gym.

We had now all been given our postings to a police station near to our homes although we'd be regularly meeting up again on courses, on training days and for Outward Bound camps. My posting, to the village police station of Wolstanton, was just a three mile bus ride from home and was going to be my first glimpse at some real police work.

THREE

Wolstanton Police Station (after conversion to private offices)

"RIGHT THEN, young Pye... Hmm… It is Pye, isn't it?"

"Yes, Sir," I replied, with an arm-quivering salute.

I was standing in the Chief Inspector's office, an upstairs room at Wolstanton's police station.

"I expect you to be smart, punctual, helpful and to learn. If you don't know ASK. We've already got one cadet here, and he's enough for anybody."

This was Chief Inspector Harry Selwyn Sturdee Philips, an ex-military man with even more military ribbons than Sergeant Haywood.

Wolstanton was a village with a main street of shops, some businesses, and plenty of houses. It was on the outskirts of Newcastle-under-Lyme where the large divisional police station was to be found.

Alan Machin, a pleasant young constable, took the time to show me around the building. I was interested to see that there was only one cell, and surprised that it was used as a storeroom for brushes and buckets. There was a small kitchen, a canteen, a CID office and some other offices upstairs. The place was old, with an open coal fire in each room. The floors were covered with the same thick khaki-coloured lino that was a feature of every police building I'd seen so far.

The cell block, with its barred window, can be seen in the photograph on the right-hand side of the building.

"Who's this, Alan?" enquired the middle aged man who had set me with a suspicious stare.

"Cadet Pye, Sarge, he's started today."

This was Detective Sergeant Arthur Pointon who was in charge of Wolstanton's CID. This was a real detective and just like the TV French detective, Maigret, he wore a trilby hat and belted raincoat.

"Can you make tea, boy?" DS Pointon asked, frowning, as though this was highly unlikely.

"Yes, Sarge, I think so." My reply included an attempted intelligent expression.

"Right, first job then, and let's hope it's an improvement on Roy."

Roy, who is Roy? I thought.

All the crockery in the little old-fashioned kitchen at the rear of the building had the Staffordshire Police emblem on it in blue. I had finished pouring out the half-dozen cups of tea which I'd calculated were required when Alan's head came around the door.

"The CID had to rush out, so keep their tea warm," he said.

I safely delivered some of the tea, but returned to the kitchen puzzling as to how I could keep the two already poured CID cups hot. A brainwave came to me – I lit the grill on the old-fashioned gas cooker and placed the two cups on a plate underneath.

Mrs Shutt, the cleaner, collared me in the passageway and gave me a long list of daily chores. One dangerous-sounding job she delegated was that of lighting all the coal fires with inflammable lino polish.

"And don't take any advice from Roy, or you'll get into trouble," she finished off.

There was that name again, *Roy*.

I watched excitedly through the window as the old grey Austin A30 CID van pulled into the backyard. Detective Sergeant Pointon and the colossal detective, Gordon Wood, hauled a protesting man from the back of the van. He was HANDCUFFED! I stared wide-eyed as he was taken through to the cell. There was a crashing sound as the buckets and brushes were flung out.

"Who keeps putting this shit in here?" shouted someone, as the heavy steel door was slammed shut despite the swearing complaints of the irate man.

WOW, I thought, *that was exciting.* Using a tray, I retrieved the two lightly grilled teas, set them down onto the kitchen table and quickly stepped back into the charge room, eager not to miss any more action.

Gordon seemed unruffled by his recent struggle, he dusted his palms against his jacket and calmly asked, "Now then, where's that tea, son?"

"In the kitchen, sir," I replied, impressed by his coolness.

Gordon disappeared through the doorway… CRASH!

"BAA-LLUDDY HELL!"

The door burst open, closely followed by Gordon, now not calm at all, his right hand pinned underneath his left armpit.

"What the hell have you done, had a bloody blowtorch on it?" he bellowed at me.

"I'm sorry, sir, I put it under the grill to keep it warm," I spluttered, backing away in fear of being hit by this giant.

"Bloody Roy, and now *you*. Grilled tea, whoever heard of grilled tea? Clear it up and make some more."

Recognising the fear in my eyes and seeing the funny side, Gordon's angry face turned into a grin as he strode into the CID office shaking his head and muttering.

"Grilled bloody tea."

I met the staff during the first couple of weeks and got to grips with my list of odd jobs as well as answering the telephone and operating the switchboard. I mastered how to fill in message forms and use the radio. I watched how some people did things – some good, some bad, and then I met Roy.

"Hello, I'm Roy… Roy Whitfield."

"Hi… John Pye," I attempted a smile, but Roy's appearance had taken me by surprise. He was wearing the same cadet's uniform as me, but additionally had a big piece of sticking plaster on his forehead, a black eye and his hand bandaged.

"Whatever happened to you?" I enquired.

"Come off me scooter, here in the backyard."

"And you did all that in the backyard?" I said in astonishment.

"Yes, I fell through the coal cellar door. Bike's okay though," he continued as he pointed through the window at a blue motor scooter, which was adorned with dozens of mirrors and lights. "I've been off sick for three weeks."

Over the next few weeks I realised why Roy had such a reputation. He trapped his fingers in the cell door and had to go to hospital. Drove his motor scooter into the side of the CID van. He vomited on secretary, Mrs Leak's, typewriter after having too much to drink the night before. Got bitten by a stray dog and on two occasions nearly blew up the CID office by putting too much lino polish on the fire. Roy made me look like a true professional. Was he on my dad's payroll, as well as Hibbo?

Gordon had forgiven me for his burnt hand; he'd had many laughs telling people about grilled tea.

"What did Sergeant Green want you for last week?" he asked one morning.

"He'd got some law homework for me," I said. "Did you know he did limbo dancing?"

Gordon's brow furrowed. "You ought to be careful what you say, he is after all your training sergeant, so I guess he has to slither under the boss's door occasionally.'

My own puzzled expression at this part explanation created recognition in Gordon's eyes. "You don't know what a *Limbo Dancer* is do you?"

Gordon crumpled into laughter at the story of my encounter with Sergeant Haywood and my vision of Sergeant Green in grass skirt.

October brought with it the first one of many Outward Bound camps that I would have to suffer. It was a dark cold morning when I met up at Headquarters with the other cadets I had joined with. We were taken off in Land Rovers to the formidably named Blackshaw Moor Army Base high up in the Staffordshire Moors. Our home for the next two weeks would be a building that was nothing more than a larger version of my dad's garage back home.

The billet was a pre-war, single-storey brick building with a corrugated asbestos roof. There were rusting metal-framed windows set into the walls, and rows of old, red-painted iron bedsteads either side. On each bed lay an old and dirty-looking candy-striped straw-filled mattress with the shape of a human being firmly and permanently indented into it.

In the centre aisle of the building were tatty looking cast iron pot-stoves, each with a pipe leading directly up through the roof. At the side of each bed stood a battered, green-painted metal locker, and the floor was bare dusty concrete. We trooped into this cold and barren-looking prison all thinking that this was set as an endurance test.

Our first amateurish attempts to get the heaters lit failed miserably. How I had wished for a few good dollops of Mrs Shutt's lino polish. But the will to live took over and we quickly became pot-stove lighting experts. It was amazing how much warmth they could generate.

We were shouted from our beds at half past six every morning for physical training and made to jump up and down clad in ridiculous navy blue shorts and white vests. We'd have breakfast in the canteen along with all the soldiers who were based there. This could be followed by a trek across the moors with a compass and map and maybe even a night's camping out.

After the first few exhausting days we started to look forward to getting back to our hovel. It had changed in our minds from a stark and barren prison cell into a haven of peace and comfort. The vile-looking torture device that was your bed was now an object of welcoming warmth and comfort. The old straw-filled mattress with sharp bits poking through the cover was superior to any Slumberland. The sight of all those tired but cheerful young faces reflecting in the glow from the cherry-red pot-stove made you feel that it wasn't that bad. Strange how you make the best of things. At the end of the two-weeks we'd all survived and I found myself back to ordinary duties at Wolstanton.

I got my name in the local paper when I went with Sergeant Cyril Buxton in the black Austin Westminster police car to a muddy pool on the old Brymbo colliery site, where a swan was stuck. I waded in and freed the bird, which showed its thanks by nearly knocking me over when I released it. The *Evening Sentinel* newspaper did a little story on the incident, which gave my dad something to boast about at the pub.

More courses would follow along with different training days at headquarters. A week or two would be spent working in the offices at Newcastle Police Station. Sometimes I'd be able to go out in a patrol car or on the beat with a constable. All the physical training that we were forced into had given me a real appetite for sport and I found myself called upon for the cross-country and boxing teams. There were also regular weekend charity performances with the cadets' gymnastics team.

The only cadets who could get out of boxing were the girls. Everybody had to box. Everybody, that is, except Jim. Jim was an experienced cadet with almost eighteen months service. He was brimming over with self-confidence, flannel and how to dodge work whilst outwardly appearing conscientious and knowledgeable. He would come up with the most amazing excuses to get out of boxing. Just as we were sure we were about to witness his demise in the ring some miraculous event would save him. The stories seemed without limit: a court appearance, a dental appointment, a sprained thumb, the dog had died at home and his mum was upset. There were numerous mysterious telephone calls enabling a last-second exit from the gymnasium. He would make the odd appearance, but only when he had his excuse ready or was sure that the boxing ring wasn't erected. Then one day it happened. Jim couldn't escape. He was trapped with the full boxing ring erected and canvas laid. Something had gone sorely wrong with his plans!

Various sweating bodies took up different corners of the room battering away at punchbags, whilst others shadow-boxed or skipped furiously. Medicine balls were heaved about and two heavyweight cadets, Les Rowe and Jock Smart, professionally slugged each other into a blood-spattered pulp in the ring – this was called sparring.

Overseeing all, and refereeing the so-called sparring, was our boxing Instructor, Mr Brown. He was a likeable former boxer and referee, painfully thin and wearing his usual grey woollen tracksuit with elasticated ankles and wrists.

Jim was hiding in the equipment store, pretending to stack rubber mats and clearly getting worried; no dental appointment, no dead dog and the mystery telephone caller had let him down.

"Okay, Jim… gloves on… Let's see what you can do," said Mr Brown with a wry smile.

Everything stopped, total silence, just the creaking of the punch bag swinging from side to side as we looked over open-mouthed… Could it be true? Was he going to have to get into the ring?

I dashed off to the canteen to round up any stray cadets who might wish to witness the best entertainment of the whole year. When I returned, followed by a jeering mob, Jim was standing in a corner of the ring with Mr Brown lacing up his enormous black boxing gloves. He could actually be seen to be shaking as the muscular Les Rowe cast a menacing scowl over from the opposite corner. A fever pitch was reached as twenty-odd blood-lusting juveniles chanted, "Jim… Jim... Jim, Jim, Jim."

The bell rang and Les shuffled confidently forward – perfect boxing stance and mean stare. Jim stepped backward, pressing himself tightly against the ropes and hiding his face behind the boxing gloves. Les, unblinking, edged ever closer, his top lip curling into a sneer as he decided on his first punch.

Thwack!

With one single straight left into Jim's gloves, behind which hid his head, it was all over. Jim crumpled to the canvas like a pile of old clothes at a jumble sale. The place went wild, cheering, shouting and whooping. Les was carried out shoulder high, as though he had won a fifteen-round grueller against all the odds. That was the beginning and end of Jim's boxing career.

FOUR

ONE ENTIRE week at headquarters was dedicated to a first aid course. Many hours were taken up with bandaging each other, applying splints and tourniquets and learning the medicinal wonders of hot sweet tea. Several sessions concentrated on determined efforts to explode 'Resussi Anne' – a life-sized plastic practice doll – designed for learning mouth-to-mouth resuscitation. Resussi Anne also had to endure numerous other indignities throughout the week.

The triangular bandage figured prominently over the whole course. This was obviously an important medical invention which would help us to save many lives in the years to come during our chosen profession.

We frequently went back to headquarters for other courses and occasionally had to spend a week or two away on an Outward Bound camp or something similar.

Another school friend of mine, Roger Joynson, had now also joined the cadets. Roger had been my best mate at school and we'd done everything together since about the age of eleven. It was amusing to us that his past life had also gone unnoticed and that he too had been allowed to join the Staffordshire Police.

"Yes… another camp," Roger said.

We were staring at each other across the two illegally purchased halves of Bents Best Bitter in the bar of the Thistleberry pub in Newcastle – still not eighteen and enjoying our weekend off.

"Where the hell is Oakamoor anyway?" I said.

"Near Alton Towers, the other side of Cheadle."

"Who's going?" I quizzed.

"It's a mixture," said Roger, "A few from your course. I was up there last week helping to set the tents up. It's a dump; a field of mud."

"But we've only just done one camp," I complained.

"Yes, but they're doing mountain and cave rescue, river crossings and that stuff… all the things you'll need in the middle of Wolstanton."

Roger was right. A dump it was. Two minibuses and a Land Rover carted us down through the tiny village of Oakamoor and then whined in first gear up almost vertical hills. We were finally deposited in a mist-shrouded farm field on a grey drizzling March morning. Our four very basic tents had been pitched on top of a sloping sea of mud. Another larger, new, and much more luxurious tent had been erected on the only level and dry area. This was the instructors' accommodation.

The field was to be our home for the next two weeks. It would be a base from where we would learn to become accomplished mountaineers, cavers, river crossing experts and much more. At least that was the idea.

To give us the appearance of being a team and possibly to allow the local people an easy means of identifying the strange youngsters, we were supplied with blue berets. These had to be worn at all reasonable times and certainly helped identify us as 'strange'.

Bob Edwards, one of our instructors, was a young PC who professed to be some sort of survival expert. We soon discovered that he had his favourites – the cadets who got the easy jobs and the privileged front seats of the Land Rover – I was not on his list.

"Pull these ropes… tighten them up," Edwards shouted, "it's all got to be really taut."

This was our first attempt at river crossing and the rain, which had not relented throughout the previous week, was still coming down. We had fastened one thick rope around a tree trunk on either side of the river. Several tension-ropes were tied onto that rope which we secured to other trees. The River Dove belied its name – there was nothing peaceful about it. It was a deep, dark, cold, raging torrent. The rope stretching across its banks was now so tight that it felt like a piece of wood – a slippery, greasy piece of wood.

Cadets crossing the River Dove. Courtesy Bill Wrench

"Right, Jock," shouted Edwards, "you've done this before, show them how it's done."

Jock Smart, obviously a Scot, was a stocky athletic lad, who was always grinning. A micky-taking shout of 'och aye the noo' and 'hoots mon' rang out as Jock removed his beret and shoved it down the front of his trousers. A torrent of cheers, jeers and rude remarks followed, including, 'don't get the berets mixed up.'

Jock was hoisted up the tree trunk around which the main rope was tied. This was several yards back from the river's edge and meant that he had a struggle to get over the knotted tension ropes and eventually out over the water. He carefully hooked his right leg around the main rope and let his left leg dangle down as a counterbalance. With both arms outstretched, he slowly started to inch out along the rope towards the river, pushing with his right leg and pulling with his arms.

There was a hushed silence as everyone watched pensively and tried to master what was taking place. One false move by our fellow cadet would be more than merely unpleasant and we all knew that our time would soon come. Each time the rope started to sway Jock stopped and became motionless until he'd regained his balance. A huge cheer went up when he finally arrived safely at the other side.

Slowly but surely others followed suit, and the crowd on the far bank grew in size. The mood then switched from willing people across to willing them to fall in.

"Girl Cadet Price, off you go," snapped Edwards.

Poor Linda was the first girl to attempt it and received no sympathy from the baying mob. She carefully folded her beret and shoved it down into her jeans – even more disgusting remarks followed.

"You won't get that back."

"I want it when you've finished with it, Lyn."

A disapproving stare from Lyn was enough to temporarily silence the culprits as she clambered onto the rope and bravely started to edge forward. Her bottom moved gingerly up and down as she got into the rhythm. This brought a further barrage of rude comments, including requests from the now accomplished river crossers, who wanted to come back via the nearby bridge for a better viewpoint.

"No, you stay where you are," Edwards bellowed, "stop being so childish. Right, Pye, your turn."

Beret down trousers, deep breath, dangling leg, and pull. God! Now I knew what the beret was for! This could ruin me forever. Pull and push, pull and push, I was beginning to get the hang of it and was soon out over the water, it looked terrifying.

A chant started…

"Pye – Pye – won't – be – dry."

Ignore them, I thought. In the middle now…

TWANG!

What was that? My whole body vibrated.

TWANG!

It didn't take me long to realise that Edwards was using his stick to pluck the tension ropes like an enormous guitar. Each time he did it my entire body vibrated and I started to sway, I felt as though I was shaking to pieces. I stopped dead, and concentrated on balancing with my dangling leg.

TWANG, TWANG, TWANG!

Edwards was determined to kill me and now loud jeering started up from the crowd who had already crossed – total silence from the other bank.

"Come on, Pye, keep moving," came Edwards' oily sarcastic voice.

"Bollocks," came my involuntary reply.

"What was that, Pye?"

TWANG!

"Nothing, Mr Edwards," I vibrated back.

"Keep moving, Pye."

TWANG!

There was no way I was moving whilst he was doing that. I decided that I was going to stay on the rope for the rest of my life rather than give him the pleasure of seeing me drown. In the end the twanging subsided and I inched my way to safety. A cheer went up as I dropped down onto the muddy bank side. There was laughter as Edwards swung around, not quickly enough to spot the gesture I waved in his direction.

"Right then, Brown, let's have you," said Edwards.

Tim Brown was thin and gangling with about as much co-ordination as Rita's marching. He looked even younger than me, and the worst swear word he was ever heard to have uttered was 'sausages'. He was wearing a thick green anorak that was enormously oversized, baggy canvas trousers and heavy hiking boots and, if he went in, he would never be seen again. Beret in trousers, Brownie shakily mounted the main rope, but seemed in danger of falling off before even getting over the water.

"Come on, Brown, don't muck about, get on with it," bawled Edwards.

Brownie was now twenty feet out over the water, a small white face dragging along a gigantic green flapping body.

TWANG, TWANG!

Brownie's features distorted as the masochistic Edwards plucked the tension ropes.

TWANG, TWANG!

Brownie now appeared to have six eyes, each one wide with terror. He was right in the middle and the raging torrent roared along underneath him.

TWANG, TWANG!

"No, no, please, no!" pleaded Brownie in a high-pitched, quivering vibrato voice.

TWANG!

Brownie was now vibrating so much he had become a blur. His counterbalanced leg waved crazily and suddenly something fell away from his trouser leg and flopped into the torrent beneath him.

"He's shit himself," someone shouted and screams of laughter broke out.

It was actually his beret. It must have worked its way down his trouser leg with the shaking. It was swept away into oblivion as the laughter continued.

TWANG, TWANG! Edwards was determined to take at least one life before the day was out.

"Don't, PLEASE don't!"

TWANG, TWANG, TWANG!

"Don't, don't, NO, NO!"

TWANG, TWANG, TWANG!

In a desperate panic, Brownie decided to make a bolt for the riverbank. Back arching, right leg pushing, he shot along the rope like a steam-driven caterpillar. All caution and balance were now gone. Only the will to live remained.

TWANG, TWANG!

"NO, AHHHHH… BASTARD!"

SPLASH!

He didn't make it. His green anorak welled up to the surface full of air. It looked as if he was wearing a four-man dinghy. A small, white terrified face looked up from the centre of the dinghy, arms flailing, trying desperately to grab at bank side roots.

"Did he say 'bastard'?" a nonchalant voice asked.

"Sounded like it… beats sausages."

Brownie was dragged out and excused beret for the rest of the camp.

Edwards seemed displeased that his day had only resulted in the near death of just the one of us and so his passion for murder was not satisfied. The following morning he shepherded us to the summit of a fifty-foot sandstone cliff. A sadistic sneer took over his features as he went through the intricacies of mountain rescue. Admittedly, it wasn't much of a mountain, but the drop was easily sufficient to kill you.

"When am I going to need to use mountain rescue anyway?" I moaned, as I looked up from ground level at the tormentors, who were standing over me.

"Shut up and stop trying to move your arms," sniggered John Bowers. "You've got the easy job. We'll be doing all the grafting."

He pulled hard on the rope that snaked around my feet and around and around the old wooden and canvas stretcher on which my blanket-swathed body lay. I was pinned so tightly to the stretcher that I could hardly breathe.

"Right!" said Edwards. "This must be really tight. He must not be able to move at all."

"No, don't do it any tighter, please, I can't breathe," I croaked as John Bowers, like a true friend, increased the tension yet more.

"Don't want you falling out, do we?" he said, winking.

"Okay," commanded Edwards, "now, this rope must go through the D-rings, like this."

He demonstrated by passing a thick, old, brown and rather frayed-looking rope through two small D-shaped iron legs that were screwed onto the wooden poles of the stretcher.

I'd been picked on because I was the lightest of the group and because Edwards' last attempt on my life had failed. I knew what my fate was – I was going to be lowered over the cliff face. I started to wonder how old the stretcher was. The wood might be rotten. Who had assembled it all those years ago? Did he use the right screws? There were only those screws holding the D-rings on, and that rope, it looked pretty old. The D-rings made a horrible grating sound cutting into the sandstone as I was pushed towards the edge. Eleven of the lads had the rope around a thick tree. I could see deep rope marks in the trunk, evidence of where other poor souls had been tortured for the crime of 'being light'. I was on a slope inching towards the cliff edge. Gravity had me, and I was now reliant upon the wood, the screws, the rope, the D-rings and eleven teenagers – so many worrying factors.

"Lower and stop, and lower and stop!" chimed Edwards.

Each time the order was given, the D-rings grated into the sandstone. My feet were now sticking out over the edge. Two of the lads who were roped to a tree, eased me further over until I was upright with just my head poking up.

"Thanks very much," were my last words before I started my slow descent to the increasingly distant accompaniment of Edwards' chimes.

"Lower and stop, and lower and stop!"

It seemed to take several years to reach the bottom. I was determined not to let anyone think I was bothered, despite the horrible creaking sound coming from my right D-ring and the spinning one way and then the other. At least if I did fall they wouldn't have to put me on a stretcher.

I recited the definition of heavy motor vehicle, moped, pedlar and even larceny, which was the long one. I was halfway through the *Lord's Prayer* when I finally touched down.

FIVE

IT WAS back to Wolstanton after the camp. Roy had somehow managed to attain the age of nineteen without any really serious injury and had gone off to the Police Training Centre as a PC.

We had a new inspector now, Albert Deeth, an ex-military man, who used to beat out a tattoo on his filing cabinet upstairs. This was a signal for me to take him up his cup of tea or fetch him a Kit-Kat, depending upon which tune he was playing.

I was now boxing for the force at my weight of ten stone four pounds, which fitted into the welterweight category. I was off to tournaments most weekends and some evenings. We'd occasionally have an overnight stay somewhere. I'd won an array of prizes, which were mostly useful things rather than cups or trophies. I'd arrive back home late at night sporting a black eye and clutching a tea set or a transistor radio to wake up my mum and dad with – "I won!"

"What the hell sort of a state was the other bloke in?" was Dad's usual question.

Dad was proud when I won, and used to boast about it in the pub. Mum didn't like it and used to say things like, 'Do they have to hit you in the face? Can't you have a word with the umpire? You're going to get hurt'.

"It's a *referee*, Mum."

I think Dad didn't go to see me box because he knew I wouldn't want him to see me lose. When he told me he was going with his mate, Harry Masters, to watch me box at the Victoria Hall in Hanley, I knew he'd finally decided I was invincible.

We were fighting an army team, and I was drawn against a lad called McIntyre. It sounded like a real boxer's name. Mr Brown, my trainer, was the ref (which should have been a good omen). The bell clanged, I edged forwards and jabbed McIntyre a few times – easy! I caught him again and again. First round over and all was looking good. Second round, jab, jab then I caught him a right wallop, he staggered.

"Finish him!" roared the crowd.

Yes, I will, I thought, as I bludgeoned him again, throwing all caution to the wind… *must win this one.* He turned his back on me and covered his head.

"Give him a bike," someone shouted from the crowd.

I chased after him raining blows.

Thump!

Stars appeared – everything was now red – he'd caught me one! My nose had exploded – what a fool. I knew I had to finish it, but I couldn't see a thing. I was now a raging windmill roaring around the ring hitting out at everything that moved… Mr Brown included.

"Stop, stop!" I heard someone shout through the bloodied fog as I flailed onwards.

You could almost feel the draught as I ferociously whirled around in ever decreasing circles chasing after my quarry. Suddenly I couldn't move my arms. They were pinned to my sides – someone was holding me from behind. Had McIntyre called his mates into the ring to help him? I struggled desperately to throw off my attacker.

"Stop, stop, John." It was Mr Brown. "Stop, Stop, John, I've got to look at you."

I turned to look at the blurred image of Mr Brown, his white shirt quickly disappearing into a speckled red hue as I blew clouds of bloodied mist all over him.

"I'll have to stop it, John, your nose has gone," shouted Mr Brown's distorted outline.

"No, no, my dad's here with Harry Masters," I pleaded. "You can't stop it now, I can win, let me carry on."

"No, John, I can't," spluttered Mr Brown, as I blasted him with mouthfuls of blood. "I'm sorry, John, it's over."

Why, tonight of all nights, when my dad had come?

The bleeding stopped after a visit to the hospital. My nose hadn't 'gone' as Mr Brown had said. It was still there, but now a different shape, sort of rugged looking.

I quite liked it.

One morning in May, fellow cadet, Ian Bruckshaw, having passed his driving test and eager to show off his Vauxhall Viva picked me up from home. It was Open Day at Headquarters and we were both helping out setting up different stalls and equipment. We were also involved in a marching exhibition and I was going to be doing some sparring in the gym.

I'd had a tough time with bulling my boots. I couldn't seem to get them right. I'd spent so long on them the day before that in the end I'd cheated. I'd sprayed them with some plastic stuff that was supposed to help you start your car in the wet. Well, they actually looked pretty good, but they were still tacky. I carefully placed them in the car's rear foot well, put my boxing kit and best uniform on the back seat and off we went.

It was a bright but misty morning as we began the journey, joking at everything and laughing at nothing. We were a few miles from Stafford when everything disappeared. All perspective and sense of distance was lost as we were enveloped in a thick bank of fog. The car lurched to the left as Ian hit the brakes. A keep-left bollard appeared like a ghost and shot past on our right… Green grass swept towards us out of the gloom.

"*Roundabout!*" I yelled, but it was too late.

The loud dull thump as the car hit the roundabout heralded my first experience of flight. We touched down briefly as we crossed the roundabout and were then airborne again before crashing down onto an embankment and hurtling towards a brick wall. It was as if I had as much time as I needed to take in what was going on. I studied the wall in detail as everything seemed to slow to snail's pace. I even had time to work out that the impending collision was likely to catapult me through the windscreen in the general direction of Stafford town centre.

The thought flashed through my mind: *What a great idea to have cars fitted with belts that you could clip on to stop you flying through the windscreen.* I didn't suppose it would catch on though and got back to reality. In the split second it took I managed to half-turn my head and hang on to the back of my seat. As this was a two-door car with tip-up front seats, this strategy was of little use.

Aided by my tip-up seat, the eventual sickening jolting crash smashed me upwards into the roof of the car rather than through the windscreen. In that instant everything returned back to normal speed. The wall was now no more, except for a few bricks on the car bonnet. I slumped back, mind racing on overtime.

"Quick, let's get out," I shouted, "before it catches fire."

Ian, still holding the now distorted steering wheel was clearly dazed. He stared vacantly through the smashed windscreen into a garden that had never been on view to the public before this moment. He then slowly turned towards me and gasped in horror. His expression, coupled with the wet feeling on my face and the blinding headache, gave me the realisation that I was injured. We kicked open our respective buckled and jammed doors, and exited from Ian's once shining 'splendid little runner'.

It was a beautiful garden, complete with goldfish pond, dwarf conifer trees and hanging baskets. The back door of the house was suddenly flung open and out dashed the worried-looking male occupant, clad in a dressing gown. The ambulance had arrived before

I had finished my hot sweet tea. Ian hadn't even had time to triangulate the bandage he intended fixing to my badly cut head.

We arrived at Stafford General Hospital and nine stitches later, through the eye-watering smell of iodine, I heard my dad's voice giving Ian his tenth telling off in only as many minutes.

"You stupid bastard, what do you think you were doing?"

"Sorry, Mr Pye, sorry," Ian repeated.

"Sorry, bloody, sorry!" shouted my dad.

"Leave it out, Dad! It was the fog," I croaked from my hospital trolley, coming to Ian's aid.

Dad muttered for the rest of the morning and had a go at Ian at every opportunity. My hospital stay lasted a couple of hours and then the three of us went down to Stafford Police Station. We had to fill in some more forms and collect my stuff, which had been recovered from Ian's ruined car.

"Come and sign for your belongings, young man," said the sergeant as I followed him through into an office. "No boxing for you for a while with that head," he said comfortingly. "And no marching," he added, with a grin, as he handed me my boots. They were no longer black and shiny, but white and hairy.

In the crash my towel must have fallen from the seat onto the still tacky boots and given them a perfect flock coating.

In August 1968, I was chosen to go on a four-week driving course at headquarters along with two other cadets. I had already passed my driving test, but the course would mean that I would be immediately eligible to drive certain police cars after being appointed PC on my nineteenth birthday. The force held only a few of these cadets' driving courses and this was the second one. I think it resulted in some bad feeling from constables who had been in the job years and were still waiting to get a driving course. This probably was the reason for these courses being phased out.

You'll see from the photograph (below) that some of the constables were getting on in years. That's me middle row second from right. The elderly chap next to me sporting his military awards is PC Ivor Sturley. Ivor was the force's most commended officer, with a total of eighteen commendations to his name. But even such a glowing record didn't enable him to get on a driving course quickly.

It was whilst I was on this course that twenty-two-year-old PC Bob Potts was killed when his police motorcycle was involved in a collision with a petrol tanker. Bob had been an impressive sportsman and always took part in the force boxing tournaments. I was horrified when I heard about this tragedy. I later saw the mangled remains of Bob's patrol motorcycle when it was transported to the yard at the Driving School during the first week of our course. Bob's parents donated a trophy in memory of their son, which was awarded each year for the best performance at the force boxing tournament.

Driving course: cadets and constables.

More courses and camping expeditions were followed by more first aid practice, drill sessions and physical training work outs. I was then told that I was to spend three months at one of the Leonard Cheshire homes at Penn, near Wolverhampton along with another cadet. We were to work as carers attending to the severely disabled people who were resident there.

Our accommodation was a caravan on some wasteland at the back of the main building. In the weeks that followed I learned how to wipe noses and bottoms, clear up sick, spoon-feed people and try to make some unhappy people feel a little happier. I probably grew up more in those three months than I had done in all my now eighteen and a half years.

Two of the residents had electric wheelchairs, which were then state of the art technology. Together with the staff, we'd regularly organise a race around the passageways inside the home. We would arrange for all the residents either to have their doors open or to be seated by their rooms. They could then watch the two competitors hurtle by to the accompanying cheers.

I became friendly with a lovely man named Jack Gill, who was severely disabled with multiple sclerosis and other illnesses. Jack had a strong Black Country accent and I would tell him jokes and funny stories. Despite him being much older than me and so poorly, we shared the same warped sense of humour. I used to push him down to the pub in his wheelchair for a pint, and we'd be laughing all the way there and all the way back. Sometimes he'd splutter in that broad accent – "Stop, John, stop, yam killing may!"

Jack wrote a letter to me a couple of weeks after I left, thanking me for cheering him up, and saying how he missed my company. I wrote back to him and was arranging to go over to visit him when I heard that sadly he had died.

SIX

MY NINETEENTH birthday had now arrived. This was the big turning point in my life, for I was now officially 'PC Pye', which had a rather stupid ring to it.

I had to be content for a few weeks at Newcastle nick helping out in the admin offices, doing filing jobs and making more tea. This would last for a couple of weeks until a course became available for me at the Police Training Centre at Ryton-upon-Dunsmore near Coventry. The only bonus was that I could now answer the telephone with, "PC Pye speaking. How may I help you?" It was usually the case that I could not help them at all. Civilian clerk, Rosemary would raise her eyebrows and smile before reaching out to take the phone from me before the confusion became too great.

The actual Ryton course was itself preceded by a two week module at headquarters (yes that's just a fancy name for yet another course!) The three other recruits who joined me were all new faces as none of them had been cadets. We were taken to Stafford Magistrates' Court to swear our allegiance to our *Sovereign Lady the Queen*, and be sworn in officially as police officers. My new chums were: Graham Woodward, a former electrician, Eric Cartwright, who had been a motor mechanic and Terry Lockett, whose previous career had been as a guardsman. The two weeks we spent on this course were devoted mostly to learning law and drill – things which I was already fairly accomplished at. We would also be properly kitted out and so it was time to hand in my old cadet's outfit. In return I was going to get a PC's uniform complete with colossal helmet.

The Staffordshire police helmet was well known in police circles for its unfashionable appearance and was jokingly referred as 'The Staffordshire Bucket'. When placed atop my still young, although by now rather battered face, it looked utterly ridiculous. Stitched inside each helmet was a brown leather band, which could be pulled down. Packing, in the form of folded newspaper could be inserted to create a tighter fit. If successful this allowed the wearer to use his eyes.

Staffordshire Police had just amalgamated with the smaller Stoke-on-Trent City Police Force. Stoke had a smart helmet with a cockscomb top, a wide leather black band and a large silver Garter Star (as shown on the front cover). There was even a night duty helmet complete with a black star.

"Can't I have one of those?" I pleaded with Mr Ryan, the store manager, as I pointed up to a Stoke helmet on the top shelf.

"No! All new recruits have to have a bucket. Those are for the Stokies. Anyway they'll all be withdrawn eventually and everyone will have the same – probably a bucket, so get used to it."

Neither the Stoke nor the Staffordshire bobbies wanted the amalgamation. There was a lot of bad feeling at the start with the different force members suggesting that their ways were better. The two forces had amalgamated in 1968, but it was several years before all officers throughout Staffordshire and Stoke-on-Trent wore the same uniform. Everyone serving within the boundaries of the old Stoke force continued to wear and be supplied with the old Stoke uniform. The differences were few, but they were subtle – the helmet being the most prominent feature.

So I got my bucket helmet and Mr Ryan showed us how to ensure that it was worn correctly.

"Bend your thumb," he explained. "Get the tip of your thumb to just touch the rim of the helmet whilst the thumb joint touches the end of your nose."

Thereafter for the rest of our police service we would go through this universally accepted little procedure whenever we put on our helmets. Constables and sergeants, the only ranks who wore helmets then, all probably did this without even thinking about it.

Mr Ryan piled us up further with boxes of trousers, jackets, white cotton gloves and a raincoat. I was also given my truncheon or 'staff' as I knew everyone called it. Mine was a second-hand one, as was most of the kit with which we were issued. Some of the stuff must have been used by Staffordshire bobbies back in Victorian times. My staff was dark brown – almost black – with a new-looking leather strap attached.

"Lignum vitae!" Terry exclaimed.

"What?" I queried.

"Lignum vitae," Terry repeated, "the hardest wood known to man. That's what the truncheons are made from."

My staff had a crack throughout its entire length.

"Cor! Someone must have had a headache, then," I said.

We were each given a chrome-plated police whistle complete with chain. These had to be worn as part of the uniform with the whistle inside the right breast tunic pocket. The chain was attached to the top chrome uniform button and was on show rather like that of a pocket watch. Different forces chose different sides to wear the chain… even Stoke and Staffs used the opposite side.

"Cuffs," said Mr Ryan, giving out three pairs of shiny new ratchet-type handcuffs to the others.

"What about me?" I said.

"Oh, hang on!" said Mr Ryan, rummaging in a box. "Here you are."

He handed me a second-hand pair of heavy, dull-looking handcuffs with a large screw-type key on the side. They looked like something you'd see at Stafford Castle.

"What's this?" I asked.

"That's all there is left, so you'll have to make do." Mr Ryan then turned to address all of us. "Right, that's your lot. If you don't get booted out, you'll get more kit when you finish Ryton."

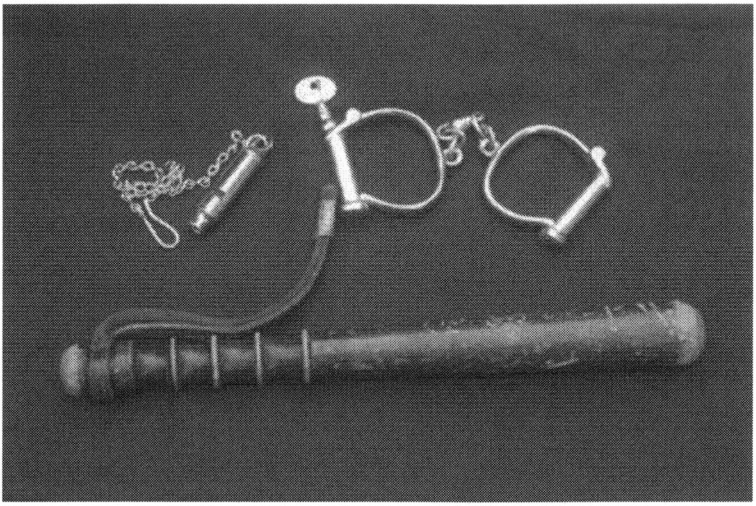

Whistle, staff (truncheon) and those ancient handcuffs

"Can't I have a smaller helmet?" I whined.

"No, that one's perfect," snapped back Mr Ryan.

"My mac's too big as well. You can't see my hands."

"Well, roll your sleeves up then. Oh, and here's your collar numbers." He handed us all a large brown envelope.

We peered inside our envelopes and saw they were filled with dozens of small chrome numerals. My envelope contained a handful of ones, noughts, nines and sixes – I had now become PC 1096 Pye – a Constable of the Staffordshire Police.

Most of our evenings for the remainder of the pre-Ryton course were spent huddled together in a dormitory room piercing holes through various parts of our new uniforms. We had each *borrowed* a fork from the canteen. With one of the prongs bent upwards as a makeshift hole bodger, we laboriously poked away at our jackets, coats and epaulettes. The reason for this criminal damage was so that we could fix our assigned collar numbers (identity numbers) in place. Each numeral had two lugs on the back and a split pin, which was to hold it in place. This meant that every single number had to have two holes made in the material of the uniform. It took hours and if you didn't get the row straight you'd have to bodge more holes until you did. By the end of the week we had all contracted severe 'bodger's thumb'.

The term 'collar number' dated back to the time when police uniform included a tunic with a closed neck design. The identity number would show around its high collar. In fact such uniforms were still in use up until the late fifties.

Collar numbers and 'bodging fork'

The course was taken up with more of the familiar pressing and boot bulling, some square-bashing and plenty of classroom work. My weekend at home was interspersed with embarrassing poses for a variety of friends and relatives invited around by mum and dad to see... 'Our John in NEW uniform'.

And so to Ryton – the Regional Police Training Centre, Ryton-upon-Dunsmore, near Coventry – May 1969.

I had my own car now, such as it was – a Ford Special – a red fibreglass sports car shaped body, underneath which lurked the innards of a 1953 Ford Popular. Its 17 inch wheels would not have looked out of place fitted to a bicycle. The tiny side-valve engine could press the car into a 0-57 mph acceleration time of several minutes – it couldn't quite reach sixty!

Arrival at Ryton was like nothing I had imagined and as I chugged along heading for the entrance I considered that it closely resembled an army camp. An enormous parade square was visible from the road and I could see a squad of twenty constables and WPCs, marching along. One figure was badly out of step in the back row. I strained my eyes to see if it was Rita… but no!

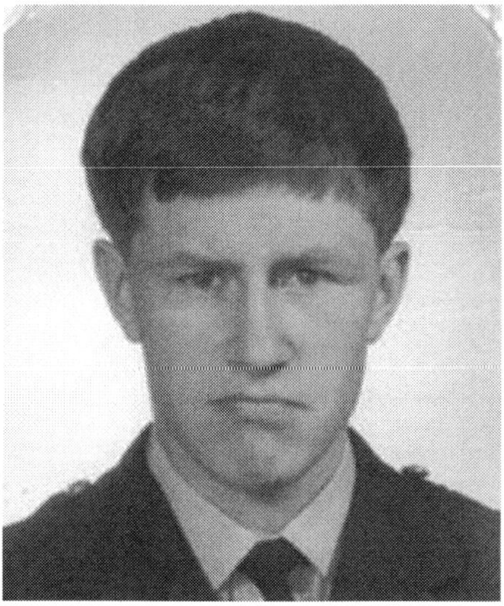

Ryton was an enormous facility catering for hundreds of new recruits from all parts of the country. Huge loudspeakers belted out a marching tune, but even above this and the unhealthy clattering of my engine, I could hear a voice. The strident, Scottish tones of William McIvor – the drill sergeant pierced through the din like a sharp sword.

The black and white barrier pole was lifted as I proudly showed my brand new police officer's warrant card to the sergeant on the gate. He examined the card and laughed out loud as he showed it to a colleague. He then barked back at me, "Pye J, Staffs, course 446B, classroom nine, room twenty-two, D Block."

The warrant card is the officer's official identification, proving that he really was a police officer. The Staffordshire Police version was a small flip open booklet covered in simulated brown leather with the wording 'Police Officer's Warrant Card' embossed in gold lettering. When opened, it revealed certification that John Pye was an officer of the Staffordshire Police. Mine also contained a photograph of a small boy with a basin haircut, broken nose and scarred face.

Ryton on Dunsmore Police Training College

SEVEN

FOLLOWING the directions given, I drove my car along the concrete roadways that criss-crossed this vast area. Dozens of single-storey buildings lined the route and everywhere I looked there were pipes – thick black metal pipes. Some came up out of the ground, travelled along at the side of the road and then mysteriously disappeared back down into the pavement. There were as many as four of these pipes in a row, with sizes varying from up to twelve inches down to six inches in diameter. Some sprouted upwards for ten feet and crossed over the road, only to disappear back into the earth on the other side. Big wheel valves were fitted here and there and steam could be seen venting out in some places. Sparrows flapped about in puddles of the brown water which had collected beneath.

After parking my car along with the rows of other wrecks, I set off, suitcase in hand and uniform over arm, to find D Block.

The complex had originally been built as a hostel for war workers employed in a nearby factory engaged in the construction of military hardware. It opened its doors as such in May 1943. Consequently, it closely resembled the Blackshaw Moor Camp where I had completed my two weeks endurance test a couple of years before. Each accommodation block had a three-foot high red letter stencilled on the wall. I was now standing outside the building labelled 'D'.

All the buildings were of the same weathered brick construction as Blackshaw Moor and again reminded me of Dad's garage back home. The tongue and groove, red painted entrance door and corrugated asbestos roof did not look inviting. I stepped inside, half-expecting to see Dad mixing some paint. But another, now familiar sight met my eyes – more of that bloody khaki lino. It was everywhere.

There was a toilet block and a room with a bath in it, but none of them were proper rooms; they were just separated by red wooden partitions with a gap at the top and bottom. There was one, long narrow corridor leading down the centre of the building with bedrooms either side. It must have been sixty feet long. All the walls were decorated with eggshell emulsion and the bedroom doors with yellow paint.

Other figures started to appear, each clutching a suitcase and with a uniform draped over an arm. Police helmets in carrier bags added to the burden along with the occasional biscuit tin of goodies from home.

I lumbered up the corridor, which seemed hardly wide enough with the kit I was carrying, nodding and smiling at my fellow students as I passed by the mostly open bedroom doors.

"Hi... Hi… Hello… Hi… How are you?"

A familiar face looked up as I passed one door. It was Eric Cartwright who I'd met a few weeks before on our pre-Ryton course.

"I've been here half an hour," Eric explained. "Terry and Graham are in E Block. They'll be in different classes from us as well. What room have you got?"

"Twenty-two," I said, making a hopeful face.

I swung open the door to room 22 to reveal my home for the next thirteen weeks, apart from weekends. There was an iron-framed bed, an old brown wardrobe, a set of drawers, a washbasin with a mirror above and, amazingly, green lino instead of khaki – luxury! A tea-towel sized mat lay on the floor at the side of the bed, and hanging on the wall, slightly askew, was a cardboard inventory notice. It spelled out the meagre room contents in bold black type:

Bed: One, Wardrobe: One, Drawers: One set, Mat: One.

There was a signature at the bottom of the notice:

L Randall, Chief Superintendent, Camp Commandant.

I mused at the term, 'Camp Commandant' and peered through the window at the distant parade square wondering if I might see a squad of goose-stepping SS Officers. I gave the inventory notice one last glance for the presence of any of Sergeant Haywood's graffiti. There was none and so I moved on to the fire drill notice that hung on the door and was printed in red. It gave precise instructions of where to assemble in the event of a fire. A fire might not have been a bad idea.

The only communal room in the building was an ironing room, which was not much bigger than the tiny bedrooms and contained four ironing boards and irons.

It was now half past eleven and we'd been instructed to meet in our appointed classrooms at midday in full uniform. I relaxed a little realising that I had some time to sort myself out. I put my things away and decided to have a quick wash before getting into uniform. I turned on the hot tap. It coughed, gurgled, coughed again and then exploded into life with such terrifying violence that I felt sure it was about to break free from the basin and embed itself in the ceiling. I backed away in terror as a torrent of dark brown boiling water roared from the tap, splashing over onto the floor. Clouds of steam filled the eight feet by six feet room.

Protected by a bath towel and my floor mat, I turned off the tap and, after mopping the floor dry with my towel, I put on my uniform.

As Eric and I made our way down to our Classroom, with other new recruits, we found out that the brown boiling water was part of everyday life at Ryton.

Sergeant Neale, our class instructor, greeted us, assigned us each a desk and in his opening speech warned us against trying to bribe him with end-of-course gifts. He went on to state that if we did, he would very much like a pair of spotlights for his Triumph Herald. We were given a timetable with meal times, class times, break times, a list of 'do's' and a long list of 'don'ts. There were twenty of us in class 446b, fifteen men and five women, and the same number in the two other classes on our course (446a and 446c). Sergeant Neale drummed it into us most days that 'A' stood for Asses, 'B' for Best and 'C' for Clowns.

Two other courses were also in progress and each consisted of three classes: a junior course (us), an intermediate course and a senior course. A four-week gap separated the different courses. The centre also catered for additional 'refresher' courses at the same time and so an estimate of three hundred fresh faced rookies at any one time would not be amiss. The catchment area for Ryton took in the entire Midlands, but because of the shortage of spaces in other training camps, there were would also be people from much farther afield.

The place seemed alive with dark-blue clockwork-helmeted figures marching in packs from classroom to drill square, from gym to canteen. Everywhere we went we had to march. A shouting voice always formed part of the regime, with bellowed instructions becoming the expected norm.

The canteen was enormous, like an aircraft hangar. Meals were at 8 a.m., 1 p.m. and 5 p.m. The silence of 'grace' was followed by the thunderous rumble of hundreds of chairs being dragged out and the clatter of knives and forks. This together with the chatter of three-hundred youngsters all filled with new experiences, new problems and eager ambition made meal times a deafening event.

After breakfast it was drill every day for all three courses and one course would then be picked for inspection. The two and a half years I'd spent as a cadet had benefited me greatly. We were all given the same little definition book that I already knew off by heart. I additionally already considered myself to be an accomplished presser, ironer, marcher and, to my mind, boot-buller. But even from the first day, no one on the camp could believe the boots of a fellow Staffordshire colleague, Terry Lockett.

Terry Lockett's boots were incredible – gleaming, shining, glowing – words could not describe. People from other courses would visit his bedroom especially to look at them, and to try and extract the secret from him. Terry, the ex-guardsman, would never fully disclose the formula of how he did it, not even to his fellow Staffordshire officers. The problem was, no matter how good ours were, Terry's made it look as though we hadn't even tried. He seemed to get a commendation at every inspection.

Eric and I, like all the other students on the camp, spent hours sitting together trying different methods and different polish. It was always easy to spot a Ryton student, even when off duty in civilian clothes. Apart from the basin haircut being a giveaway, everyone also had those two black stained fingertips. It could take several 'bulling-free' days for these to fade and so it meant that you were stuck with this little trademark for at least three months.

'Cherry Blossom is the best,' was an opinion often voiced.

'Terry uses Kiwi, I've seen it in his room,' would be a regular counter to the argument. The camp stores immediately sold out of Kiwi boot polish. I imagined a sales rep from Kiwi coming to interview Terry for an advertisement. Posters would then go up everywhere with a picture of him pointing, in Lord Kitchener style, saying, 'Your Boots Need Kiwi'.

Eric had overheard gossip that instead of water or spit, methylated spirit should be used – no good. A heated spoon should be rubbed over the toecaps before applying the polish – disaster. Leave half an hour between layers of polish – no improvement. A bottle of liquid for renovating patent leather shoes turned up…

you only had to paint it on. It looked good, but then McIvor rumbled it. It was deemed cheating and anybody caught out was put on 7.30 a.m. staff tea duties for a week. Terry then slipped out a tip about 'candle wax'!

"Pour melted candle wax over the toecaps, rub it down until smooth and then bull with polish and water."

The trouble was you could never be sure whether Terry's intention was to help or sabotage.

I spent several hours that weekend, melting, pouring, polishing and rubbing until I could contain my secret no longer and had to ring Eric.

"Is Eric there, please, Mrs Cartwright? It's John."

"Just a moment, love, I'll get him. *Eric… telephone*!"

"I've done it!" I said.

"Done what?" replied Eric.

"My boots, you should see 'em, brilliant. I used the wax method and they're absolutely amazing!"

Monday morning brought a queue of inquisitive boot polishing fanatics to the door of room D22.

"Bloody hell!" was the most common phrase as they viewed a large pair of boot-shaped black diamonds nestling on my bed in a cardboard box, which was lined with tissue paper.

"Must have taken you years. That's a commendation," someone commented.

Eventually D Block inmates formed up and we marched down to the parade ground for Monday inspection. I was almost tiptoe marching so as not to catch my boots on anyone's foot and cause damage to the gleaming masterpieces which also doubled as my footwear. We formed up in our now familiar fashion along with all the other classes. McIvor's distant figure, complete with polished wood and brass pace stick could be seen strutting backwards and forwards. His mouth opened as much as twelve inches as he shrieked abuse at late-comers and people whose turn it was to be shrieked at anyway.

"PAAARAAAADE… SHUN!" bellowed the massive voice from the distant, tiny figure.

With a form of proud violence I stamped my right foot down into the concrete, thrust my arms down by my sides and stuck out my chin. This was the first time I was actually looking forward to a face to face encounter with McIvor. My mind raced as I imagined his eyes narrowing as he scanned my trouser creases, haircut, and impeccable uniform. The delight I would have as those eyes widened in astonishment upon landing on my boots. His jaw dropping open with the sight of his own reflection staring back.

I decided on one last crafty admiring look down at the weekend's handiwork and with the slightest movement of my head I glanced down.

My own eyes must immediately have become as big and wide as McIvor's mouth. 'OH NO!' I shouted inside my head, almost wanting to shout it out loud. My right toecap was now like a piece of crazed and broken pottery. Almost the entire wax covering had parted company with the boot. It was lying rolling from side to side on the concrete like a piece of broken chocolate Easter egg.

"WHAT'S THIS, LADDIE?" roared McIvor directly into my face, as though he was communicating with someone half a mile away.

"An accident, Sergeant," was my feeble reply.

"ACCIDENT, LADDIE, ACCIDENT," he bawled, as he crushed the Easter egg with his pace stick.

"SEVEN THIRTY TOMORROW MORNING, LADDIE, STAFF TEA DUTIES."

"Yes, Sergeant."

I wanted to kill him, snatch his pace stick from him and chase him across the parade ground beating him around the head.

EIGHT

A practical exercise at Ryton (see the cast iron pipes in the background)

SPORT played a big part in our training and a session was usually included in the daily schedule. It was a hot summer and that didn't always go too well with the five-mile cross-country run we'd sometimes have to finish with. I'd done okay one day and had come in fourth.

Sergeant Neale was always there cheering on his class. "Well done, Pye, I'll buy you a half in the bar tonight."

"Thanks, Sarge," I gasped, face like a beetroot.

I was now looking forward to a long soak in a deep hot bath of dark brown water. I swilled a family of large spiders from the huge cast iron bath and went through the hot tap ritual which all experienced Ryton dwellers knew well: *Turn on hot tap and quickly retire to a safe distance.* The coughing and exploding was followed by a steady stream of what resembled stewed tea. I opened the ground floor window slightly to ventilate the steam-filled room, and fished out the larger pieces of rust along with a spider I had overlooked. After clambering over the side of this gigantic bath, I lowered my aching body into the mire – it was heaven. I smiled, remembering someone in class saying that the rust was therapeutic due to the iron content. I then closed my eyes and floated back home to Mum's cakes, clean water, ironed shirts and toilet paper that didn't give you a sore bottom.

A trickling sound caused me to jolt back to reality. Had I left the tap running? No! A hand had appeared through the open window and was just finishing emptying the contents of a large bottle of blue ink into the bath. I jerked upwards causing a tidal wave.

"Bastard!" I shouted, as the villain casually shook out the remaining few drops and disappeared as deftly as he had arrived.

The brown water was now black, and I had to start all over again with fresh brown water. This sort of prank was pretty routine and mostly taken in good part.

After our evening meal we'd lie on our beds with doors open, studying. It was quite normal for someone to wander in and a discussion over a point of law would ensue. Six or more people would cram into the room sitting on the bed, the floor and the drawers, and we'd test each other on definitions.

As the halfway mark on the course arrived and we were now 'intermediate students' the time had arrived for some practical court work. One of the buildings was authentically fitted out as a magistrates' court. There was a bench, a dock, seats for the public, seats for the press and probation officers, and even a large coat of arms above the bench.

Sergeant Neale had given everyone a different offence to research. We had to make up a set of circumstances as though we'd reported a lawbreaker. Our task was then to write a report and give evidence in the court. The other instructors would pretend to be solicitors for the defence and prosecution. They would then switch to become the accused or a magistrate whilst the students sat in the public gallery.

Sergeant Neal had clearly spent some time going through the law books trying to find the most obscure and ridiculous crimes possible. I was to report a shopkeeper for the misdemeanour of: *having a shop blind lower than eight feet.*

WPC Tomkins was given the offence of: *disturbing public worship.* Eric was lumbered with: *selling or exposing for sale English hares out of season.*

We all wrote up the reports during the weekend prior to the event, some of us putting in daft sounding names and stupid circumstances for a bit of a lark.

"*Call PC Pye*," a voice shouted.

I nervously strode into the 'court' as a titter came from the public gallery.

"SILENCE IN COURT," bellowed Sergeant Neale, who'd now also become the court usher.

I climbed into the witness box, gave the oath, announced myself and was duly coaxed through my evidence by the solicitor for the prosecution – Sergeant Neale.

Sergeant Stevenson, a tall, bald man, was now the defence solicitor.

"Thank you, Officer, and you measured this shop blind, did you, from its lowest point to the pavement?"

"Yes, Sir," I said with confidence.

"How did you come to receive this complaint, Officer?" quizzed Sergeant Stevenson.

"Several members of the public reported to me having banged their heads on the blind, Sir," was my reply.

"And what was the distance measured between pavement and blind?" Sergeant Stevenson asked as he rocked slowly back and forth on his heels whilst holding both his uniform jacket lapels between fingers and thumb – in true 'barrister' fashion.

"Seven feet, Sir," was my reply as another titter went up from the public gallery.

"Are they all giants in this locality?" pressed Sergeant Stevenson.

"There are some very tall people, Sir," I replied firmly.

"Thank you, Officer. No further questions."

Other offences were found to be proved. This included Eric's *'selling hares out of season'*. Another fictitious wrongdoer was convicted of *'shaking a mat outside a house at the wrong time of day'*. The case against the *'incorrigible rogue'* was sound enough for a conviction. The dreadful sin of an *'uncovered meat wagon where offal and blood could be seen'* was also evidentially in order.

Unfortunately, WPC Tomkins didn't manage to press charges for the person who *'disturbed public worship'*. She went to pieces at the last moment and the case was adjourned indefinitely.

There was a good swimming pool at the camp, which was probably the only new facility to have been built since the war. We'd get an hour or so in the pool each week. Most people could swim already and some of us had done some life-saving. On the other hand, some were hopeless. One poor chap, whose home town was Rhyl, couldn't swim at all. He thrashed about in the pool with a rubber ring around him. Sergeant Willey, the swimming instructor, would shout in that echoing voice that you hear in swimming pools. "Let's hope no one falls in the sea at Rhyl for the next thirty years."

One of the girls never used to make a proper job with the razor before swimming sessions and couldn't work out why her nickname was 'Spider'.

We were instructed in self-defence holds and some judo throws. One of the holds was called 'the hammer lock and bar', which was an effective way of restraining a person from behind. We were taught how to use our truncheon to best effect by striking at the shins or breaking the shoulder blade. If things got out of hand, we were trained to use the 'staff' as a sword to lunge at a person end on.

Some handcuff instruction followed and as a matter of course we were shown how to restrain a prisoner by handcuffing him with hands behind back.

In extreme circumstances a violent prisoner could be 'cuffed' bent over with the cuffs at the back of one of his legs. This method was banned in later years.

Everyone except me learned how to quickly snap their shiny modern handcuffs around a struggling prisoner's wrists. I had to make do with being last to finish every time as I unscrewed the key from my museum piece cuffs.

We were strictly forbidden to go off the camp to the only local pub, The Blacksmith's Arms, although we often ignored this rule. In fact there was a students' bar on the camp which was busy most of our evenings (swotting permitting). It was common for someone to have much more than his, or her, fair share of alcohol, especially if the definitions were proving too much.

There was always an instructor on duty in the bar, ready to pounce on anyone who was close to overstepping the mark. Other students would rally around and whisk the miscreant away to their room before they could get themselves in trouble.

On one occasion when it was Eric's turn to get blind drunk, I safely delivered him to his room. He became a little morose and made a verbal disclosure that, as he was about to die, he would like to make out his last will and testament. He wanted to leave me the brown wardrobe from his room. By the end of the course I was also due his drawers, mat, bed, inventory and fire drill notice.

Back in D Block, as we now neared senior status, everything was running like a well-oiled studying and bulling machine. Loud laughter would always be heard from someone's room with daft comments and practical jokes.

"What's this stuff, Stan?" I enquired, picking up a small canister from his sink.

"Shaving foam," Stan replied.

"What, in an aerosol can?"

"Yes, it's new, dead easy to use and saves a bit of time in the mornings, no need for a brush and soap."

I squirted a small blob onto my hand.

"Hmm, it's good! I'll have to get some."

I spied my chance as Stan momentarily left his room and put my artistic skills to use. I drew a three-foot long penis in shaving foam on his eggshell wall, carefully replaced the can and quickly made my exit.

"Pye… what have you done?" Stan yelled as he returned. "There's about ten shaves there."

This was followed by howls of laughter as the rest of the block visited his room for a look at my handiwork.

It was probably twenty minutes later, when Stan appeared in my room with an anguished expression.

"I can't get it off," he said.

"What?" I asked, looking up from my law notes.

"That bloody thing you've drawn on my wall – it won't go."

"What d'you mean, 'it won't go'? It's only shaving soap."

"Yes, but the wall wasn't very clean. I've wiped the soap off and it's cleaned the wall underneath and left a perfect picture of the dick in clean eggshell."

I dashed to Stan's room, but found I'd been beaten to it by the rest of the block. They were all doubled up at the immense glowing eggshell penis picked out against the grubby background. It took Stan's entire can of shaving foam to clean the wall; it was the only way to remove his new mural.

Stan had the last laugh. He beamed with pride a few days later when, following room inspection, he received a commendation for his initiative in cleaning his room so thoroughly.

NINE

THE PRESSURE of the course steadily increased as we entered the third stage and became '*senior students*'. We were still expected to attain the highest of standards in appearance and this meant that the pressing and bulling were as intensive as ever, but there was now even more law to learn and a lot of practical exercises as well. On top of this we knew that we were all heading toward the end-of-course examination. Providing we passed that we would also have to take part in a passing out parade. This meant that even more time was spent on the parade ground as we learnt our routines for the big day.

Throughout the entire course two different students from the senior course were delegated to perform night duty security for two consecutive nights each. It was a form of practical exercise and Eric and I teamed up to do our stint together. One person had to remain in the reception office to man the switchboard whilst the other went out on patrol around the camp. We swapped over every hour to wander around the empty classrooms, admin blocks and down to the deserted car park. Whoever was on patrol would occasionally ring through to reception using one of the internal phones. It was of course a little 'taster' for us all – an insight into what lay ahead in the years to come as a beat bobby.

It was 2 a.m. as I entered the ghostly gloom of the swimming pool. I looked over to the opposite wall… and FROZE! There was a darkened figure standing looking back at me. Was this my first encounter with a violent desperate criminal? I lifted my torch and started to stagger backwards, only to see the figure imitate me. It was a mirror… I was looking at myself! I phoned Eric and reported the incident to him. He was still shaking his head when I made my way back in for a brew. Apart from this incident it was a fairly uneventful night, but there had been incidents in the past. Someone from an earlier senior course had chased and rugby tackled a suspicious figure seen leaving one of the female blocks at three o'clock one morning. It turned out to be one of the instructors!

On another night the whole camp and surrounding residents were woken up to the sound of a loud marching tune being belted out over the parade square loudspeakers. Two figures were seen running away… last seen somewhere near G Block. There was hell to pay, what with complaints from the public as well, but the crime was never solved. After completing our two night-duty shifts and necessarily missing out on two mornings of lectures by catching up on our sleep we had to work hard to catch up.

Fridays meant an early finish and the weekend at home. I would travel back in my tatty old car and after a bit of leisure time between more bulling, pressing and studying I'd make my way back to Ryton on the Sunday evening. The Americans had landed on the moon. It had taken place as I completed those last few weeks at Ryton on Sunday 20th July. I journeyed back that evening with clouds of exhaust smoke belching out of the back of my car, twiddling the knobs on the old valve-radio to get an update on the landing. My thoughts were: *They've just landed on the moon and I can't even get the Home Service.*

The last week of the course was taken up with exams and practical exercises. Almost everyone had done okay. Eric, Stan and I were awarded Joint Top Sportsman in the camp sports making B-class top dogs. Sergeant Neale was chuffed to bits by this, even more so when he got the spotlights for his Triumph Herald.

The day of the passing out parade came at last and the weather was wonderful. The camp gates were opened up for the afternoon to all the proud parents, relatives, wives, girlfriends and some kids. My mum and dad came, together with my nan and everyone seemed to be clutching a camera.

We had become so good at drill that we actually enjoyed it. We looked good and we knew it. But the passing out parade involved much more than just being good at marching and doing drill on command. There were two main features. The first was a traffic signals exhibition lasting two minutes. All three senior classes did this together to a rousing marching tune. It entailed us in unison, carrying out the different police officers' traffic direction signals. These included 'stop from the front' (right arm raised) and 'stop from the rear' (left arm out in line with the waist). All the waving on signs and several elements of drill also formed a part, such as marching on the spot, left and right turns, about-turns and saluting. It was done by memorising the moves and doing them in time to the music. In 1976, twelve of the students from Ryton appeared on the television programme *The Generation Game* where they performed this procedure, which the contestants had to copy. The results were judged by the then Chief Instructor from Ryton.

Passing out parade day with my Staffordshire 'bucket'

The second feature of the parade was a marching exhibition based on the same principle and again lasting two minutes. This was accomplished without any music or orders other than a starting command. We had to count out in our heads the number of steps we had taken before making the next move. When we first started to practise it even Sgt McIvor and the class instructors could not contain their laughter. Arms, legs, heads and bodies were all shooting off in different directions and total disarray. We considered this exhibition to be impossible, but come the day we had, without exception, mastered it and I've never seen so many ear-to-ear grins.

There was a dinner dance on the last night and we all had to hire dinner jackets. I don't think there was a sober person on camp that night. The next day, even without the help of the giant hangover, would have been a sobering experience. It was time to say goodbye to so many good friends. Obviously I would be bumping into the other Staffordshire officers once in a while, depending upon where we were posted in the county. But as for all the other faces, this might be the last time I would see them.

I collected all my belongings and the bits and pieces that had helped to make D22 almost comfortable for the past thirteen weeks, and loaded up my car. I'd managed it in one go when I unloaded on the first day, but now it was going to take me three journeys to the car park.

After all the goodbyes, Eric, Terry, Graham and I would have one week at home before meeting back up at Stafford Headquarters. Yes, you've got it – another course!

My thoughts during that week off were consumed with wondering where I would be posted to. I managed a night out with my old schoolmate Roger, who was preparing for his own Ryton course and I tipped him off as to what to expect.

When the next Monday came I met up with my other three Ryton colleagues and it was clear that we'd all spent the week with the same thoughts – postings. Now we would learn our fate.

A Chief Superintendent came into our classroom and the four of us shot up from our seats. I had remembered the static electrical chairs and so, not wanting the sack at this late stage, I kept my hands well away. Terry let out a small, but fortunately, unnoticed grunt as he received a minor shock.

"Good morning, gentlemen," said the senior officer. "I've come to welcome you back to your force and give you your postings."

"Right, PC Pye, you're the ex-cadet?"

"Yes, Sir."

"You are going to Longton Division, part of the old Stoke-on-Trent force."

"Thank you, Sir." I said… not knowing if this was good or bad.

Most of the people I knew were from Staffordshire. I didn't know much about Stokies, apart from their helmets being better than the Staffs' ones. I did know, though, that Longton was a hell of a place to get to every day – a traffic nightmare. It could have been much worse; I could have gone to somewhere miles away, meaning I would have had to live in digs.

"Yes, Pye," he continued, "Longton Division, but you'll actually be at Stoke, which is a sub-division."

This was much better, quite easy to get to.

As Eric's mum was a widow he would be working in his home-town of Stafford, and Terry and Graham were told they were going to police stations in the old Stoke force area. We had all been lucky and as we marched over to the stores, I realised I would now be getting a Stoke helmet.

"There you are," said Mr Ryan. "You wanted one and now you've got one… and a night helmet with a black star. Make the most of 'em. There's no doubt they'll be withdrawn soon. They're planning to go over to buckets force-wide with a new badge for Staffs and Stoke."

"What about these handcuffs?" I asked. "They're bloody useless. By the time I've unlocked them to put them on a prisoner he'll probably have run off or died of starvation."

"No, I've no more new ones," said Mr Ryan. "You'll have to make do."

He handed me another box. "Here you are… leggings, for when it's pissing down, and one of these." He pulled something else off a shelf.

"What's this?" I asked, looking at the iridescent looking, quilted, armless jacket he had given me. "Looks like a bulletproof vest."

"No, it's Tropal lining," laughed Mr Ryan. "It goes under your coat for when it's really cold. Here you are… a greatcoat."

I was now disappearing under a vast pile of blue serge.

"Cape," snapped Mr Ryan as he reached up to place yet another heavy item on top of the swaying tower of clothing behind which I had disappeared.

I wasn't expecting a cape and I wasn't sure what it actually was. I hadn't seen one before. It looked really smart with two brass lions' heads and a chain where it closed around the neck.

The loading continued. "A Gannex mac like the Prime Minister, Harold Wilson, wears…different colour though," he added as he grabbed more and more uniform.

A flat peaked cap and a pair of black leather gloves were followed by four blue shirts and a box of collars. A first aid book (giving even more uses for triangular bandages) increased the size of the mound. The war-duties' manual would be helpful in the event of a nuclear attack. A six-foot steel measuring tape and pocketbook cover came next along with a stolen motor vehicle book. A wanted persons' book, a red accounts book, even more trousers and two more jackets… the voice inside my head was now shouting *STOP, STOP.* All this was on top of what I'd had before I went to Ryton. I wondered if it would all fit into my car. Last on the list was another bulging envelope full of more chrome numbers.

We had a few more lectures that week learning about local procedures and bye-laws and found out who our new bosses were to be. We spent even more hours making little holes in our various new jackets, coats and epaulettes, and fixing numbers.

We would be on probation now for two years. The only thing considered lower than a probationer was a cadet. Even a police dog had a higher standing than a cadet, so I looked upon it as a promotion. Each of us would have a senior constable assigned to the task of tutoring us through our first month of proper police work and then we were on our own.

TEN

The old Copeland Street Police Station at Stoke (demolished 1974).

IT WAS AUGUST 1969 when I finally arrived in the real world. Stoke Police Station was a faded, but beautiful Victorian structure built from sandstone blocks which had taken on a grimy black patina from years of pot-bank smoke. Above the doorway, carved into the ornate pediment in stylised two-foot high characters, was the word POLICE, together with the construction date of 1897.

An archway, which looked more suitable for a coach and horses than cars, led from the road into a cobblestone yard at the back. This separated the main part of the building from an annex which had originally been built as the Superintendent's house. It had since been taken over as council offices.

"Hello, young man," said a friendly voice. "I'm Rodney, but everyone calls me Bill."

I never did find out why!

"I'm your tutor constable for the next month."

Bill was on a 9 a.m. to 5 p.m. shift for this first day and it was his job to show me around the offices, introduce me to the staff, and explain the different departments. After this relaxed start I would be on regular shifts. Each shift was eight hours in length: 'Earlies' – 6 a.m. until 2 p.m. 'Lates' the afternoon shift, also called 'Noons' ran from 2 p.m. until 10 p.m. and 'Nights' from 10 p.m. until 6 a.m. The only way you'd get off shifts was for court appearances.

Various room titles were displayed on the doors: *Parade Room, Report Writing Room, Chief Inspector, Inspector, Admin Office.* The building was a maze of passages, with steps and corridors everywhere. There was a newly built toilet block with a locker room, kitchen and canteen at the back of the old building. On top of this fairly new extension, stood the CID. The canteen was really nothing more than a kitchen along with a small dining hall. There were no official canteen staff – you had to bring your own food with you each day.

Two cleaners worked at the station, Ethel and Elsie, and a janitor, Harry, and yes… khaki-coloured lino!

"Ethel or Elsie will cook your breakfast on early shift except on Sundays," Bill explained. "All other meals on the different shifts you'll have to sort out yourself. Sandwiches, soup, chips, it's up to you."

Bill led me through into the Enquiry Office. It was the first room that any visiting member of the public would see – the sub-divisional nerve centre. There were half a dozen stone steps leading off the street up to the huge front door. Each one had been worn away with a dip in the centre caused by feet walking, running or being dragged up and down. Once a visitor had climbed the steps he would find himself in a corridor and a sharp left turn would place him on the public side of the enquiry office desk.

The room was a scene of antiquated chaos. It seemed that the building had changed little since Victorian times. The solid brick walls were not plastered, but had been transformed into a lumpy smoothness through countless layers of paint. The current colour scheme was then a pale eggshell blue. The counter was high, as it doubled as a stand-up writing desk. There were dozens of devices and structures bolted to or leaning up against the walls.

A big window looked out onto Copeland Street and directly opposite I could see the Copeland Arms pub which I soon gathered was an after duty watering hole. Next to the pub was a yard which was shared parking for both the police and the next-door council workers. A makeshift green wire fence down the middle split our area from theirs. "DO NOT park on their side," Bill said firmly. "Or you'll be in trouble."

Beneath the window stood an old, brown wooden table supporting the radio equipment for speaking to and receiving messages from officers out on patrol. Also on the table was a strange-looking, two-tone grey, metal square-shaped device with a loudspeaker grille at the front and an on/off volume switch. The device was entitled 'WB400' and when switched on would emit a constant, *'pip,pip,pip'*.

If a wailing noise followed by a voice should suddenly come from the speaker then you'd have to take notice. This was the nuclear attack early-warning system receiver. The fact that I am writing this book indicates that the device never went off apart from tests.

The radios used by the outside patrols came in pairs – a transmitter and receiver each of which was powered by rechargeable batteries. Screwed to the wall for this purpose were four rows of chargers, taking about twenty batteries – small yellow ones for the receivers and long red ones for the transmitters. There was also an ageing telephone switchboard similar to the one at Wolstanton. The cell passage led directly from this room where there were six cells, each with a heavy steel door and crazed white tiled walls.

Bill reached over and took a tatty looking sheaf of crumpled papers on a clip board from a hook on the enquiry office wall. "THIS," he said, as he placed the board down onto the counter and patted it with the flat of his hand, "is the duty pad. It gives the details of what tour of duty you will be on. You must check it every day. It doesn't matter what you *think* you should be on… it's always subject to change. You may be taken off your normal shift to appear at court, or for some other job, so keep your eye on it."

I nodded as I gazed at the square of tattered hardboard with its large aluminium bulldog clip and clump of papers. This pretty nondescript item was to dictate the 'life and times of PC 1096 Pye', for the next few years.

"Right, let's introduce you to the inspector," Bill said and beckoned me to an office door in the corridor.

"Yes," came the eventual and rather sharp reply to his knock.

"Good morning, Sir, PC Pye to see you," Bill announced as he opened the door.

I marched in, helmet wobbling, crashed my right foot down onto the stone floor and flung up one of those arm-quivering salutes. Inspector William Holdcroft, or 'Wild Bill' as he was nicknamed was sitting on a frayed, old green armchair at a desk piled with papers. He looked up at me over the top of his glasses.

"Right, you'll soon learn your way around. Stick with your tutor constable and you won't go far wrong. Smartness and punctuality. If you don't understand, *ask*…" I'd heard similar words back at Wolstanton.

Upstairs in the old part of the building there was an admin office, and a snooker room complete with full-sized snooker table. It was only half past two, but there was a game in progress. The curtains were drawn and the green baize was brightly lit by a heavy-looking wooden lighting system that hung by chains from the ceiling.

“These are some of the lads from our shift," Bill whispered. “They've just finished earlies.”

I strained my eyes in the gloom, trying to focus on the two silhouettes bent over the table with snooker cues. I then noticed a third figure lying prostrate on one of the red leather bench seats apparently fast asleep. Familiar features began to emerge as my eyes became accustomed to the dark. There was no doubt it was definitely… ROY! I thought I'd seen the last of him at Wolstanton, but here he was at Stoke, now a PC and on my shift.

My lecture about the duty pad had revealed that our shift for the next day was to be earlies.

“We parade at 5.40 a.m., so you'll need to be here for five thirty at the latest,” Bill said.

I hated getting up early, but didn’t want to be late on my first day. I had a real battle with my mum, who suggested setting her own alarm and making me some breakfast.

“No, Mum, I'll only have a cup of tea and then I'll be gone,” I said for the tenth time.

“No, no!” she said. “I don't mind… If I get up at half past four I can have a nice breakfast ready for you. You can't go around arresting people on an empty stomach.”

“No, Mum, honestly!” I pleaded. “Just pack me something up – some bacon and stuff. I can get it cooked later on at my meal time. It’s half past nine now, I'm going to bed.”

“All right,” Mum said, “now you’re sure you don't want me to get up? Have you set your alarm and got your uniform ready? What about that awful car? Will it start, do you want your father to get up and take you? Ron, you'll have to get up with him, he can't be late on his first day.”

“Leave him alone, woman,” Dad mumbled from behind his newspaper.

I lay in bed trying so hard to go to sleep, but to no avail. I tried different positions. I read a bit – light on, light off – looked out of the window wondering if my car *would* actually start. I counted how many strips of wallpaper there were around the room. I checked that both clocks were still working and made sure the alarms were set correctly. Suddenly there was a fire engine coming down the street with its bell clanging. I sat bolt upright. No, it was one of those stupid dreams where a noise is waking you from a deep sleep and you somehow instantly have a dream that involves the noise. I slammed my fist down onto the alarm clock and sent it crashing to the floor still ringing. I stumbled from bed and accidentally kicked the still spinning clock into the skirting board, silencing it.

I sat on the side of the bed scratching various parts of my anatomy as I came to terms with the fact that it really was quarter to five in the morning. I slowly dragged myself into the bathroom. I'd never realised what a loud noise the toilet flush made before. Oh, the other alarm clock was now going off. I could hear muffled voices from my parents' bedroom as I dashed back to smash the other clock into silence. I then clumped thoughtlessly downstairs in my gleaming size tens. After several more trips up and down the stairs for things I had forgotten I now seemed all set. No! I'd left all the lights on upstairs; one more trip should do it. I collected the huge sack full of food that Mum had left me on the kitchen table and slammed the front door as quietly as it is possible to 'slam'. My car started okay and I was there in good time for parade. Everyone was there in good time. Everyone that is, except Roy.

Vincent Turner was our shift sergeant and when he came into the parade room he seemed enormous; six foot three and heavily built, with a strong Potteries' accent.

"Nar then troops, wane got a new un wi us this moanin, young constable Pye, fresh from Ryton and a berra time kayper than Roy. Thay needst a nickneem… theers too many Johns here. Thay't now answerable t' the neem O' Porky… Porky Pye."

And so it was, in spite of my slim ten-stone four-pounds that I became *Porky*, sometimes *Pork* for short!

Roy turned up at half past seven with all sorts of daft stories about spark plug leads, punctures and the like. He was whisked off into an office with Sergeant Turner. I couldn't hear properly, but part of it was something like, "they't a bloody weest o' time, they't even late fer naytes".

Bill took me out on foot patrol around the town centre; almost everybody seemed to want to say 'hello' and 'good morning' to us. Every once in a while someone would leer at us, or make some mumbled remark. Bill would tell me the person's full name and address, and add something like, 'You won't get a smile out of him. I had him in court the other week for drunkenness', or 'remember his face, he's a good cat burglar'. *Why would anyone want to steal a cat?*

Bill showed me a few addresses that I would undoubtedly be visiting and one or two short cuts through back alleys. We stopped a car and I wrote out a form to make the make the driver produce his documents and then it was soon time to go in for breakfast.

"Fried or boiled?" chirped Elsie.

"Pardon?"

"Fried or boiled – your eggs, how do you want them?"

"Oh, fried, thanks."

"Are you really going to eat all this?" she said, looking at me, shaking her head.

I surveyed the large array of items Elsie had extracted from the bag my mum had packed up for me. The banquet included four rashers of bacon, two eggs, a lump of cheese, two sausages together with a pile of mushrooms. A small tin of beans, two tomatoes and four North Staffordshire oatcakes finished off the list.

"I'll do my best thanks, Elsie."

Elsie cooked the enormous feast to perfection on a white metal plate with a blue rim.

"Don't touch the plate, it'll burn you," she added as she placed the feast down in front of me.

Sergeant Turner folded the top half of his *Daily Express* over and looked at the sizzling mountain I was about to munch my way through. "Dust know, Pork, he said. "I was held prisoner by the Germans and they'st got on that plate my rations fer a fortnight."

I ate the lot.

It had been an interesting day; nothing exciting had happened, but I'd made a start, and after my initiation into how NOT to play snooker I arrived home in the mid-afternoon. Mum came in from work just after four o' clock looking rather tired. I was puzzled when Dad eventually got back home himself and said, "We'll be getting up with you tomorrow."

"No, don't be daft, there's no need."

"Yes," Dad replied, "your mother and me will get up. Mr and Mrs O'Neal from next door are coming around. Mr and Mrs Hancock from over the road along with your Aunt Lily from around the corner, we'll all be there. We were all awake this morning, so we might as well make a regular thing of it."

"Did I make a noise then, Dad?"

ELEVEN

BILL USED to take every opportunity to remind me of the need for smartness and punctuality. It seemed that every boss I met would give me the once-over, checking the sharpness of the crease in my trousers, my haircut, or how bulled my boots were.

Bill went further with this. "Your smartness gives you that look of authority and discipline. It will give you a psychological advantage in a tricky situation. You must look the part; a scruffy bobby never gets anywhere."

We had to do point duty (traffic duty) each weekday on certain busy road junctions at peak traffic periods. These were junctions that should, by rights, have had traffic lights. Some were easy when you got the hang of it. The junction of Copeland Street with Glebe Street for example was a busy T-junction, but not much of a hardship for point duty. Others were much worse: Whieldon Road was a nightmare – a busy multi-junction – an hour on there and you were exhausted.

One day Bill pointed out a battered old Ford Anglia car to me.

"That's Fred Hails' car, he's Stoke-on-Trent's Coroner, an important man. You'll have a lot to do with him over Form 12s."

"What's a Form 12, Bill?"

"A Form 12 is the number of the form you use when you deal with a sudden death. Fred Hails is constantly in touch with the Chief Constable and what he says, goes." Bill went on. "You'll have learnt at Ryton that 'Her Majesty's Coroner' should be saluted by police officers. If you don't salute him, and he's in a bad mood, he'll report you."

Considering the Coroner's high status and his frequent involvement in road safety concerning road accident deaths, his car was astonishing. It was a complete wreck – a Ford Anglia with rust literally everywhere. Bill explained that on the radiator grille of the car a small plastic rose was fitted that had a light bulb inside it. This was wired to light up every time he turned the ignition on. The light enabled any constable to spot the distant oncoming Coroner and be ready with a salute. Fred expected a salute in virtually any circumstances, and point duty was no exception.

"When you see the oncoming rose," explained Bill. "Stop all traffic except the lane he's in, wave that lane on, come to attention and throw him up a smart salute as he drives by."

I got caught with Fred on most occasions on the Copeland Street junction. It must have been a puzzling sight to other motorists, as I brought the traffic to a standstill and then rigidly saluted the elderly monocle-wearing driver of the rust-encrusted car. They had probably presumed that it was en-route to McGuiness's scrapyard.

There were only a few traffic light systems controlling road junctions in the sub-division back then. It was the responsibility of the police to ensure that everything was working correctly. If a bulb had gone out or even worse, the entire system had gone dead, it would be up to us to contact the council. They'd come out, day or night and put things right.

The lights were controlled electronically from a large metal cabinet which would be mounted somewhere nearby on the pavement. A thick raised rubber strip ran across the road which would act as a contact breaker. Whenever a vehicle ran over it, a signal was sent through to the cabinet. The electronic brain inside would change the lights accordingly, or that was the idea.

Breakdowns were regular and the keys to all the cabinets were kept at the police station. In the event of a snag we could open up and use a switch turn the whole thing OFF! There were other buttons inside as well which allowed for remote control. We would use this method if traffic conditions were unusual, such as on a football match day. The electro-mechanical wizardry inside the cabinets was temperamental and would frequently stick on one phase or another causing traffic chaos. There was a knack to restoring normality. This entailed standing with your back to the box and slamming the sole of your boot against the metal plating. The lights would flicker for a few seconds before getting back into their rhythm – the performance often squeezed a few laughs from motorists.

My month with Bill came to an end as the winter of 1969 closed in and I was allowed to patrol on my own. I still had the peace of mind knowing that he was usually never far away to help me out and give advice.

I had already been involved in a variety of incidents, including thefts, burglaries, assaults and a few Form 12s and as a bonus was becoming fairly fluent in police jargon. It was like another language which was made up from certain phrases, abbreviations and ways of saying things that meant something to us, but nothing at all to other people.

'You've got to deal with a Form 12', was a prime example. An 'RTA' was a road traffic accident. A 'Domestic' was a family argument that was getting out of hand and a 'Cough' was, of course, an admission of guilt.

The different types of assault were usually referred to with a nickname derived from the section of the old Offences Against the Person's Act which was most likely to apply to that particular assault. 'Come back into the nick, there's a Section 47 in here for you to deal with', meant that somebody had been injured in an assault. The more serious types of assault were nicknamed accordingly with the most serious ones being a 'Section 20' or a 'Section18'.

The victim in any crime was the 'IP' (injured party), and if you arrested a 'D&D', it was a case of drunk and disorderly.

Any offence that was classed as a crime had to be recorded on a form 34. These were blue foolscap-sized documents in triplicate with old-fashioned carbon paper in between. The detail which was required seemed endless and unnecessary.

Each crime had to be given a detailed 'MO'. This abbreviation was taken from the Latin term 'Modus Operandi' (how the crime had been carried out or Method of Operation). Once in while a rookie constable's description of the MO would become a source of laughter and almost always included another overused police phrase – 'As opportunity arose'.

An amusing example would be: 'Removed left-handed man's shoe from display, as opportunity arose'. Another hackneyed expression was: 'And made good escape'.

Each crime had to be given a 'Motive'; the motive for sexual offences would be 'LUST'. Any description of an offender was never allowed to contain the word 'MEDIUM'. If you were daft enough to slip a 'medium' in anywhere you could expect to be called up to Detective Inspector Dodd's office for a grilling. "What the bloody hell is medium height?" or "what is medium coloured hair?" he'd say.

I had arrested a man for theft one afternoon and was puzzled when the DI told me:

"You'll have to do a MIPPY for him."

"Oh, right, Sir," I said as I wandered off thinking, w*hat the hell is a Mippy?*

"Where can I get a Mippy from, Joe?" I foolishly asked the CID office mickey-taker.

"Oh, do you want a male or a female one?" was Joe's reply.

Immediately smelling a rat, I ignored Joe and turned my attention to Dave, a more helpful detective. Dave explained that the word Mippy was a nickname for the acronym MIPYW. "It stands for… 'May it please Your Worships'." He said.

At this point I was still none the wiser and Dave enlightened me a little more. "It's for when we need to remand a prisoner in custody because of the seriousness of the offence or to make more enquiries.

We have to present him before the court charged with an offence and apply to the court that he be remanded in custody."

Still none the wiser!

"But what's this bloody MIPPY thingy then, Dave?"

"That, Pork, is how the prosecuting solicitor starts off his appeal to the magistrates; 'May it please Your Worships. The defendant stands before you charged with blah, blah, blah.' They don't say it much anymore, but that's where the term came from and it's stuck."

Another police expression was the word 'Cuffed'. Cuffed could mean 'handcuffed', but it was also a police adjective for idleness or for failing to deal with an incident correctly. Certain officers were renowned for cuffing to get out of having to do the paperwork, or so that they could finish duty on time.

Some people were such 'Cuffers' that they did more work by Cuffing than they would have done had they dealt with the job properly. The text in the 'action taken' column of a message form was occasionally a giveaway to a cuffed incident. Overused phrases such as 'advice given', or 'drivers exchanged names and addresses' could be a clue.

Another well-used phrase was 'The Job'. This had become a generic term for 'The Police Service' and would be used regularly in conversations between colleagues of all ranks: 'How long have you been in the job?' was a predictable question. Even former serving officers would be referred to as: *Retired Job*. But a similar phrase: *Ex-Job*, was more likely to refer to someone who had left under a cloud or been sacked.

One of the oddest things was the way we talked about individual criminals and troublemakers. They were always identified in any conversation, by their full name. Dave Woodward for example, would never just be called Dave Woodward, he would always be David Ronald Woodward. If the person actually had a criminal record, his full name would be spoken and then be followed with the acronym 'C.R.O.'. This stood for 'Criminal Records Office'. Dave

Woodward would, therefore, become 'David Ronald Woodward C.R.O.'. The term C.R.O. would often be used on its own to describe someone who had a criminal record... 'He's a C.R.O.'

It was strange that the worse a criminal was, the more names he seemed to have. Henry Kent C.R.O. for example, was nothing more than a drunk and petty thief. Melvin Edward Kenneth Cooper C.R.O. on the other hand was a prolific safe breaker and burglar. This didn't always apply though, as some people deserved many, many more names than those with which they had been christened.

Words which were useful to use on official forms and records tended to become a standard part of the everyday police vocabulary. Two good examples were 'frequents' and 'associates'. It would have been puzzling to any outsider listening in to a robotic conversation between police officers… 'I saw David Ronald Woodward C.R.O. the other day. I've heard he's been associating with Melvyn Edward Kenneth Cooper C.R.O. and they've both been frequenting The Bridge Inn. Cooper got locked up for a Section 47 last week… Jimmy Spicer C.R.O. was the IP'.

As I started patrolling on my own I became more familiar with the Potteries dialect and the odd sayings and characteristics which had developed in the community over many years. I lived less than four miles away in Newcastle-under-Lyme, but the differences and use of strange words and phrases left me needing an interpreter.

'Keep on the bricks, young man.' This is a Stoke-on-Trent farewell, often kindly given to me as I left someone's house. It means *stay on the pavement – stay safe.* Someone who was *Yampy* was daft. A *Hurst* was a funeral car (a hearse) and that nearby city of *Birningham* was of course Birmingham. A certificate (medical, death or otherwise) was always a *Sustificate,* whilst a skeleton in Stoke became a *skelington.* Mushrooms were almost always *Musherooms and* the Hanley store of Debenhams was known to most as *Depenhams.* If a darkening sky suggested poor weather, the phrase: 'It looks black over Bill's mothers,' would be an opinion on the subject. Who Bill, or indeed his mother was, no one could tell me. There were dozens more.

Some of the well-used police phrases could actually be ambiguous until you became accustomed to them. One good example in Stoke when dealing with a Form 12 (remember that's a sudden death) was the sentence: *The body has been moved.* This actually meant that the body had been REMOVED from the scene, and in those days this was done by the ambulance service (not a hurst!). Form 12s were a common feature of a PC's job in Stoke, certainly as a rookie you would find yourself dealing with probably two per week. There was a lot of paperwork involved and that one case could take up most of your eight-hour shift.

Fred Hails, as Coroner for Stoke-on-Trent, was thorough and was constantly complaining to the Chief Constable when things were not done in exactly the manner he liked. There is no doubt that the public benefited from his passion for detail in the way of compensation to relatives and the alteration of work practices.

Industrial disease was the main cause of premature death in these times. Both the mining and pottery industries which were the chief forms of local employment were hazardous to health. A first consideration though, would always be to establish if there were any suspicious circumstances. If there was the slightest suggestion of anything unusual the CID would have to attend and satisfy themselves that there was nothing untoward before 'muggins' could get the paperwork done.

Sometimes, in the case of an elderly person dying alone at home, quantities of cash would be found in the house. All this would have to be carefully collected, recorded and kept safely at the police station to be later handed over to the next of kin.

Such was the case one summer Sunday morning. I had been on fatigues, which meant that I had to slop out the cells and cook everybody else's breakfast – Ethel or Elsie did not work on Sundays. I was now becoming fairly accomplished at cooking the breakfasts in the manner which was apparently an age old tradition. This entailed frying the entire meal on the metal, white enamelled plate from which it would be eaten. I'd had only one complaint that morning, which was from Dennis, the senior shift PC, who seemed as old as my grandad.

"I don't remember my missus putting these black bits in for my snappin'," Dennis remarked.

Everyone's breakfast had to include North Staffordshire oatcakes and melted cheese. If it didn't then you were clearly a stranger.

I was chomping through the last mouthful of my own breakfast, when Sergeant Turner came in.

"Pork, there's a Form 12 to be dealt with down at West End. It's an old lady dead in the bedroom, looked a bit dodgy at first, but everyone seems satisfied it's okay now. The CID are still there at the moment. I want you to deal."

"Okay, Sarge," I said, trying to be as nonplussed as possible whilst inside my head I was thinking, *Why me again?* This would mean working overtime, which we didn't get paid for.

I arrived at the house at half past eleven and found Dave the detective was there with the mickey-taking detective named Joe. The police surgeon, Dr Wood, was also there. Dr Wood was an ordinary GP who was also employed by the police. He would carry out various medical tasks such as certifying death and examining and patching up prisoners. He would get called out at night time to take blood samples in breathalyser cases and that kind of thing. Doc Wood – as he was known – lived nearby in a street of rambling Victorian houses and always had a slight aroma of whisky about him. I climbed the stairs to the bedroom where I could hear the voices. Dave greeted me.

"Hi, Pork, you're dealing then?"

"Yes, Dave," I said, with a resigned expression.

"Another balls-up then, Porky," chimed in the sarcastic Joe. But I'd already learned to ignore him.

The old lady lay fully clothed on her back on the bedroom floor. Doc Wood was bending down near to her with his legs shielding her head from my view.

"I'm satisfied that she's died from natural causes," said the doctor, "obviously there will be a post-mortem, but I should say it will be a heart attack."

As the doctor stood up I was horrified to see the woman's face and throat coated in what seemed to be thick congealed blood. The doctor looked around at me and, seeing my expression, spoke calmly. "Oh, don't worry about this, officer, there are no injuries. This is the lady's stomach contents that have come up, which can happen. I think she's been eating beetroot."

My God, I thought, visualising the row of jars of beetroot my dad had put on the pantry shelf only the week before. *I'm not sure I'll touch the stuff again.*

"Right then, Pork," said Dave. "Doc's certified death at quarter past eleven and we've had photos taken just in case. We've had to move the body about from its original position a bit for the doctor. All the doors and windows were secure," he continued, "everything seems okay. There's a lot of money about and no relatives on hand, so PCs Banks and Mack are downstairs starting to make an inventory of the cash. The ambulance is on the way to collect the body, so we'll leave you to it."

"Can you write Porky?" came the expected remark from Joe.

"Yes thanks, getting the hang of it now," I replied, as I followed the three back downstairs.

I entered the front room where the other two officers were searching for the cash as the doctor and detectives made their way out through the front door.

PC Dougie Banks, a senior PC, and PC Steve Mack, fresh from Ryton, were both rummaging through cupboards and drawers.

"There's a lot of cash about, Porky!" exclaimed Dougie. "It looks like she's been hoarding her pension money up; most of these haven't even been opened," he said, as he showed me a handful of little brown pension envelopes. "We're up to £230 already."

There hadn't been much happening that morning, so I wasn't surprised when another officer arrived at the scene to see if he could help out. It was Sam, the panda driver.

"Hey up, need anything doing?" Sam enquired.

"Well, there's cash everywhere, so we've got to search every room," I replied.

"Okay," said Sam, "I'll start upstairs then. Has the body been moved?"

Being engrossed in what I was doing and only thinking of Dave's information that they had disturbed the body slightly for the doctor, I unthinkingly answered, "Yes."

I subconsciously heard Sam tramping up the stairs and a few seconds later dived towards the hallway as a loud yelling came from upstairs. This was immediately followed by an almighty crash as Sam leapt from the top to the bottom of the stairs. He landed against the front door smashing a jardinière that contained a huge cheese plant.

Lying on his back Sam looked up at me with his terrified face covered in soil and leaves. "There's another one up there with its throat cut," he spluttered.

I had to buy Sam a pint next time on late shift to make up for my misuse of police jargon.

TWELVE

ON ANOTHER Sunday morning, when still new to the job, I was told to visit a house on Leek Road. It was in the middle of a row of other terraced houses and close to the railway line.

The chap who lived here hadn't been seen for a few days and a neighbour was worried as yesterday's milk was still on the step. The circumstances had a familiar ring to them. I tried the usual knocking on windows and doors, but all to no avail. Eventually, on the second attempt, I shouldered open the rickety front door. The now familiar, sickly sweet smell of death met my nostrils as the door swung open revealing a tiny and gloomy hallway. Evidence of a lonely, elderly person was everywhere; faded family photographs, clutter and dead flowers. I pushed open the door to the darkened front room where the heavy dust-laden curtains were pulled together and switched on the light to reveal a horrifying scene.

The long-since dead man lay on the carpet, a thin and shrivelled excuse for a human being. Red spatters of blood covered most areas of the pale yellow wallpaper, and some splatters could even be seen on the lampshade. The body lay on its back staring wide-eyed and open-mouthed at the ceiling. Around the corpse was a black outline which was vaguely in the same shape as the outstretched body. On the left wrist could be seen a blackened indentation.

As I moved a little closer my foot squelched down into a part of the black outline – this was blood, thick congealed blood. The only recognisable red blood was that which had been spattered around by the man in his death throes. A razor blade could be seen still pinched between the fingers of his right hand. A brief pencil written note stood helpfully on the mantle shelf against the clock. It simply read:

I can't go on any longer.

The black indentation in his wrist was the site where he had lacerated his veins and arteries, first starting with tentative cuts and building the courage to cut deeper. My radio report brought the attendance of the CID, Doc Wood and a police photographer. A sergeant and an inspector also paid a visit. An hour passed before I was left to get on with the paperwork.

It was fairly late in the day before the ambulance service arrived to take the body to the city mortuary. I'd had some difficulty tracing a relative to perform the identification and was relieved to hear that a cousin had finally been found in Newcastle-under-Lyme. I arrived back at the police station to be told that, as it was a Sunday, there would be no mortuary staff on duty. I was instructed to collect the keys from Hanley Police Station to get the job done. My eyes must have widened with concern as I was given more information on what this entailed. I had to unlock the deserted mortuary, find the body and get the relative to identify it. I was a little relieved when I discovered that I would at least have the company of young policewoman, Jacky, to help me through the task.

Together with the relative, a middle-aged and rather nervous chap, we made our way by panda car to Hanley Police Station. I dashed inside and found the station sergeant.

"Sarge, PC Pye from Stoke. I've got to do an ID at the mortuary, so I need the keys."

"Yes, I've been told to expect you. Have you done this before?" he asked, furrowing his brow.

"No, Sarge, I don't even know where it is."

"Right, here you are." He handed me a bunch of large keys on a giant steel ring weighted down with a lump of shiny lead. "Each key is numbered and all you have to do is look for the corresponding number on the door. The rest of it is simple," he finished with a wry smile.

Following the directions and thankful of such intricate and helpful advice (I don't think), I drove around the back of the police station.

Thoughtfully positioned, right next door to the abattoir, stood the dilapidated, crumbling Victorian building that served as the mortuary for the City of Stoke-on-Trent.

I asked the relative to sit tight in the police car whilst Jacky and I got things ready for him. Spying the number ONE on the outside door, I rummaged through the bunch to find the right key. The tall, green painted door swung open easily and we found ourselves in a small porch with another locked door, this one with the number TWO on it. After another three doors, we arrived inside a bleak, white-tiled, lofty echoing room. Four huge, eight-feet high, cream-painted fridges stood against one wall, making a constant unnerving humming sound.

In the centre of the room stood a vast, porcelain slab which was used for performing post mortem examinations. In a corner against a wall rested a heavy-duty, metal surgical trolley. A large metal table was in another corner and a galvanized metal bucket stood nearby with a wooden handled mop poking from it. Two pairs of white rubber wellingtons lay near the bucket.

"What do we do now, Jacky, any clues?" I asked.

"No," came Jacky's shaky reply. "I've not been before either, and wish I wasn't here now."

I resigned myself to the fact that the job had to be done, walked over to the first of the fridge doors and pulled down on the handle. The heavy door swung silently open and was followed by a small cloud of cold-air vapour, which tumbled out and down towards our feet. Inside the fridge were four sturdy looking tubular metal trays mounted one above the other. Lying on the top three trays was a white, linen covered cocoon, in the shape of a corpse.

"Oh, God," I said, "which one's ours? I mean, how are we supposed to know?"

"I don't know," Jacky said with a slightly trembling voice, "but surely they're labelled?"

"Yes, they must be," I agreed, and peered down inside the fridge alongside one of the bodies. "Yes, I think you're right, there's something tied around this one's feet." I tugged at the tray and it felt it effortlessly move toward me a few inches with a metal castor sound similar to my old roller skates. The cocoon's head now stuck out of the fridge. "That's it!" I exclaimed, delighted that my discovery of how to pull a human body from a fridge appeared to be the nicest thing that had happened all day.

Confident that we would soon be able to complete our task, we stood either side and pulled. The tray rolled out with ease until about three feet was left inside the fridge. Suddenly, and without warning it slid completely out and downwards. Both Jacky and I dived for our lives as the immensely heavy tray and body crashed to the ground. We both looked at each other open-mouthed, wide-eyed, in total disbelief and despair. It was a full minute before we started to pull ourselves together and realised that we should have wheeled the metal trolley under the tray. The small hydraulic arm on the side was to raise its height so that the tray could be pulled out onto it. Too late for that now though, as the body of who knows who lay on the floor and had partially parted company with his metal tray.

The only solution appeared to be for the two of us to load the body back onto the tray and slide it into the remaining lower empty slot. With considerable difficulty this is what we managed to do. After all our efforts, when we opened the fridge next to the one where we'd been playing 'musical bodies' we discovered that the suicide victim was there. He had not been wrapped in a linen cocoon and was instantly recognisable. Only the bodies which had been the subject of a post-mortem had been cocooned. Because this one arrived on a Sunday when there were no mortuary staff on duty he had simply been put into the fridge by the ambulance team to await attention the following day.

We completed our task in a rather unsatisfactory way by merely pulling the front of the tray partially out of the fridge. We then invited the relative to come in and complete the identification, a duty which the poor man duly carried out.

It wasn't until we got back to Stoke, that we discovered that we should have used the trolley to roll the tray through a small aperture in the wall. This would have placed the body in the Mortuary's private Chapel of Rest (of which I had no idea existed). After draping the body with a purple robe (of which I also knew nothing about) the relative should have been invited in to perform the identification. We both spent a few anguished days wondering if any of the mortuary staff would notice that someone had been moving bodies around.

I had been lucky with my posting to Stoke, which allowed me to live at home with my parents, but my old schoolmate Roger had drawn the short straw. He had been sent to Burton-on-Trent. It was over forty miles from Newcastle and had utterly changed his life. He had to live in digs in Burton and had a landlady who was horrible to him.

Roger told me that on his first early shift he should have been at the police station for 5.40 a.m. and he had overslept. He quickly threw on his uniform and then ran out of the house into the street in a panic. It then became very clear to him that he wasn't absolutely sure where the police station was. Imagine the dumbfounded look on the face of the passer-by when a uniformed policeman ran up to him asking for directions to the police station!

Speaking for myself, I'd got the hang of getting up quietly for early shift by now, and so far I'd always been in good time. Poor Roy, on the other hand was hopeless; he was late every day. He'd moved out of his parents' home and was living with his large girlfriend somewhere in Longton. He had no telephone and if he overslept we'd have to ring Longton Police Station and ask them to go and knock him up. There were lots of jokes as to why he was late: *He was trapped beneath the girlfriend,* was one overused quip.

At half past five, one frosty winter's morning, I pulled into the car park and manoeuvred up to the green wire fence. It was bitterly cold and still dark. A council gritting wagon trundled past, amber light flashing, spraying rock salt everywhere except on the road. I waved to the driver and made my way up the front steps and into the nick. I couldn't believe my eyes – there was Roy. Not only was he NOT late, he was actually EARLY!

"What are YOU doing here, Roy? Have you changed shift? Are you on nights?" I joked.

"Very funny," Roy said, sneering a little with annoyance. "No, I made a special effort. I hitched a lift on the gritting wagon."

Sergeant Turner strode into the parade room holding the duty pad in his hand. He staggered against the wall in emphasised sarcastic astonishment clutching his heart as he saw Roy.

"It's a bloody mirage, I dunner beleeeve it."

"Special effort, Sarge, got a lift on the gritting wagon!" Roy proudly exclaimed.

Sergeant Turner flipped the pages of the duty pad back and forth squinting over the top of his glasses and furrowing his brow.

"Well, Roy, special effort it certainly is, because you are three and a half hours early, you shouldn't be here till nine o'clock, they't in court!"

Roy went up to the snooker room for a sleep until he was due to start at nine, but I think the laughter probably kept him awake.

Our forty-five minute meal breaks on the noon shift would sometimes be fish and chips from one of the local chippies. Watch out though. If Inspector Wild Bill Holdcroft caught you openly carrying your goodies in uniform you could even get put on a charge for something as simple as this. I cottoned on to how we got round the problem when I saw PC Dougie Banks climb the station steps for his meal break one evening. Steam could be seen drifting from the two small vent holes in his helmet. Dougie removed his helmet to reveal a newspaper package of fish, chips and mushy peas.

There was a large wet-fish wholesaler in a back street off the town centre. We used to buy fish from them cheaply, so it wasn't a rare thing to see someone unloading a helmet full of wet fish to take home.

I remember seeing Sergeant Turner walking back towards the nick along Glebe Street one evening just before Christmas. He was wearing his helmet and cape, and I thought that he looked even more rotund than usual. As he drew closer I could see the two legs of a very substantial turkey poking through the front of his cape. After unloading his cape he then emptied his helmet of four large pieces of Finnan haddock.

THIRTEEN

I WAS NOW getting into the swing of things with the shifts. I enjoyed nights; there was always the chance that something exciting might happen. I got on well with the rest of the shift and had managed a good number of arrests by now, mostly for everyday stuff like shoplifting, drunkenness and fighting. We were in the depths of an icy winter and I'd never realised until then how cold it could be at night. All that harsh weather uniform that Mr Ryan, the stores' manager, had heaped upon me was now much appreciated.

I was on town centre foot patrol. There could be as many as six constables patrolling the town centre on nights, each with a different beat to look after. I was on Number One beat and so my radio ID, (or call-sign) was 'Sierra One'. The police station call-sign was 'Lima Alpha'. Correct radio procedure was supposed to be followed with full use of the call-signs. At the end of each transmission you had to use the word 'OVER', indicating that you had finished speaking.

It had been a quiet evening so far. I'd had to turf someone out of the Talbot pub, and had dealt with a domestic in Water Street on the outskirts of the town. A bloke had been having a right argument with his missus over him coming in drunk, and the neighbours had called the police. So there I was, not yet twenty and looking about fifteen, telling these people who were the same age as my parents how to behave. I told the bloke that it was about time he grew up. Anyway… 'all quiet on departure' (no, I didn't cuff it).

As I came out of the house I spotted Bill waiting in the shadows across the road. He was still keeping an eye on me.

"Okay, Pork, you handled that all right," he said.

We strolled back to the town centre chatting. Bill must have been listening outside the window, as he seemed to know everything that had gone on. We separated on to our different beats as we neared

Church Street. It must have been about four thirty as I strolled alone along South Wolfe Street. The main post office which stood halfway along was a beautiful old building called Majestic Chambers. This name was carved into the stonework over the main door. All the windows, which were of the small mullion type, were opaque, apart from one. This, Bill had pointed out to me, was a special window designed for no other reason than for the night duty policeman to look through. The windowpane was the same as the others, but the centre of the glass was a clear polished circle, so that we could look through. It was of course known as 'The Policeman's Window'.

The window gave you direct line of sight to a small mirror on the ceiling through which you could see the big safe. It was supposed to be checked several times on nights. Each time I approached the policeman's window my imagination would race. *What would do if I saw a shadowy figure sticking the gelignite onto the safe, ready to 'blow it'?* It never did happen.

It was so cold that night that I must have been wearing nearly all my uniform. Two pairs of socks, boots, trousers, a vest, shirt, pullover and jacket. The Tropal lining that I had thought was a bullet-proof vest was snugly fastened under my greatcoat. My helmet, gloves and a scarf finished off the ensemble. I was cven wearing a pair of long johns… everybody wore them on nights in winter, but nobody ever admitted to it – they were really warm!

I was further laden down with my long rubber torch, my staff, handcuffs and my two radios.

One of the radios was for receiving messages and you would wear this clipped to your lapel; the other was for transmitting, which you'd keep in your pocket. It had a button on the side, which you pressed when you wanted to speak. A little spring-loaded aerial would shoot up, which you'd push

back in when you'd finished. I was only ten stone four pounds wet through, but now must have weighed in at fourteen stones. I could barely shuffle along, but I was warm.

As I came to the darkened back entry to Woolworths I stepped into the gloom to check all the rear doors. I'd noticed earlier that the fruit and veg man had been and made his delivery. He just used to pile the boxes up outside the rear entrance. It was asking to be pinched, so it came as no surprise when Sergeant Turner had told us at the beginning of the week that someone had been helping themselves. As I shuffled away towards Kingsway, I caught a glimpse of a distant figure. It was the first person I had seen for ages, and I slid into a doorway and watched as he drew closer. It was a young man wearing the familiar white overalls of a pottery worker and carrying a small knapsack over his shoulder.

A cigarette machine was fitted to the outside wall of Preedys tobacconists opposite my hiding place. The man stopped by the machine, fiddled with the lever, looked up inside the slot and then started to pull at the top of the machine. He didn't try hard and stopped short of doing enough for me to arrest him, but he was definitely up to no good. Should I nab him now and at least find out who he was?

As I considered my dilemma, he crossed the road and started to walk away up South Wolfe Street, with the occasional furtive backwards glance. I sneaked across the road and slithered into a doorway, now certain that I was about to witness the commission of some heinous crime. Spying my chance to gain further ground I tiptoed, helmet under arm, into yet another entrance and peered carefully out. YES, there he was at the back of Woolworths rummaging through the wooden crates. This was the Woolworths fruit thief actually in the act!

"Sierra One to Lima Alpha control – Over," I whispered into my transmitter. My fumbled attempt to turn down the volume on the receiver was hampered by my heavy duty gloves. I didn't want the answering voice to alert my quarry.

"Yes, Pork, what's up – Over?" crackled back Sergeant Turner's voice, barely audible.

In my hushed tones I hastily outlined the situation and then decided to move in closer. Fit as I was, I wouldn't be able to run fast weighed down under all the clothing and equipment. Stealthily, I moved up another ten feet or so and moulded my bulbous blue serge into another recess. I could now clearly see the shapes of apples and bananas being stuffed into the knapsack. I still had some fifty feet to go before I was within grabbing distance and the evil deed now appeared to be finished. The young man slung his bag over his shoulder and started to walk nonchalantly away in the direction of Minton's pottery.

I now commenced a running, tiptoeing, darting into doorways strategy. This lasted about five seconds before the youth turned and spotted me in full tiptoe without a suitable refuge in which to dart. I was caught – seen – spotted, right in the middle of the pavement. I stopped dead with one foot still off the ground and onc arm outstretched holding my radio. The thief also stopped – mouth open and arms in the air. I almost expected him to point at me and send me back to the end of the street. It was a bit like playing 'statues' as a kid. But he didn't send me back… in one swift movement he had turned and was in full flight.

As I slowly started to gain traction with the pavement I blurted some garbled message over my radio. I could not seem to get going, I was so laden down with clothing and other cumbersome items. My staff in its special trouser pocket was clonking against my right knee and I could hardly lift my legs up with my greatcoat buttoned. I threw away my helmet and caught a glimpse of it bouncing across the road as I started to pick up speed, then a glove went, then another. I was fast approaching the end of South Wolfe Street and the swiftly disappearing figure had turned right.

By this time I was travelling at an alarming speed and seemed to have to bank over as I negotiated the corner. A familiar looking figure came into view as I hurtled onwards. The dark blue uniform and peaked cap the man was wearing filled me with smug confidence. *What a stroke of luck… one of the lads, he's bound to gather what's happening and cut the thief off.* But NO… as the fruit thief sped away from me the figure just stopped and gazed open mouthed.

"You prat," I bellowed, as I steamed along, "why didn't…" It wasn't a policeman at all. It was a bus conductor. It was time to lighten my load a little more. As I closed in on the bemused bus conductor I threw my heavy rubber torch in his general direction.

"Look after that," I spluttered.

The long black torch flew from my hand with the velocity and accuracy of a heat-seeking missile and homed in on the bus conductor's testicles. I heard the dull thud as it embedded itself between his legs, and saw him crumple to the ground as I sped by like a runaway train.

The Woolworths' fruit thief had escaped. I gave up the chase about two hundred yards away in Spark Street. It took me another two hundred to come to a stop, and he'd vanished. When I finally got back to collect my belongings I found the conductor sitting on the pavement still hunched over with both hands buried down his trousers.

"You bloody well hurt me," he said, looking up and grimacing.

"Sorry, mate."

Roy hadn't been too well of late. He'd been trying hard to get to work on time as he'd had several warnings and was concerned that he could be sacked. He looked pale and was making a bigger botch of things than normal. We reckoned that his girlfriend wasn't feeding him properly, or was wearing him out.

"You look like death warmed up, Roy," I commented as I made my way up the station steps looking forward to the pile of chips that were burning the top of my head. It was a noon shift on a Wednesday, and Roy was going back out on his town centre patrol after his own meal break.

"Yes, I feel a bit off, something I ate."

I scoffed my chips and after potting two reds, a yellow and the white in an attempted game of snooker, made my way down to the enquiry office to see if there were any jobs for me.

"Yes, Pork, a death message in Bath Street, the details are on the pad," instructed Sergeant Turner.

He'd hardly finished his sentence when Roy's voice came over the office radio.

"Sierra Two to Lima Alpha… Over."

"Yes, Roy, go ahead… Over," returned Sergeant Turner.

"Sierra Two to Lima Alpha, can you send me a car down to Campbell Place, please, Sarge… Over."

"Yes. What's the problem, Roy?... Over."

"I… I… I… wonder if you could send me a panda car down to Campbell Place, please, Sarge… Over."

"Yes, Roy, I got that bit, but what's the problem?... Over."

"Sierra Two to Lima Alpha, can you get a car down to Campbell Place, please, Sarge… Over."

"YES, ROY, but WHAT is the problem?... OVER."

"I could do with a lift into the station, please, Sarge. Could you send me a car down?... Over."

"For the final time, Roy, WHAT is the problem?... OVER.

"I've shit myself, Sarge… Over."

It wasn't too long after this when Roy decided that the police wasn't for him and packed it in. I don't know what happened to him after that. It was rumoured that he'd got a job with the council working on the gritting wagons so perhaps that helped him to get to work on time.

A few weeks after Roy's unfortunate accident, a Spring afternoon in 1970 my radio directed me to deal with something else that I hadn't bargained for when I joined the job.

"Go to Liverpool Road Porky," instructed Sergeant Turner. "A swarm of bees has landed on a car."

My first thought had been: well what the hell am I supposed to do about it?

As I arrived at the scene I was astonished to see a large crowd had gathered. They were watching (from a considerable distance) a huge swarm of bees, numbering tens of thousands. It had completely engulfed the cab of a bright yellow Morris Minor pick-up van.

I later discovered that swarming happens when the colony grows in size and the older Queen leaves, to be followed by more than half of the worker bees.

I was surprised to learn that this was not that unusual and that the details of local beekeepers were kept at the police station. The expert soon arrived and seemed remarkably pleased and enthusiastic about the affair. This turned out to be the easiest piece of crowd control I was ever to be involved with. The gathered watchers, were all clearly interested in what was happening, but as the bee keeper made his approach the buzzing increased to a low roar and they needed no prompting to move back.

Armed with only a wallpapering brush and protected with nothing more than a net covered Stetson hat, he laid out a large white sheet on the road. He then delicately but swiftly brushed the dark brown mass into a large cardboard box. For a moment the bees went crazy and both the crowd and I seriously considered a further retreat from our ever more distant view point.

What happened over the next fifteen minutes was astonishing, as almost every bee seemed to be drawn into the box by the presence of the Queen.

The keeper then slowly closed the lid on the box making the gap narrower and narrower. When he was satisfied that he had collected all that was possible he taped the lid down and popped the box into the back of his van. He drove away with a beaming smile, but not before promising me a jar of honey from the captured bees which he would introduce to one of his hives.

I later learned that swarming bees are often attracted to yellow objects, hence the cab of the pick-up.

The Hollywood pop festival with Grateful Dead onstage. (yes that blow-up at the side of the stage is supposed to be what it looks like!)

On Saturday 23rd and Sunday 24th May 1970 one of the country's first open air pop concerts took place in a farmer's field in an area known as Hollywood, near the village of Madeley. It was a spot I knew well and only a few miles outside my home town of Newcastle-under-Lyme. The event attracted forty-five thousand people. Some famous names were on the bill including Mungo Jerry, José Feliciano, Keith Moon, Spencer Davis, Black Sabbath, Grateful Dead, Eric Clapton and many more.

I was ordered to do a special duty (paid overtime!) for one of the days and spent a pleasant afternoon strolling around chatting to students and hippies. There was little trouble and not much for us to do except wander about and enjoy the entertainment. I can remember seeing a young student girl sitting in front of her tiny little tent playing a guitar during a lull in the real entertainment. She sang a bluesy soulful version of Gershwin's 'Summertime'. She was brilliant and got a well-deserved round of applause from me and two other constables; I always think about it every time I hear the song... maybe she became famous.

It was amazing how little trouble there was throughout the two-day event, with only a couple of minor theft reports and two suspected drug overdoses.

FOURTEEN

HAVING NOW served almost twelve months, I was overdue for my one-month attachment to the Criminal Investigation Department.

I knew most of the detectives, a real mixed bunch, but mostly long serving and experienced. Detective Inspector Tommy Dodd was the man in charge and chain-smoked small cigars. He seemed to know all the personal details of every crook on the patch and was obsessed with detail.

I'd had a suit from Burton Menswear especially for this month. All the detectives wore suits and Burtons, as it was known, was the place for cheap, off-the-peg clothing back then. My first job was predictably making a large pot of tea. I'd now had plenty of practice and as the grilled tea story had not reached Stoke this went without a hitch. We had a one gallon metal teapot and the ritual was to pour the milk into the teapot rather than individually into the cups. It was hard luck if you particularly preferred weak or strong tea.

I was given my own desk complete with wire IN and OUT trays. I noticed that the IN tray was already distorted from the bulk of papers, documents and brown folders that were stuffed into it. As I started to sift through the six inch wad, I quickly realised that this was all the time-consuming, boring work that no one else in the office wanted.

"Yes, it's not all robberies and burglaries, there's tons of that rubbish," commented Dave, whose desk was opposite mine.

"Hmm," I said, "it's going to take me the whole month just to get through this lot."

"Well, no time for that now," Dave said, "I've had some info. Davis's Bottling Stores is going to get screwed this evening by Edward William Ray C.R.O. With a bit of luck, we're going to catch him in the act."

It was almost 10:30 p.m. as Dave drove the battered Ford Anglia CID van onto the waste land at the side of Davis's Bottling Stores in Leese Street. For some unknown reason our CID van had no gear knob, just a gear stick with a sharp end on it, which gave you a sore left palm. The whole area was littered with run-down and partly demolished buildings. Davis's, was still operational, but was no exception to the derelict looking theme. Two heavy-looking six feet high wooden gates hung at a slant between the crumbling brick pillars which formed part of the high brick perimeter wall. Crazily tilted skyscrapers of wooden beer crates were silhouetted above the wall; Davis's was a drinks supplier to pubs and clubs.

"Let's get in here," Dave whispered, pushing me into the yard of an abandoned house.

As I peered over the wall, I could pick out the gates in the dim light of a street lamp.

"When's it going to happen, Dave?" I asked, expecting a long wait.

Dave checked his watch with a quick flash of his torch.

"Well, it's gone closing time, so any time now."

The words had barely left his lips when a figure rounded the corner at the top of the deserted street and slid into a doorway.

"Right on time," whispered Dave.

A silhouetted head peered around the doorway, looked one way and then the other, before creeping unsteadily along against the wall in the shadows. My heart was now pounding with excitement. The figure stopped by the gates, lurched back and forth, fell against the gates and slumped to the ground. One of the beer crate skyscrapers on the other side was dislodged by the shaking. It swayed as though made of rubber and toppled, sending two crates of empty bottles smashing over and down onto the pavement inches from the drunken prostrate burglar-in-waiting.

Dave shook his head. "Pissed again." He muttered.

"I don't suppose he'll do it now will he Dave, what with all that noise and everything?" I asked.

"Oh, that won't put him off."

The figure staggered to his feet crunching the broken glass underfoot and then piled the two crates on top of each other. With one last look over his shoulder he clambered up and hoisted himself over the gates. There was a sickening dull thump as he landed on the other side, followed by all manner of crashing as several more of the skyscrapers disappeared from view.

After about twenty minutes the gates started to shake and rattle.

"Right, Pork, get ready to nab him," said Dave.

Two hands appeared shakily on the top of the gate. A few seconds later a quivering head popped up and a fierce rattling commenced as the pickled perpetrator attempted to hoist himself upward. The strain of heaving up the weight of his beer soaked carcass, which was additionally laden down by pockets full of bottles was pitiful. A leg eventually swung up to join the hands and head. Ray let out a low almost ghostly moan as the sensation of pain started to filter through the anaesthetic of twelve or thirteen pints.

"Is that him, Dave?" I whispered excitedly.

"What?"

"Is that him… Edward William Ray C.R.O?" I said, trying out my newly acquired police vernacular.

Dave shook his head at me and made no reply. Ray was now astride the top of the gate, perfectly silhouetted against the night sky. Both his hands pushed downwards trying to alleviate the obvious pain caused by perhaps fourteen stones pressing down onto his genitals. The moans turned to a high-pitched squeal as he started to fall to the pavement.

"Right, Pork, go get him."

I shot out of my hiding place like a sprinter from the starting blocks and virtually caught Ray before he'd hit the ground. He didn't struggle – not with fifteen half-pint bottles of Bass and three bottles of Babycham jammed into his pockets. Edward William Ray C.R.O. denied everything, which he always did, even when caught red-handed.

I visited Davis's the next day and took a witness statement from Mr Morley, the warehouse manager. I carefully included all the required detail. I included the time he had left the premises the night before and how he had returned much later after a call from the police. The statement gave all the details of how the property had been broken into and of the several bottles of missing drink. I also detailed that he had noticed that a large pile of excrement had been deposited on the office floor. I was pleased with my wording in Mr Morley's statement: *I discovered a pile of excrement on the office floor, which appeared to be human and of recent origin.*

True to form, Ray pleaded not guilty. The court broke out into stifled laughter as the defence solicitor, George Tiler quizzed poor Mr Morley about his 'expert' knowledge on human excrement. Edward William Ray received three months' imprisonment.

Lenny Fowler C.R.O. wasn't much of a crook either and if it was possible for a criminal not to warrant even one Christian name then this would be Lenny's position. Lenny's forte in life was to be a pain in the neck with his petty crimes. Pinching people's lead waste pipes from outside their kitchens was his favoured trick. Stealing milk from doorsteps, drunkenness and just being a pest summed up Lenny. Consequently, his all-time big heist wasn't too well planned.

The lead he'd decided to steal from a house in Shepherd Street would have been easy money when weighed in at the local scrapyard. Lenny's capture, however, was inevitable, in spite of a certain amount of planning.

He had 'cased the joint' before clambering up onto the top of the bay window of the house and starting to hack away at the lead with a small hand axe. Unfortunately his recce had not been too thorough –

he had not checked the property well – the occupants were at home and watching television!

As the police arrived the annoyed homeowner was standing inside his front door with an anguished looking Lenny staring down, no doubt thinking: *I wonder if they've seen me?* Lenny's getaway vehicle, a large wooden wheelbarrow, was spotted on the pavement right outside the door to the house.

Lenny received a small custodial sentence and after his release it was realised that his wheelbarrow still stood taking up space in the CID property store. A bemused and nervous Lenny was shown up to the CID office to be met with a fanfare as half a dozen detectives loudly hummed the theme tune of the *This Is Your Life* program.

DC Geoff Virgo took up centre stage holding the large red leather bound property register in both hands. He welcomed Lenny into the gathering with a superb rendition of the Irish brogue of 'This Is Your Life' host, Eamonn Andrews.

"Lenny Fowler," twanged Geoff. "You thought you'd come here tonight to collect a wooden wheelbarrow… but tonight… Lenny Fowler… ace lead thief, drunkard and general everyday pain in the arse… This Is Your Life."

The fanfare continued as Lenny was requested to sign for his wheelbarrow.

FIFTEEN

THE CID did not do the same regular shifts as uniformed officers. They usually worked days (nine to five) or lates, but would hardly ever finish duty on time. Someone would also have to arrive at 8 a.m. to start work on any prisoners who had been arrested in the night. There was always a CID officer working a night shift and it was his responsibility to cover the entire division. He would be called back and forth to crimes throughout both Longton and Stoke until his shift was supposed to end at six in the morning.

Police officers didn't get paid overtime back then. Detectives were actually expected to carry on working on a particular job if it was serious, or involved an impending court appearance. They were paid a small addition to their pay called 'Detective Duty Allowance'.

There was always a variety of new jobs to do on each shift on top of all the enquiries that you already had. Each day would bring more thefts, burglaries, assaults and so on, and there were piles of mundane enquiries which filled your in-tray.

As most criminals were known to 'frequent' public houses, (note the use of the police lingo) it was accepted that detectives would visit pubs. Whilst performing this tedious duty, and in an effort to appear inconspicuous it was often (always) found necessary to drink beer. It therefore seemed reasonable that we would receive some recompense at the end of each month for performing this onerous task. This would be covered under the official guise of *cultivating informants* or *making enquiries re burglary*.

Dave often came by juicy info that he'd picked up in one of the local pubs and so I was excited when he beckoned me over to his desk one morning. "Right, Pork… job on this afternoon."

I gathered that this meant we were in for something similar to the Davis's bottling store episode, or hopefully even better.

"You know All Saints Church down West End?" Dave continued.

"Yes," I said exercising my local knowledge. "It's derelict, going to be pulled down."

"Correct," continued Dave. "There's a lot of lead on that church roof, or there *was*. Somebody's been systematically stripping it off every afternoon and weighing it in at Moore's scrapyard. Now I know who that someone is – Gerrard Ivan Derek Bedson C.R.O."

We used Dave's car, as Bedson, a seasoned criminal, knew the registration plates of all the CID vehicles (both of them) off by heart.

It was two o'clock on a bright sunny afternoon as Dave parked his car a short way up Vinebank Street. The pair of us sat in the front seats looking down onto London Road. We had a pretty good view of All Saints Road and the church building. It wasn't long before Dave raised an eyebrow and chuckled.

"He's here, the cheeky bastard, he looks like he's going mountain climbing."

Bedson was a swarthy, well-built, thirty year old who'd been in trouble for everything from parking on the pavement to house burglaries and serious assaults. Here he was in broad daylight striding along the pavement with a large coil of rope slung around his neck. There was a certain audacity about the man as he nonchalantly made his way in through the church gateway. He stopped and looked up at the lofty height of this mammoth crumbling edifice, his intention being to strip away its last remaining valuables. With one furtive over-the-shoulder glance he then disappeared from view.

"I could think of a better use for that rope," Dave muttered, "and we wouldn't even have to take it off his neck. We'll leave him to it for a while, we've got to get him bang to rights or it's a waste of time."

After ten minutes or so we could hear a distant, repetitive, dull banging sound.

"Right, we'll give him a bit longer to be sure that he's cut some pieces off and then we'll take a look," said Dave.

After another ten minutes we left the car and walked over towards the church, looking up towards the towering roof. There was no sign of Bedson anywhere, but the dull *thump, thump, thump* of his hammer and chisel could still be heard coming from somewhere up on high. There was no sign of the rope or any clue as to how he had got up there. The noise seemed to be coming from the valley between two steeply-pitched tiled roofs. Dave explained that the lead would run along this divide to where the tower joined the main building. The church had once been a magnificent structure, but its sandstone block walls were now black due to its lifetime in the Potteries. The stained glass windows had become victims to stones and the graveyard was waist high in grass.

"Okay, Pork, a bit of initiative here, see if you can borrow those ladders." Dave said pointing towards a large, green GPO lorry parked down the road.

Two other detectives, Joe and Derek, had arrived by now.

"Hope you don't mind heights, Porky," said Joe, in his predicable sarcastic manner.

The three GPO men were happy to let me commandeer their enormous, three-storey wooden ladders and even offered to set them up for us. The noise this made seemed certain to alert Bedson as they reversed into the church gateway and clattered the ladders up against the wall. But the dull thumping carried on relentlessly and was interrupted only when Bedson presumably had a little rest or piled up his booty.

The ladders were positioned just below the eaves so that Bedson would not be able to see them, but also because they were at their absolute limit.

"Okay, Pork, up you go then, go nick him," said Dave, grinning.

Oh no, I thought as I started off upwards. Normally I was okay with heights, but this was a CHURCH – it was enormous – really high! The ladders were bending and shaking badly. Visions of the mountain rescue escapade flashed into my mind as I neared the halfway mark. If I was to fall off even at this point I would surely die, so there was no point in showing my fear from now on.

Joe had been positioned at the base of the ladder and gave it a little shake.

"Mind you don't fall, Pork," he called out.

"Cut it out," I replied, "because if I do, I'll make sure I fall on *you*."

Suddenly the thumping stopped, everybody froze. Had we pushed our luck too far with the noise? No, it started again. Bedson still hadn't a clue and was no doubt having another rest.

It was scary when my hands were on the top rung. The slightest movement seemed to make the ladder move in and out, and I had visions of it snapping. I now had to take hold of the edge of the building and climb farther up until my head was poking up above the floor of the roof valley and looking along. It was an immense building. The flat lead covering the floor of the valley was some four feet wide and stretched for about thirty-five feet to where it joined the tower. There, at the far end, was Bedson, with his back to me kneeling down, banging away with a hammer and chisel. Three or four large pieces of lead were piled up on the tiles next to him. I took a deep breath; I was now shaking with fear, but did not want anyone to know.

"OY!" I shouted.

Bedson spun around, still on his knees. He dropped his hammer and chisel and with a look of total disbelief shouted: "F***ing hell, you're tall!"

"Police, you're nicked," I shouted back in a quavering voice.

I wasn't even going to attempt to give him the police caution until I was on safe ground. I was shaking so much I would have got the words all mixed up.

Bedson walked over and casually looked down at my petrified face.

"Want a hand up?"

I hoped that he hadn't decided to kill me. I desperately wanted to get off this ladder and so I took hold of his outstretched hand and he hauled me up onto the roof.

"Thanks," I said, "you know I've got to caution you… you are not obliged to say…"

"Yes, yes," Bedson interrupted, "I know all that crap backwards, mate, no need to bother."

"But how did you get up here?" I asked.

"Through the window then up the steps in the tower," Bedson explained. He nonchalantly pointed towards a small hatch door in the side of the tower. "It comes out there… easy."

How pleased I was to hear this, as there would be no way in the world I could have climbed back over the eaves and down onto the ladder. I had resigned myself to living out the rest of my life on top of a derelict church.

I directed Bedson down by his own much safer route and he was then rather unnecessarily handcuffed and taken away. I remained on the roof and following Dave's instructions went back to the pile of cut lead and selected the smallest of the pieces to use as evidence. It was a tremendous weight and I had to drag it the full length of the roof valley. Joe was standing below right in the line of fire, but I thought better of it and shouted a warning before heaving the mass over. It landed with a dull *flop* as it hit the concrete. I gave a sigh of relief when I finally made my way back down to the ground, via Bedson's safe route. No one on the day ever found out how terrified I had been.

At the court hearing several weeks later, the stipendiary magistrate, Mr Geoffrey Smallwood, was visibly seen to stifle a laugh. The comedy of the situation was almost too much for him as I related from my pocketbook Bedson's reply… 'F***ing hell, you're tall'.

One of the cases I had to investigate during my first CID stint was a series of indecent exposures. These had been happening around the Hancock Street area. The 'flasher' always wore an imitation sheepskin coat, and reports suggested that the same man was now responsible for up to five incidents. He had typically become known in the CID as the 'Hand Cock Flasher' and it was usual for him to do this first thing in the morning when he could be sure of catching the pottery girls on their way to work. His last offence had gone a step further as he had caught hold of a girl by the arm and there were worries that another attack could be even worse.

I'd made an early start that morning to do 'Obs' (observations) and was hoping to catch the culprit. It was half past seven as I wandered along trying to look inconspicuous with my Burton's suit hidden beneath a duffel coat. I strolled to the end of Hancock Street and slipped in under one of the Seven Arches railway viaduct alcoves with my snapping bag (sandwich bag) over my shoulder. I was hoping to look like just another pottery worker.

Then I spotted him – mid-thirties, five feet seven, receding fair hair, overweight and wearing that all-important imitation sheepskin coat ('medium' did not enter into his description). It all fitted. This was the man. I radioed in and alerted the station to what was happening. A flurry of radio activity followed as other patrols were warned. I didn't want to allow the suspect to go as far as upsetting another girl, but would have liked additional evidence. I couldn't be absolutely certain this was the man at this stage but I'd got enough to nick him whether he flashed or not.

Suddenly the suspect bobbed out of view into an alleyway at the side of the houses. This was exactly what he had done before – it was his MO – he'd always flashed at a girl from an alleyway as she'd walked past. Then a new figure caught my eye – a pretty twenty-year-old blonde complete with a shopping bag. She had turned the corner and was heading away from me towards 'Flasher's Alley'. Without doubt this was his target.

I allowed a few seconds to pass before stepping out from my hidey hole and then followed the girl at a discreet distance as she drew closer to where the man was lurking. My eyes drifted towards the end of the street and focussed on a new figure. The outline of a uniformed colleague was unmistakable – PC Hawley from the early shift was heading in my direction and clearly unaware of the unfolding drama.

The flasher had no clue that the net was closing in and had been busily preparing for his latest attack. This action, chiefly involved the unbuttoning of trouser flies, the unfastening of belt and the dropping below hips of trousers and underpants. He peered around the wall to be horrified at the sight of PC Hawley heading in his direction. He could never have known that the constable was oblivious to everything except his impending breakfast.

The panicking flasher darted out into the street clutching at his falling trousers. He stumbled forward in a hopping, jumping gait past the startled girl. He was definitely trying to 'make good his escape' away from the alarmed and puzzled PC Hawley. The Flasher's rapid, but ever-decreasing in-length, staccato steps were now taking him in awkward comedy straight in my direction. I lurched from one side of the pavement to the other, both arms outstretched as he blundered towards me. His jacket and shirt flap billowed out behind him as his trousers dropped ever downwards. PC Hawley was now also chasing the man, but didn't know why.

"POLICE, STOP." I shouted, as the flapping, toppling figure crashed to the pavement in front of me with trousers now below his knees and backside on full view.

"I was only having a piss, Officer," the man gasped in desperation as he looked up at me.

PC Hawley arrived, also panting, but with trousers intact.

"What the hell's going on, Porky?" he shouted.

I described the circumstances to my bemused colleague, who had been told nothing of *Operation Hand Cock*.

The culprit was reunited with his trousers in time for a panda car ride back to the police station. It turned out that he had a string of previous convictions for sexual offences. He was a genuine 'C.R.O.'. Astonishingly he stuck to his story that he had gone to the alleyway to relieve himself, and denied anything to do with all the other incidents. I now had to prove his guilt.

"Right then, Pork, now the work starts," said Dave, "we're going to have to put him on an ID parade."

This was something new. I'd been taught about identification parades at Ryton, but not in great detail as they were really a CID matter. What I had learned from anyone who had ever been involved with an ID parade was that they were a real headache.

"Okay, Dave, what do we do next?"

"*You*," said Dave, "have got to go out on the town and anywhere else that looks likely, and find at least twelve 'stooges' to stand in on the parade. I am going to organise the room and the paperwork. I want you to get the stooges all to report here for say…1 p.m., and remember they must to look a bit like him."

A 'stooge' was, of course police jargon for the people who would stand in on the parade alongside the suspect. The regulations stated that the stooges had to be of a similar description and position in life. It was recommended that they were similarly dressed. So I needed: TWELVE… forty-ISH, five feet seven-ISH, fair-ISH, balding, plump-ISH men with sheepskin-ISH coats!

This was not going to be easy. It would be hard enough just getting twelve look-alikes from the crowd at Stoke football ground on a Saturday. Attempting this feat at ten o'clock on a dull wet morning in the middle of the week seemed more than doubtful. It was also pretty clear that when I told them how much they'd be paid they would NOT be interested – 2/6d, (12.5p) for several hours of their day.

"Here are some lists," said Dave, handing me an orange-coloured folder. "These are pottery firms and other employers who've helped in the past. You could also try the Sally Army as well. Some of the blokes there will welcome the money."

The 'Sally Army' was the Salvation Army hostel in Lovatt Street. The location of this particular hostel for the homeless was, unfortunately, one of the main reasons why the town of Stoke was the gathering place for such a large number of vagrants.

Any new visitor to Stoke would have been surprised, when driving or walking through the town, to see so many drunks and down-and-outs in one small town centre. It was a sad fact that most of them had long criminal records. Many were hopeless alcoholics who had taken to a life on the road, walking between one town and another with a preference for anywhere that had a Salvation Army hostel. Only a few of the chaps were local to the area. The real hardened alcoholics would drink surgical spirit because it was cheap, but you could always tell who had been at it for any length of time as it caused blindness.

Inside the folder were details of other stooge sources: The pottery factories of Minton's, Carlton Ware, Bilton's and others. The wet fish suppliers in Welch Street was listed and few more big employers who had helped out in the past by loaning an employee or two. I duly telephoned through the list, but my persuasive powers mustn't have been too good. I ended up with only three possible stooges, and these would only be used if their descriptions were close.

I trawled the town centre with a uniformed PC, but between us we had still managed only six possible stand-ins in total. A vivid imagination would be required to consider any one of these was even vaguely similar to the flasher.

The captain of the Salvation Army hostel was waiting at the door as we arrived outside.

"I've assembled all the men who wish to help out," he said and showed us through to the canteen.

About a dozen men were sitting at tables or standing about. This was a mixture of the most bizarre specimens of the human race I had yet encountered. But things were now getting desperate and I simply had to get the stooges together. It was almost one o'clock and Dave had already postponed the parade until two. I hastily picked out seven of the men who, it has to be admitted, bore no resemblance to the flasher, and arranged transport for them. You would have thought that the chosen men had won the pools; they were so elated at the thought of earning 2/6d. The remaining downhearted few wandered away.

Back at the nick things were getting busy as people started to arrive and had their details logged by the uniformed inspector whose job it was to actually manage the parade. All the stooges were instructed to line up in the locker room, whilst the photographer, Detective Sergeant Mellor arranged his large and complicated brass and wooden tripod and camera. The regulations stated that photographs had to be taken of the stooges, and then the suspect would be allowed to select his own position in the line-up. He was also allowed to object to any of the stooges.

As the stooges assembled in the line-up, the faces of the detectives and other officers assisting could be seen to be fighting back uncontrollable laughter. This was a bizarre scene as not a single one of the men vaguely resembled each other. Detective Sergeant Mellor, had to leave the room supposedly to fetch some more equipment, but could be heard laughing loudly in the corridor.

The flasher was shown into the room and he selected a place in the line-up in between two of the totally dissimilar Sally Army men. DS Mellor took the final photo, trying his best to control his laughter. All the men in the line-up, including the suspect, blinked and rubbed their eyes as the camera flashed.

The five young ladies were shown in and all picked out the man without hesitation. After the parade, statements were taken and each stooge was paid his 2/6d. This delighted the Sally Army men, but the other men all looked a little disgruntled. The flasher made a full confession and admitted to other offences and indecent assaults he had committed. I gave a sigh of relief because if he had contested the parade I'm pretty sure it would have been thrown out of court.

The photographs of the parade arrived a few days later, so that they could be submitted together with the file of evidence. DS Mellor had thoughtfully included several spares copies, which were immediately posted on the office noticeboard and became a source of laughter for months to come. The main photograph showed that the line-up consisted of two very tall men, one of whom was bald. A short fat man aged about sixty-five stood at one end, whilst a young man with a Beatle haircut took a place next to him. A fifty year old with a gaping mouth filled with bad teeth and a bus driver in uniform were included. The man wearing a polo-necked sweater also had a deformed leg and this made him stand at an odd angle. Other stooges varied in height, weight and clothing. Two of the Salvation Army men were so suntanned from their life outdoors, that they appeared to be of a different race. Right in the middle of the parade was a giant wearing a white boiler suit. To cap it all, it was later noticed that the flasher had chosen to stand in front of the only locker that had a policeman's helmet perched on top. It was like 'X' marks the spot.

It was rumoured that the training department used the photograph for years to come as an example of how NOT to conduct an ID Parade.

SIXTEEN

MY ONE MONTH in the CID was extended to six weeks so that I could clear some of the extra paperwork that had been generated. I'd enjoyed it and felt my future lay in that part of the job, but now it was over. It was back to uniform for me and the regular nights, noons and early shifts.

I was still involved with boxing and represented the division at the Force Boxing Tournament at The Borough Hall, Stafford, on Wednesday, 18th November 1970. I won two hard matches in one night to become force welterweight champion. My arrival back home in the early hours was greeted with my dad's usual comment. "What the hell sort of state was the other bloke like if you won?" – I had two perfectly matched black eyes!

The next day the Chief Inspector told me I was not allowed to go out on patrol until my black eyes had gone. "Can't have you wandering around in uniform looking like that," he said.

I enjoyed the uniform work, even though there were a lot of mundane jobs – so many forms, books and booklets, each one with its own identifying number. A lot of these documents had to be revised following the introduction of decimal coinage in February 1971. This including the payment to ID parade stooges, from 2/6d to twelve and a half new pence.

Great importance was still placed on some things that in the modern world may seem of little significance, such as swearing and dropping litter. If anyone was foolish enough to swear in the street within earshot of a constable they could expect at best the most fearsome and public humiliation possible and at worst – arrest. A similar line would be taken with anyone seen dropping litter.

Many of the jobs that we were expected to do were time-consuming and boring. We even had to check on people's houses when they were away on holiday, or when the property was empty for some reason or other. People would come into the police station in droves as the potters' holidays approached and fill in the small blue cards that were used for this purpose. Predictably the forms were titled, 'Void Premises Forms' and on the back were columns in which we were supposed to record our visits. We had to try to get a few visits listed before the people were due back home. With the pressure of other things there must have been a few imaginary visits as there were hundreds, particularly in the summer.

One of the things about these menial jobs was that you were always out and about, lurking in the shadows, or in some back alleyway. You'd find little known short cuts and get to know all sorts of people. As a result you would spot things that you might otherwise have missed.

I was using up some spare time one evening whilst on foot patrol trying to get a few void premises visits done. It was half past seven and already dark when I emerged from an alley at the back of an empty shop and started to walk down towards the main road. In front of me on the other side of the road was the gloomy and deserted loading bay of Minton's Pottery factory. I was surprised to see a figure, the silhouette of a man, lifting something down from the concrete loading bay shelf. I crossed the road, keeping in the shadows and trying to walk quietly. As I came up behind the bending figure I could see he was shuffling a heavy-looking cardboard box along the ground and against the wall.

"What are you doing?" I demanded.

It might have been the sudden fright of looking up from almost ground level to see this seemingly seven-foot tall helmeted policeman (who was only five feet ten). Perhaps it was the way I demanded an explanation, or maybe it was a bit of both. But as the man spun around and dropped even closer to the ground he immediately, and without any hesitation, shouted out in full voice. "It's tiles… I've pinched 'em… I'm guilty. I'm pleading guilty." This must have been the quickest cough any policeman had ever received.

I wasn't able to appreciate the humour of the situation as something else had caught my eye. Swivelling on the spot I saw a second figure step out from a darkened doorway. The tall, well-built man clicked on a powerful torch as he strode towards us. I took a step backwards and reached for my radio. The thought went through my head that I had interrupted an international gang of tile thieves, who were now about to 'do me over'.

"Where in hell did you spring from?" the man shouted towards me, as he drew closer.

"Who are you, is more to the point?" I quizzed.

"I'm the security man for Minton's," he went on. "This fellow is one of our employees; I've been after him for weeks. I reckon he's stolen enough tiles to do Stoke Baths. I've spent hours trying to catch him and just when I've got him bang to rights, you suddenly materialise in front of me and nick him. I might as well have stayed at home."

Later, a search of the man's house revealed a veritable tile warehouse. He had a nice little side-line in kitchens and bathrooms, which subsidised his job as kiln man.

The security man became a good friend and the security lodge became a 'tea stop'. The tile thief lost his job, but after a short prison sentence went into business full-time as a tiler.

Form number 121 carried the heading 'Complaint Form'. It was a very wide reaching description to cater for everyday minor, but frequent, ongoing difficulties people were experiencing. Footballing in the street became an expected evening time complaint. On many occasions I've used my police whistle to blow full-time and signal the end of a complete eleven-a-side match. Pretty well anything that wasn't actually a crime could go down on a 121; noisy neighbours, thoughtless parking, prowlers and Peeping Toms were all included.

Prowlers and Peeping Toms would generally get more attention than other 121s. Nine times out of ten, the complainant would be a young lady and the offender had located a good vantage point from which to peer. Stories would sometimes filter back from visiting officers and not all of these were written up on the form! There is no doubt that on some occasions a report that: *The prowler was back again*, was actually due to the presence of a conscientious constable taking advantage of a good viewpoint.

Henry Kent was a petty thief and local drunkard. Henry's single Christian name is a clear indicator of his position in the league table of criminals. But he was funny. He was a diminutive figure probably no more than five feet four and as thin as a rake. He would smoke rollups created from flakes of tobacco picked from discarded fag-ends (gutter-flake) which would be mixed with any other available combustible substance. The scrapings from his trouser turn-ups would sometimes be used and it was quite normal for the cigarette to burst into flames and disappear before the first drag was taken.

I was once sent to a scene of traffic chaos in Stoke during the evening rush hour. As I stepped around the corner into Liverpool Road the sound of angry horn blaring filled the air. Henry was standing upright in the centre of the road, blind drunk and apparently fast asleep. He was wearing a tattered evening dress suit complete with a pair of immensely oversized black shoes. The shoes, in point of fact, were not a pair, they were both left feet. This feature was in keeping with Henry's standard 'shoe-theft MO'. The footwear without doubt been stolen from a shoe shop display stand.

I attempted to lead Henry out of harm's way but he seemed riveted to the spot. After a few seconds I decided it would be easier and quicker to lift him by the waist and carry him to the pavement. As he weighed less than nine stones it was a simple task, and in no time I put him back down – still standing upright. I was expecting to hear the sound of the traffic getting back into its stride but quickly about-turned to the sound of several drivers laughing. There, still in the middle of the road from where I had lifted Henry, were his gigantic shoes.

The arrival of 1972 introduced Staffordshire to the motorists' scourge – the 'fixed penalty ticket'. Every constable was supplied with a booklet containing twenty-five of the tickets. These could be issued to motorists or attached to cars when certain minor traffic offences had been committed. A bundle of little plastic bags would also be handed out to us for fixing the ticket to the windscreen of the offending vehicle. The tickets, when they first came out, were for a £2.00 penalty. I guess this must give some insight into how the cost of living has changed over the years.

Copies of all fixed penalty tickets that had been given out by a constable during a 24 hour period had to be submitted for processing before midnight on the day of issue. One little perk on a cold wet evening would be to make out a ticket for an offending vehicle just before the stroke of twelve. This ruse required you to then stroll into the nick to hand in the ticket. It also allowed you to join the office staff for the twelve o' clock brew.

Burglar alarm calls on nights were always enthusiastically attended by patrols and although a lot were false alarms, there was always the chance of a 'hit' resulting in arrests. Each police station had dozens wired directly into their respective enquiry offices (later called control rooms). At Stoke the alarms were all mounted on a six feet square wooden board near the doorway to the cells. Dozens of metal boxes were fixed to it and each box was wired up to as many as thirty different properties. These included banks, clubs, shops, warehouses, and dozens more properties in the area. Every individual alarm had its own set of winking lights and buzzer which would start up if it was triggered. A thick file kept records of activations, false alarms and problems with different alarms. Each alarm had to be tested every morning by flipping the test switch, which caused a buzzer to sound. The buzzers all had a slightly different tone, so with a little musical skill, 'Jingle Bells' or 'Happy Birthday' could be played, and frequently were.

Police station burglar alarm system (in use up until 1980s)

When a radio call went out to a patrol to go to a burglar alarm call during a night shift, it could mean catching burglars in the act. It would not be unheard of for several other cars and even foot patrols to also make their way without even being instructed. This was particularly the case if the alarm was at a pub or club as the licensee would switch the pumps on and serve up a half for everyone.

London Road Sports and Social Club in Shepherd Street had regular alarm activations. Bill Cope, the secretary, licensee and keyholder, lived in a terraced house next door to the club. Bill liked a drink very much indeed and was often the worse for wear when it came to shutting up in the early hours. He was an expert at one-liner jokes and instant summaries on any situation. On many occasions he would press the wrong button on the alarm panel at the club, or leave a door open. In no time at all several keen policemen looking forward to a free half would surround the place.

At two o'clock one Saturday morning the call went over the radio that the burglar alarm was going off at the club. I was only a one-minute sprint away and shouted back that I was on my way. To my amazement as I got there even I had been beaten to it by a panda car and another foot patrol.

Silhouetted intermittently via the blue flashing light of the police car stood Bill. He was swaying back and forth by the club's door holding his left hand to his ear against the deafening ringing of the alarm. In his right hand he held the keys and was making badly aimed lunges at the keyhole. Obviously, in his drunken state, he had made a bodge-job of setting the alarm, but had heard the bell before he'd got in through his own front door.

"Slorry lads, done it again," Bill slurred, as his long-range tactics eventually paid off and the door opened up.

We entered the foyer to the wailing sound of an internal siren, the extreme volume of which threatened to burst eardrums. Bill staggered through to the bottle store where the alarm panel was to be found and his little band of thirsty personal protection officers trailed eagerly behind. With the foyer door closed to keep some of the painful sound out, our eyes settled on where the panel was fixed high up on the wall. This was a metal box complete with pulsating red lights and a small chrome keyhole. The box was issuing yet another, but not so painful, wailing sound.

Bill, only a short man, started to climb up onto a strategically placed metal beer keg on the floor beneath the alarm. On his second attempt he managed to mount the keg and shuffled about, arms waving for balance in his inebriated state. He now had to get the right key into the tiny silver keyhole on the panel. His attempts were similar to his performance with the front door. After a number of poor tries at the keyhole the additional strain on his drunken sense of balance increased his arm waving and leg wobbling tenfold. The empty beer keg now joined in with the vibrations and started to rock back and forth. Bill's imitation of a humming bird seemed likely to achieve unpowered human flight at any moment.

The required co-ordination and balance was far too much for the brain of a drunken man. He lurched forwards, arms desperately scrabbling for any available handhold. The three of us who were nearest instinctively attempted to break his fall, but to no avail. The beer keg shot out from beneath him, suspending him momentarily with legs churning in mid-air as he frantically made a grab for the alarm box.

Bill crashed to the floor, legs still kicking, with the entire alarm box ripped from the wall and now clutched tightly to his chest. A silence came over the room as we all looked down at the prone, but uninjured licensee. The box was still held tightly to his chest with dozens of broken wires poking out of the back and was now emitting a feeble distorted peeping sound.

Bill looked up at us and summed up the situation with his best one-liner to date, "That's f***ed it."

Anyway, we all managed a free half pint. There was a note in the burglar alarm book the next night saying, *London Road Club alarm out of action until further notice.*

SEVENTEEN

SATURDAY, February 12th 1972 had been a bitterly cold day. I pulled my cape around my shoulders for a bit more warmth as I trudged my lonely town centre beat on night duty. A distant church clock chimed midnight signalling the arrival of Sunday. It looked like I was in for a pretty boring six hours before my shift was due to end. There was simply nobody about – that was until a group of middle-aged men came into view. They were hurriedly walking along Church Street on the opposite side of the road. The group were all wrapped up well against the cold and animatedly chatting between themselves.

The strange thing about this was that they all seemed respectable, well behaved and stone cold sober. Most certainly not normal behaviour for a Saturday night. It would have been rather unjust to have stopped and checked them out for being well behaved. I shook my head in puzzlement as they quickly disappeared out of sight. Barely a minute passed when another similar group came into view, heading in the same direction. The quietness was disturbed even further as vans, cars, motorbikes and pushbikes appeared, and more and more people started to emerge from every alleyway and side street. Within a matter of twenty minutes there were crowds of people and traffic jams filling the main roads.

I found myself briskly walking alongside one of the groups as I posed the question: "What the hell's going on?" There was no way they were going to stop or even slow down to give me a reply – they were all on a mission.

The bewildered expression the man gave me, as he answered, implied that that I should already have known. "League Cup Final, application forms for tickets, on sale this morning."

Of course! Stoke City FC had won through to the final of the League Cup and, as they'd never won anything before, this was a big thing for the Potteries.

For some reason, the police hierarchy had overlooked making any arrangements. The car park of Stoke's Victoria Ground was swiftly filling with thousands of people intent on getting their hands on the application forms for tickets.

I radioed the situation in, and after a moment the radio clicked back on with the despairing voice of Sergeant Turner.

"Just what we need. Right, Pork, get around to the car park and I'll start organising more troops."

As I arrived on the large black ash space at the back of the stadium the sight was amazing. There were already thousands of people queuing. Everyone was wrapped up warmly with coats, scarves and gloves. Some had flasks of hot tea and others even had sleeping bags and blankets. Two braziers had been lit by some of the more enterprising fans, who had been there since the Stoke match against Ipswich on the Saturday afternoon.

In no time at all police officers from different stations started to appear, and an inspector took charge of the impromptu crowd control situation. All the traffic patrols had been called in and their crews turned out of the warmth of their patrol cars. By the time the sales started, the crowd had swelled to twenty thousand and every single ticket was spoken for. We were all told that we would have to work overtime until the sales had finished. As we were there anyway, we considered it only fair that we should join the queues and buy tickets for ourselves – so that's what we did.

Temporary lighting had been set up by the traffic boys. It was an amusing sight to see the long snaking queues of overcoat-clad people interspersed here or there with a uniformed policeman. I finished duty at ten o'clock that morning, tired, cold and hungry, but happy in the thought that I would get my two tickets. Another bonus was that we would all be paid overtime for the extra four hours – a rare thing indeed.

I made it down to Wembley with my fiancée, Gladys, on Saturday 4th March that year to watch Stoke win the League Cup 2-1 against Chelsea. What a day!

I was called in for a special duty the next day. I took my place outside Stoke Town Hall in Kingsway as the team arrived in a red and white coach. They had left their train at Barlaston Station, a few miles outside Stoke. The coach journey from there gave the team the opportunity to show the trophy as they passed the thousands of people lining every foot of the way. There were fifty thousand people in Kingsway alone, and I even got paid for the privilege of being there.

PCs Ken Hallam, Alan Stevenson and Alan Steele with the Football League Cup Trophy in Cell number one at Copeland Street police Station.

That same night, worried officials from the triumphant club contacted the police station. There were no proper security arrangements in place at the ground for the safe keeping of the coveted League Cup. They wanted to know if it could be left overnight with us whilst better arrangements were made.

The cup was brought around from the ground and placed under lock and key in one of the empty cells. It was positioned on top of a cardboard box on the floor in cell number one. The big steel door was locked and the viewing hatch kept down, so that it could be checked on every so often.

Later that night when there were no bosses about, the cup was given temporary police bail whilst some of the lads posed for a photograph with it.

At the 2 a.m. meal break, the shift had a brew of tea ceremoniously poured from the League Cup. It was returned to the ground the next day with none of the officials any the wiser as to its recent use – safe custody.

Back in the day Woodhouse Street, Stoke, was the home of Stoke-on-Trent's motor taxation authority offices. There were numerous similar such offices throughout the country whose job it was to keep all the records of motor vehicles registered to owners living in their own particular areas. Each authority was allocated certain two-letter codes and these would form a part of the registration number of the vehicle. By checking the lists, you could tell in which part of the country the car you were interested in was first registered. Stoke-on-Trent, for example, had VT, FA and EH as some of its codes. The rest of Staffordshire used RE, RF and BF. If a crime or incident took place anywhere in the country involving a vehicle, the police would need to find the owner. It would mean telephoning the motor tax office where it was originally registered in order to find out the owner's address. In the case of a car, for example, with the number

OVT 123 the interested police force would have to start with Stoke-on-Trent motor tax office.

It was a long-winded system, which was made even worse if the owner had moved to another area, or lived in another area and had bought the car from someone in Stoke. In such cases the records would no longer be held at Stoke, although the officials there would be able to track down which motor tax office had them.

It could take several days and sometimes even weeks just to find who the supposed registered owner was. If something serious had happened and someone needed to know out of office hours we would have contact the on-call motor tax man. He would then have to go down to the offices and dig out the file. It was always the same chap who was on call. He didn't even have a telephone or a car and so it was a regular job to bang on his door (typically in the middle of the night) and take him down to open up. He'd access the relevant files from a card index system in countless metal filing drawers. He did get paid a call-out fee and did eventually manage to afford a telephone.

In June 1972, I started an intermediate driving course at headquarters. This was the step between the initial driving course that I had completed as a cadet and the coveted advanced course. It was four weeks in length and our accommodation would be in the old and historic Baswich House building within the grounds of headquarters at Stafford.

Downstairs were the driving school classrooms and the most incredible permanent exhibition of *How the Motor Car Works*. This included a 1950s Sunbeam Talbot 90, which had been cut in half to allow an understanding of how things worked.

There were nine of us on the intermediate: three cars, each with a sergeant instructor and a crew of three constables. Other courses, including both the 'initial' and 'advanced' took the number of students up to twenty-seven in nine cars. Motorcycling scholars increased the headcount and so the place was always busy.

There was a lot of classroom work to do as well as driving. We were given a thick blue book with the old Staffordshire County Police emblem on the front entitled, *The System of Car Control.* The book was full of diagrams and definitions which had to be learned off by heart.

On my first day in class I realised there were a few familiar faces. PC John Cornes was a former Stoke City cadet. He had a wide, slightly toothy grin and always had a joke to tell. He spoke with a broad Potteries' accent and called everybody 'youth'. Another old mate was Scottish former cadet, Jock Smart, who had been the first to demonstrate the river crossing method and the importance of pushing your beret down your jeans.

Staffordshire was one of the few forces with its own driving school, and so constables from other forces would also take part. The course was great fun, although mentally and physically taxing. At the end of each day's driving, we all took part in the cleaning and polishing of our car. An inspection and form of drill followed this with each student standing alongside the open door of our highly polished car. On the given command we would attempt to shut all twenty-seven doors with one bang.

Our last week was taken up with several written exams as well as two stressful practical driving tests. The end of the course was heralded at half past four on Thursday 20th July with the simultaneous final door-closing. All that now remained was the announcement of our exam results, which would be given after breakfast the next day. This last evening together would be an opportunity for a laugh and to let our hair down, but was tempered by the hope of good results.

It was around midnight as I drove back towards headquarters with colleague, Alan, a constable from Lichfield. We were laughing over the evening's events as I slowed to a halt wondering why police traffic cars were blocking the main A34 which ran in front of headquarters. We took a detour and drove in through the rear entrance.

"Must be something pretty serious, Alan," I said.

As we entered the old Baswich House and started to climb the stairs, a feeling of gloom descended upon us. There was the sound of muffled voices and sobbing. A terrible accident had happened. John Cornes, Jock Smart and PC Daniel Burnside from Nuneaton, all from the advanced course, had been killed. They had been in a head-on collision with a disqualified driver, who was driving a stolen car. He too had been killed. The news was devastating. These were young fit men with everything to look forward to, good friends who had so much to offer. I was close to tears as I thought how this would affect their parents, and I knew that John, just twenty-two years old, had only recently married.

The following day should have been a time for broad grins and congratulations, as everyone had done well, but the dreadful events dominated our thoughts for a long time to come. So with this awful memory it was back to Stoke and to a little more driving rather than walking.

EIGHTEEN

AS I'VE ALREADY mentioned, the yard opposite the police station was split into two halves by a green wire fence supported by wooden posts. The left hand side was used as our car park, whilst the right was given over to the council employees. They worked from the part of the police station which had originally been built as the Superintendent's house.

This green wire demarcation line frequently became a cause of friction between 'us' and 'them' should either of the two factions stray into enemy territory. The fencing was extremely makeshift and the wooden support posts were merely slotted into holes where a cobblestone had been removed. It swayed about in the slightest breeze, but represented the power of the Iron Curtain.

Inspector 'Wild Bill' Holdcroft was a man who, as his nickname suggested, had a temper. He didn't suffer fools gladly, but was always fair and helpful after he'd first boiled over. He was also one of the most atrocious drivers I have ever known. His manic revving of the engine of his old black Morris 1000 was legendary and often turned alarmed heads when a huge explosion seemed likely. One swift flick of the ankle would follow this display as the clutch was released to catapult the ancient vehicle out from the car park and hurtle it away down the road. He is the only person I've ever seen make a 'Moggy 1000' burn rubber.

It was a surreal sight that met my eyes as I pulled into the yard one morning to see a wide-open expanse of car park. Not a sign of any green fencing or posts anywhere. Was the cold war over? Had the iron curtain been removed? No! The night before some mischievous constable had hooked the fence onto the Inspector's rear bumper.

Eager for a quiet evening at home Wild Bill climbed into his car after a hard day at work. The story has it that he turned the ignition key, revved up to maximum and spun the wheels out of the car park and away down Copeland Street. He took with him the entire fifty feet of fencing and eight five-foot-high wooden posts halfway to Burslem. He remained oblivious to the horn-sounding drivers and arm-waving pedestrians until he was flagged down by a puzzled traffic officer.

Police wages at this time were appalling. We were much worse off than most factory workers. Both new recruits and experienced officers were resigning and taking up anything that was on offer to try to pay the bills. Staffordshire Police lost a lot of staff, who went to work at the Stoke factory of the Michelin Tyre Company. Many of us who remained tried to subsidise our meagre wages by secretly taking on jobs outside our police work. There were a lot of ex-tradesmen who would be out on their days off or between shifts trying to earn a few extra quid. One colleague, who had been a plumber before joining the police, was busy fitting central heating for almost everybody in the division. Another PC doubled as the TV and radio repair man. There were decorators, electricians and someone else who made a few extra pounds selling cut-price Durex.

PC Peter Williams was a uniformed constable in the old Stoke City Force serving at Hanley. He became a successful stand-up comedian in his spare time. But back then it was considered a serious disciplinary offence for a police officer to have a second job. Pete had to be careful where he performed so that the bosses would not find out about his 'other life'. His use of the stage name *Pete Conway* was an essential part of his act in more ways than one. Pete's son followed his dad into show business – Robbie Williams is, of course, an international singing star.

As for me, well I tried to make a few extra pounds by repairing cars together with a couple of colleagues. It didn't last long and we were soon back trying to make ends meet by getting our names down for special duties.

Pete Conway (right) with singing star Frankie Vaughan, doing a bit of dressing up after a police function they had performed at in 1974

The special duties were extra duties in addition to ordinary shifts, for which we would get paid overtime. In normal circumstances we didn't get paid for overtime, but had to record it and have it as time-off instead. Often these special duties came in the form of policing at the football matches of Stoke-on-Trent's two local teams: Stoke FC and Port Vale FC. Other opportunities came with big dances or the appearance of a celebrity entertainer. Stoke's town hall was one popular venue. We all clamoured to put in for this extra work, which would put a few more pounds in our monthly pay packet.

On one occasion PC John Moss and I had been given special duty. The venue for our task was the outdoor swimming pool in the leisure complex of Trentham Gardens on the outskirts of the city. A local entrepreneur had organised the event. The Tremeloes were playing, there was a barbecue and people could use the pool if they wished. It was a red-hot summer evening and the place was absolutely packed with youngsters, all not much younger than we were.

The organiser had told us that it was a condition of the licence granted to him that he must have special duty constables at the event. He explained to us that he didn't really want us on display, as he thought it might spoil the atmosphere. He showed us to a small shed and sat us quietly out of sight, hoping that our services would not be required. It wasn't long before some idiots started throwing fully clothed people into the pool. It was dangerous, as the deep end was well over twelve feet deep. We emerged from our shed to the obvious astonishment of the troublemakers and strolled over to the pool to lay down the law without trying to spoil everyone's fun.

I was in the middle of threatening the trouble makers with removal from the event when I caught sight of my colleague's warning of approaching danger. It was only a half-raised arm and widening eyes, but enough for me to brace myself – I was about to be launched!

The lad seemed to come from nowhere and hit me in the back like an express train. I shot forwards, arms waving for balance, feet trying to get some purchase on the slippery tiles. In the microseconds that this took, I imagined the embarrassment of wallowing about in the pool with all my dignity and authority diminished to zero. No doubt an ear splitting cheer from the crowd would follow. I came to an arms-waving halt right on the very edge of the pool desperately trying to stop myself from going in. The momentum jerked the helmet off my head. It flew through the air and landed several yards out into the water as I continued my bird impressions. I stubbornly overcame the forces and sat down with a bump in a puddle.

As I was down on the ground it seemed likely that I was in for a second attack and quickly sprang back to my feet with adrenalin now joining forces with anger. I was determined to get my attacker and to prove to the baying crowd that this had been a bad move. The young man was away like a rocket as a game of water polo started to develop with my helmet. The chap had little chance of escape as this was one prisoner who simply had to be caught! I was on him within seconds as he violently forced his way through the crowd.

I brought him to the ground in a tangle of arms and legs. *Got him!* I thought, as I fumbled for my antiquated handcuffs. Stars exploded in my head as someone kicked me in the temple. I felt my prisoner being wrenched free from my grasp as his mates pulled him away and another sickening kick slammed into my ribs.

I looked up to see the blurred image of my workmate standing over me and lashing out at the seven or eight thugs who had decided to make the best of the opportunity. It looked bad for a moment as we were well and truly outnumbered, but from nowhere several familiar, determined-looking faces emerged from the crowd and came to our aid. These were all off-duty colleagues from Stoke and Longton, who were making use of the free tickets the management had given them.

My cowardly assassins turned out to be well known for assaulting police officers, and several of them would come to my attention many more times in years to come. A nice young lady returned my prized, but now sodden, Stoke helmet. My attacker, complete with bleeding head, and all the other thugs were taken away to be fined a few weeks later at Eccleshall Magistrates' Court.

It was routine for town centre foot officers to go out in pairs on Friday and Saturday nights until the pubs had closed and the drunkenness and domestics had finished. It was a sensible precaution in view of the violent incidents which were predicable during these times.

Constables on night duty had to check the security of vulnerable property, both before and after meal break. The problem was that the term 'vulnerable property' included pretty well anything that was locked up overnight. This meant that all the shops, business premises, clubs, offices and the like had to have their front and back doors and windows checked. This rather mundane activity occasionally uncovered a previous break-in and once in a while interrupted a burglar in the act.

It was surprising how often you would find the front door to a shop unlocked. Almost every night would result in a back door or window being found wide open. All these incidents had to be reported in by radio. The constable at the police station would then sift through a list of key holders to get the person in charge to come and check the place and lock up. Even a light that had been left switched on, which was out of the norm, would require similar attention.

Every incident that happened in the area covered by that police station had to be recorded in the Occurrence Book (sometimes referred to as the 'OB' or 'Book Number One'). If the previous night's entries included a few reports of insecure premises or unusual lights, it showed that the property was being checked. If there were no such entries, then the day inspector would take a closer look to see if there was some reason why property had not been checked. A busy night with serious incidents could be the answer. One of the worst things that *could* happen was that a 'break' (break-in) was reported after you'd finished duty and that you had not found it. If you appeared to have no excuse, you could expect a telephone call, or even a visit from the inspector, waking you from your sleep, demanding an explanation. It was a harsh regime, but it did mean that you got to know the different areas that you worked like the back of your hand.

One Saturday evening on nights, I was paired up with shift member, Mick. We'd been sent to the Talbot and the Sea Lion pubs to sort out a spot of bother. We'd also had the regular Saturday evening domestic at a house in Lonsdale Street. The ninety-two-year-old father had fallen out with his sixty-year-old son – again! But that was about it. Mick was due for an early finish and offered to help me out with a bit of property-checking for his last hour. "Yes, cheers, Mick, maybe I'll get chance to do a bit of paperwork later, if it stays quiet," I'd replied.

A stroll down South Wolfe Street took us past the post office and gave a chance to peer in through the policeman's window at the safe. We then stepped into the narrow alley that led to the rear of Woolworths. This was always in complete darkness and a torch was vital. There were three levels to check: ground, which was narrow and full of rubbish bins and the other two which meant a climb up the rusty iron fire escapes giving access to various doors and windows.

After starting along the first few yards, I clicked on my torch, but immediately stopped dead in my tracks.... The hairs on the back of my neck stood on end. I was stuck dumb for a second and held out my left arm to prevent Mick going any further. He didn't appear to have seen what I could see! There, clearly picked out in the beam, was the lifeless shape of a woman's leg laid on the ground in the mud. I could see the leg from the knee down sticking out from around the corner; a stiletto heel shoe was half on the foot, the heel broken almost off.

My voice came as a trembling whisper. "My God, Mick, this looks bad."

"Yes, we'd better take a closer look."

I was amazed at his coolness, for I was still trying to collect my thoughts as he strode forwards.

"Slow down, Mick," I gasped. "We must be careful... you know, the evidence, not disturbing anything."

We edged a little closer and then something about the skin texture made me start to think that things were not as they seemed. It was a shop dummy leg used for modelling stockings and shoes. Mick was doubled up with laughter. I was also elated that the situation was not as I'd thought, but couldn't believe the speed of Mick's recovery. I was still in shock, and then the penny dropped that Mick had set me up.

Whilst writing this story I've been reminded many times of the idiosyncrasies which formed an everyday part of being a copper back in the seventies, eighties and nineties. A prominent feature which has stood out is the use between colleagues of nicknames. Many of these probably first had their origins back in the First and Second World Wars. Chalky White, Nobby Clarke, Tug Wilson and dozens more would be examples of these and I knew lots of workmates who were so-named.

There were at least two officers named Dean. They were both quickly nicknamed 'Dixie'. This was a nickname which was cadged from a celebrity. The original Dixie Dean was the Tranmere Rovers and Everton footballer William Ralph 'Dixie' Dean. So yes, we had all of those and some more! My own nickname 'Porky' had been derived from nothing other than my name 'Pye' – I was Porky, but never porky!

The nicknames which stand out are the ones which were cleverly created from a flaw in the subject's character. Perhaps some peculiarity or strange habit would be behind the name. Sometimes a particular failing or even a good quality could be the root. It may have been nothing more than an unusual surname which was waiting to have something humorous attached to it. Here are a few:

'Cutter' – a particular Superintendent who considered himself 'a cut above everyone else.'

'Handbrake Harry' – a Chief Superintendent who put a stop to everything.

WPC Hoyle was known as 'Olive.'

DI Drayton was 'Thirsty' (think about it).

'Bungalow Jack' apparently had nothing upstairs!

The 'Coward of the County' was a constable who was not eager to get involved in a rough house.

The 'Olympic Torch' referred to a PC who 'never went out' (of the Police Station on nights).

There were several Jones', and so the Welsh custom of using their profession as a name was adopted in an altered fashion – 'Jones the Ball' – a good footballer. 'Jones the Beard' – obvious, 'Jones the Ticket' – a constable who was extremely zealous about the issuing of fixed penalty tickets.

'Punchy' – don't mess with this man!

A constable named 'Alfie' was called 'What's it all about.'

'The Poisoned Dwarf' – a disliked and rather diminutive Assistant Chief Constable.

'Satchmo' (after Louis Armstrong) – always blowing his own trumpet.

'Moggerdon Ron' took sleeping pills each night.

'Whicker' (after Alan Whicker) was an officer who claimed to have travelled the globe several times.

'Jungle Jim' served in the Jungle during the war.

'The Electric Pen', was a man noted for his non-stop report writing.

The list of one-liners was truly without end and many require no explanation, but others had subtle foundations: Bodger, Stumpy, Lurch, Chopper, Mr Pastry, Captain Bluelight, Doom and Gloom and The Bishop. I knew and worked with them all.

The canteen manageress was known as 'The Head Poisoner'. A certain Chief Inspector, who originated from the Black Country, could not shake off his broad accent and was dubbed 'Chow Mein'. This came about through his use of the phrase "Wot Chow Mein?" (translated as: "what do you mean?"). A rather disliked inspector had the misfortune to have been christened by his parents with the forenames Terence William Arthur. His surname regrettably began with the letter T. The resulting full initials clearly spelled out not only his nickname, but also what most of his colleagues considered him to be! But then of course there was the infamous and much celebrated 'Reg' who we shall meet later….

NINETEEN

FRIDAY, November 24th 1972 was to be a landmark day in my police service. I could never have known as I started my shift on that chilly winter afternoon that this day would result in such recognition. PC Pye's exploits in the grimy Potteries' town of Stoke were about to become front page news around the globe. They would be the subject of television and news reports on an international scale and later the subject matter in various books and magazines.

It was about 6 p.m. when I had the radio call. My ambition on that evening had been to finish on time and have a pint with my colleagues. Sergeant Turner's message outlined the circumstances and I quickly guessed that my goal was unlikely.

Number 3, The Villas, Stoke

"Go to 3 The Villas," his voice came over the radio. "It's a lodging house and the landlady says that one of her tenants has been ill. She's not seen him for a few days and now he's not answering his door."

I suspected the worst – another Form 12.

The Villas is an avenue of enormous Victorian mansions and had originally been built for the millionaires of the day, who were mostly pottery barons. The road itself had never been adopted by the council and, consequently, was unmade. It consisted of rocks, pebbles and potholes, no doubt looking similar to how it had been one hundred years before. Some of the houses had been kept in good condition, but many had deteriorated and been turned into flats.

The property was owned by Mrs Eugeizig Rodaziewicz, a Polish lady who had lived in Stoke-on-Trent for thirty years. She rented out rooms, mostly to Polish immigrants who had fled their country from the German occupation in the Second World War. The building was a particularly large, dark and eerie-looking place with a gabled porch over the front door. A large rusting iron spike was fixed to the porch roof as a form of architectural embellishment.

There were several large trees in the street, which was poorly illuminated by old-fashioned gas-style lamps. I stood pensively in the shadows outside the porch door waiting for a response to my knock. As my eyes adjusted to the gloom I could make out a figure shuffling along the darkened hallway. Mrs Rodaziewicz squinted through the opaque glass and then hauled the vast door open. She gestured me in and in her strong accent told me what she knew.

It was as Sergeant Turner had said… the lodger of several years had not been out of his room for a number of days. The landlady started back down the hallway and led the way up a flight of narrow dark stairs to an equally dark landing. She whispered the Polish lodger's name… "Demetrious Mykicura."

A passageway, dimly lit by a low wattage bulb, led to the man's bedsit. The roughly made tongue and groove door brought back memories of D Block at Ryton. I knocked lightly in a friendly manner and called out a pretty hopeless attempt at his name.

"It's the police, Sir, are you okay?"

Silence…

I increased the volume and tried the door – Silence – Locked. After a few repetitions the dreaded inevitable moment arrived "I'll have to break the door open," I said as I turned towards the landlady. She was a few feet behind me, her hands clasped and a worried, but knowing expression illuminated slightly in the dimness.

"Yez, Offizer, it haz to be done."

I firmly shouldered the door, which easily broke free from its lock at the first try. The room was in total darkness and a musty, sickly smell crept out. I fumbled my hand inside to find a light switch. There was no way I was going over the threshold until I knew what to expect. My fingers stumbled across the switch, but in spite of my repeated attempts the darkness prevailed.

"Zere iz no bulb," the landlady announced. "He iz frightened of elektrik, thinks it vil cauz expolzions."

My God, I thought, it gets worse. I pulled my torch out from where I kept it lodged between my greatcoat buttons, and clicked it on. The powerful beam revealed a sorrowful sight – wallpaper hanging in leaves – a cramped space barely big enough for the single bed and tiny wardrobe. A small mound lay piled on the bed – sheets, blankets and maybe a pillow. I swallowed realising that it was more than just bedlinen. Taking another breath of the stale air I called out the chap's name again and then slowly pulled back the covers. Demetrious lay wide-eyed with congealed froth around his mouth, his arms up by his head, his fists clenched. He'd obviously been dead for several days.

I pulled the covers fully back and my torch picked out several small cloth bags lying with the corpse. Each bag was tied with string and seemed to contain a powder. The contents trickled out from one torn bag. "Salt," I muttered and was even more puzzled as the light also reflected back from dozens of silvery parchment-like fragments. I picked one up and felt how crisp it was as it crumbled between my fingers. It was garlic skin, and sure enough, there, also in the bed, were several garlic cloves.

I showed my findings to the landlady.

"It woz for ze vampire," she said. "Demetrious believed in ze vampire, zeese things would protect him."

My God, what next?

"Vampires, you say, Pork?" crackled back Sergeant Turner's reply to my radio summary of the situation. "You'll be needing Doc Wood then. I don't know whether it's for you or the corpse, perhaps you could send a bat over to him… he only lives over the road."

CID came; it was Dave and Joe again, and both smelling as though they'd already had the pint I was looking forward to. Joe was full of his customary sarcasm.

"Hope you've got this one staked out then, Porky."

As Sergeant Turner had said, the doctor lived directly opposite and very quickly joined us. From the aroma on his breath this call-out had interrupted his wee dram. The numbers were swelled with the arrival of a SOCO (Scenes of Crime Officer) and a police photographer who had a terrible squint in one eye. This unfortunate deformity was frequently blamed for 'misaligned' photos.

Dave and Joe were satisfied that, although odd, there was nothing suspicious about the death. They left me to get on with the Form 12. Doc Wood could find no sign of injury that could have caused the death. "It will be up to a post-mortem," he said.

I went through the usual rigmarole of making a detailed plan with measurements and a thorough search of the room. I had almost finished, when for an unknown reason, I pulled up the sash window and shone my torch out onto a small area of flat roof. There, twelve inches beneath the window, was an upturned plastic washing bowl. I reached out, lifted it and was puzzled to see a piece of human excrement. The sight triggered the memory of my recent court appearance. It entered my head that this new found addition to my vocabulary was cropping up more than I would have liked.

As my torch illuminated the find I was even more puzzled to see that it had numerous garlic cloves sticking out of the surface. These were clearly additions and had not been digested. If this was to continue, perhaps I would become the 'expert on human excrement' that Mr Morley had been questioned about in court. I took statements from the landlady and the other lodgers about Demetrious's background. They told me about his job and when he was last seen. I carefully included all the things known about his obsession with vampires. Eventually the ambulance service came and took the body away to the mortuary. After writing up as much as I could, I finally managed to get off home at one thirty… pint free.

The case was extraordinary and had raised a ghoulish interest in me. I visited the library the next day and borrowed a book entitled, *The Natural History of the Vampire*, by Anthony Masters.

I was in for some mickey-taking at work over the next few days and additional temporary nicknames were bandied about for me. 'Vampye' and 'PC Dracula' took the place of 'Porky' especially when I was spotted reading my vampire book at meal break.

On the following Tuesday I took a phone call from Mr Hibbert, the Coroner's officer, who told me that the post-mortem had been carried out. "He died from asphyxiation," he said.

"What, you mean he was strangled?"

"No, no, he choked to death," said Mr Hibbert. "The pathologist found a pickled onion stuck in his throat."

"Wait a minute," I cautioned. "It's all here in the book… I'll bet it's a bulb of garlic, not an onion."

There was a puzzled silence from the phone as I described what I had learned. "Sleeping with a bulb of garlic in the mouth to stop the vampire's spirit entering the body… salt bags and garlic cloves scattered about; I've read all about it."

Mr Hibbert's silence continued and I visualised his increasingly furrowed brow as I added more disgusting details. "Vampires love to eat human excrement." (That word seemed to be coming into my everyday use.)

I explained in detail the theory that a potential vampire assassin would mix a few garlic cloves in with a strategically placed piece of dung. The garlic – a poison to the vampire – would go unnoticed as the blood sucking beast tucked into the other savoury offering. The hoped-for outcome of the cunning trap would be the death of the vampire – killed by the garlic rather than the possibility of salmonella. I've heard of bad breath but this idea takes things to the extreme!

"I'll speak to the pathologist, straight away and get him to look at it again," said Mr Hibbert.

I'd met the pathologist before and had noted that he had as many names as a good bank robber. Mr John Alexander Hunter Brown had been the humorous and clever man who had performed the first post-mortem I had witnessed. For some reason it was considered part of police training that we all had to go to see a post-mortem being carried out. I was later proud to have stayed conscious throughout the ordeal.

It wasn't long before Mr Hibbert rang me back.

"You were right, young man, a bulb of garlic it is. Mr Brown sends his thanks and The Coroner says he wants a full report, as he will be holding an inquest."

Coroner Fred Hails loved a bit of publicity and this one was a sure-fire thing. I wrote up the report in detail, picking the brains of my old tutor, Bill. He was still on tap to help me out when needed, and then Sergeant Turner could always be relied upon to fine-tune things. Eventually the masterpiece was submitted. This was complete with numerous witness statements, detailed drawings, photographs and extracts from Anthony Masters' *Natural History of the Vampire*. That was the last I heard about it until Monday, 8th January 1973 – the day of the inquest.

The Stoke-on-Trent Coroner's Chambers occupied the former Hartshill Police Station, an area about a mile from Stoke town centre.

A new purpose-built Coroner's Court had been constructed at the side, together with a small car park.

As I arrived I saw that the courtroom was packed with journalists and television and radio reporters. Doc Wood was there together with Dave the detective and the squinting police photographer. Mrs Rodaziewicz and the other lodgers had also been called to give evidence. Fred Hails was very interested in the incident and examined all the evidence in detail. At the conclusion he said that it was 'this poor man's obsession with vampires that had led ultimately to his death, so perhaps they got him in the end'. He awarded me a commendation for such a thorough inquiry.

The press and TV were clicking and filming as I came out of court and the next day each national newspaper had a column on the story. My mum and dad were delighted. It had been some time since they'd had an 'oh-by-the-way' subject to mention in the pub! The Mykicura case was to follow me around for years to come, and featured in many books, magazines and even a film.

It was only a few months after the inquest when a chap from the BBC phoned me at work. He told me that they were doing a programme on Bram Stoker, Mary Shelley and all things associated with vampires, Dracula and Frankenstein. He said that they intended doing a piece about the case and wanted me to take part. Not being in charge of my own destiny, I duly reported the request and the next week was summoned to see the Chief Constable at Stafford Headquarters.

Chief Constable Arthur Morgan Rees was a big man with a big smile. As his name suggests he was a Welshman, a sport crazy former rugby international who represented his country during their 1935 victory over the 'All Blacks'. It was amazing how many Welshmen were employed as police officers in Staffordshire at this time. Many were brilliant sportsmen and some, as a bonus, were also good policemen.

"We… ll, young man," said Mr Rees, with his strong accent. "I've heard from the Beee Beee Ceee and I knoww they want yooo to go on the tellee. But I don't reeeally like the idea of my officers being associated with vam… pires. So I caan't allow it, but never mind, you'll be on the tellee one day."

The Chief's broad grin signalled my departure and with a mechanical-style salute, wobbling helmet and a floorboard splitting right turn, I marched from his office. My first chance at the silver screen shattered. "Well done, young man, well done," echoed his voice, as I marched off down the corridors of power and headed back to the gloom of Stoke.

I watched the programme on the black and white telly when it was broadcast several months later. Fred Hails was there in all his glory, complete with his monocle, and smoking a cigarette in a long holder. There was so much smoke billowing out of him that I wasn't too sure if he was still there. Every so often the smoke would swirl away as if someone, just out of camera shot was fiercely wafting.

Arthur Morgan Rees, Chief Constable of Staffordshire, 1964 to 1977

TWENTY

THE NEXT TIME I would get to hear from the Chief Constable would be in September 1973. I had been on night duty and at 5 a.m. my patrol had taken me into a church yard. Hiding between gravestones I came across a well-known and particularly vicious criminal in possession of stolen property.

As I told the thug that I was arresting him on suspicion of theft, I fully expected him to attack me. Fortunately this didn't happen and so I took him in. It turned out that he had burgled a ladies' outfitters.

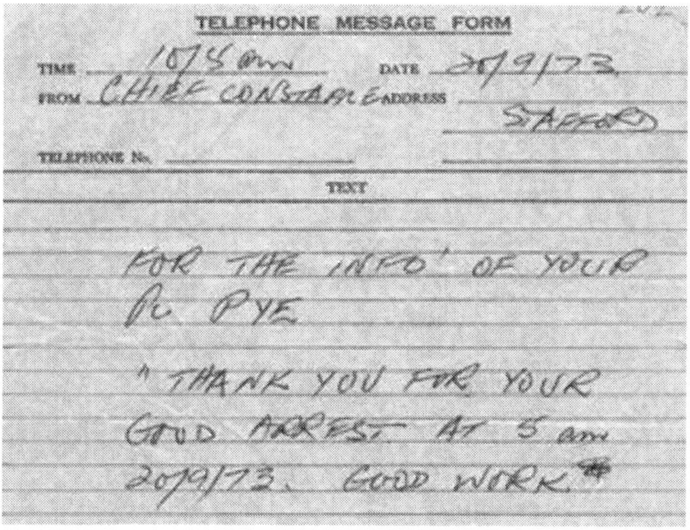

TELEPHONE MESSAGE FORM

TIME 1045 am DATE 20/9/73

FROM CHIEF CONSTABLE ADDRESS STAFFORD

TELEPHONE No.

TEXT

FOR THE INFO' OF YOUR
PC PYE
"THANK YOU FOR YOUR
GOOD ARREST AT 5 am
20/9/73. GOOD WORK"

The Chief Constable's message

The next night when I came on duty there was a telephone message waiting for me from the Chief Constable himself. In his message he thanked me for 'a good arrest'. I cannot say how much this little scrap of paper meant. To think that he even came to know of such a minor incident was a surprise. The fact that he went to the trouble of ringing up in person to thank me was the most encouraging action anyone could have taken.

There were many different characters in the job, and Stoke Police Station had more than its share. Sergeant Douglas Mathews was a complete 'one off'. Most of the sergeants and inspectors all seemed to me to be as old, or older, than my dad, and 'Dougie' fitted this category. He was a tall man, about six foot four and slim for his height. Dougie was no pushover and would stand nonsense from no one. He was a station sergeant on a different shift from me and a brilliant snooker player – unlike me.

All the police stations then had a snooker table. These were well used and a game would always be in progress at meal times. As a consequence there were several police officers who were pretty good players. Ray Reardon, who later became world snooker champion, served as a PC in the old Stoke-on-Trent force. Maybe he could thank some of his time as a PC for the practice he managed whilst at work.

Dougie would boast about how many times he'd beaten Ray. His main claim to fame though – albeit unknown to him – was his extremely noticeable speech impediment. This was coupled with the use of his own home-made vocabulary. It consisted of words *similar* to words which would have been appropriate in the sentence. Those slight differences turned Dougie's attempts at a serious conversation into farce with onlookers stifling laughter until the opportunity arose for full-blown hysteria. Hardly a day would go by without somebody saying, "Have you heard Dougie's latest?"

Dougie had an extremely high opinion of his own abilities. He was never one to hold back on telling everyone around him about how good he was at football, driving, swimming, card-playing, or any subject that cropped up.

PC Ray Reardon, complete with Stoke helmet
(photograph with kind permission of Ray Reardon)

Dougie could not sound his Rs and sounded all his Ls as Ws, so this, coupled with his home-made words (known as Dougie-isms) caused his fame to spread.

Dougie would affectionately refer to his wife as, 'the pwincess' and his two-up, two-down terrace house in Wharfe Street, Stoke, as, 'the wickle pawace' (little palace).

A famous Dougie-ism occurred one year during the summer police station outing to Blackpool. Dougie told the lads that there was nothing he liked better than to, 'whi (lie) on the beach and watch the seagulls hoovering in the sky'.

On one occasion a German lorry driver came in needing directions for the Michelin factory. As the office staff struggled to overcome the language barrier Dougie muscled in and said he'd deal with the matter as he 'spoke a wickle German'. He leaned over the counter and shouted, 'Vot iz your name?' He then asked the man to, 'Sit down on those tubercular chairs'. His other language skills were no better, as when trying to impress an attractive Italian lady at the counter, he greeted her with, 'Bournevitta, Senorita'.

I later learned that such remarks actually have a dictionary definition. A 'Malapropism' is: *The use of an incorrect word in place of a word with a similar sound resulting in a nonsensical, often humorous utterance.*

Dougie's malapropisms were certainly both humorous and nonsensical. I would have loved to have heard his attempt at the word itself.

I was now a regular panda car driver. I never worked out why they were called panda cars because they were a kind of greeny blue and white, not black and white like a panda. There were three Panda Areas on Stoke's patch with radio call signs of Panda Six, Panda Seven and Panda Eight. Along with a panda car, two constables were also assigned to each area as patrol officers (Area Men).

The Area Constables were generally PCs who lived on that patch and it was supposed to be their job to get to know the locals. As a panda car driver I spent a lot of time working with the different Area Men. They were allowed to go home for meals and I would often pick them up and drop them off for this, or when they'd finished duty.

The pranks and mischief continued when time allowed and Area Man Roger Owen caught me out a couple of times in his efforts to teach me well-deserved lessons: *Always lock your police car.*

The first time came during a night shift when I was taking the chance to check some property. I'd reckoned that I would only be a few minutes and had no idea that Roger was nearby. He came across my parked but unlocked panda car in a side street, climbed in, released the handbrake and coasted the car around the corner (we didn't have steering locks back then). My face must have been a picture when I returned to find the car had gone. I was about to radio to the police station to report what had happened when Roger appeared from the shadows saying,"I'll teach you, Porky."

It took another occasion to cure me though, as a few weeks later in the early hours of one morning, Roger found my police car unlocked yet again. I returned after a short while, unaware that my misdemeanour had been spotted. I climbed into the driving seat and was about to clip on the seatbelt as a figure rose up from the back seat and grabbed me around the throat. "I WILL teach you, Porky," Roger affirmed. This time it worked!

Bertie was another Area Man and frequently asked me in for a cuppa when I dropped him off. Sadly Bertie and his wife were having marital problems and so there was always an atmosphere. They'd both talk to me, but not to each other. One evening I dropped Bertie off and then made my way back to the Police Station. As I entered the enquiry office I could hear the sound of a drunk in the cells shouting obscenities at Sergeant Turner.

"Flattery wunner get you bail," Sergeant Turner shouted down the cell passage, in reply to the drunken man's vile comments. He was interrupted as the base station radio crackled into life and issued an unending hiss as though a patrol was trying to transmit a message.

"What's up with it, Sarge?" I said, slapping the metal casing.

"I don't know, Pork," replied Sergeant Turner, slapping it even harder.

"*Right, I've bloody well had enough of you,*" shouted the radio.

"What's this, Pork? Who is it?" said Sergeant Turner as he twiddled the radio's knobs.

"Go back to your bloody mother then, and the sooner the better," shouted the radio.

"Is someone on a domestic, Pork? Who the hell is it?" Sergeant Turner said, with a puzzled expression.

"No, Sarge, it's Bertie and his missus. It sounds like his transmitter button's stuck in."

There then followed a detailed account of Bertie's fifteen years of married hell. This diatribe was interspersed with colourful descriptions of all the things he hated about her. His wife's own broadcasts summed up what 'a useless bugger' he was. We were subjected to a full five minutes of this as I frantically fumbled through the list of officers' phone numbers to find Bertie's. The argument was interrupted by the sound of my telephone call ringing in the background. Bertie's last words were: "If that's your bloody mother tell her from me to sod off."

Bertie was rather subdued for a few days after the incident.

TWENTY ONE

WE WERE still using the original breathalysers back then. We'd keep a box in the panda cars. They were sealed glass tubes containing amber crystals; there was a halfway mark on the centre of the tube. Each of the small green plastic boxes would contain half a dozen tubes. There was a tiny hacksaw blade fitted into the side of the box. This was used to score the sealed ends of the glass tube and then push them into a tiny hole in the box to snap off the ends. Inside the box was also a folded plastic bag that had to be pushed on to one end of the tube. There were also a number of disposable mouthpieces that went on the other end.

Staffs Police 1100 Panda Car of the day

After going through a piece of legal jargon with the suspect, they would then have to blow into the mouthpiece and completely inflate the little bag. If the crystals changed colour from amber to green over the halfway mark on the tube then you could arrest the person. A second attempt was allowed at the Police Station and if that also turned green the person would be asked to give a blood or urine sample. It was a lengthy procedure and, coupled with getting the police surgeon out for the blood sample, could take hours. 'Blowing in the bag' and 'blowing a green one' were stock phrases then. Probably most police officers now would struggle to understand the connection with the electronic breath test of the modern era.

In May 1974 I started another week of nights. I had been married almost twelve months now and my wife Gladys and I had only two weeks to wait for the holiday in Cornwall that we'd been saving for all year.

It had been a warm evening and even as 3 a.m. approached it was still mild. The old Panda areas 6,7 and 8 had been changed to 41, 42 and 43. I suppose there must have been some logical explanation, but no one knew why, so I was now 42 instead of Panda 7. I felt no different.

I'd breathalysed a driver earlier in the evening and needed to drop the blood sample in to the main postal sorting office. The samples had to be sent for analysis to the laboratory in Birmingham by recorded delivery and although it was out of hours, the sorting office staff always obliged.

The radio startled me out of my holiday daydreams as Sergeant Turner's voice announced, "Four-Two… burglar alarm activated at Wengers, Cliff Vale… usually a good 'un, Pork."

"Okay, Sarge, on my way… over." I gunned the frisky Austin 1100 and sped away hearing the engine thump back into the bulkhead in between each gear change.

Sergeant Turner was right. This was a good burglar alarm, which had resulted in a few arrests; Wengers was a firm involved in the pottery trade, specialising in colour for glazes and decoration on crockery. The building itself was modern, but a bit isolated. One of the things worth pinching from these places, apart from a bit of petty cash, was the liquid gold that was used in glaze colouring.

I heard Sergeant Turner's voice directing other cars to also attend, and as I pulled into the large front forecourt, I realised I was first on the scene. At the rear of the building lay a compound enclosed by a six-foot-high, concrete sectional wall. During other break-ins, burglars had broken in after climbing over this wall.

Two other police cars arrived and I waved a greeting as I flashed my torch over the front of the building. Suddenly there was a metal clatter from inside the compound and with no thought other than 'burglar', I ran headlong towards the wall. I was a fit twenty-four year old and a six-foot-high wall was no obstacle at all. I took hold of the top of the wall with both hands and heaved upwards, jumping at the same time and hooking my left foot over the top. I started easing myself up and readying for the drop down to the other side when everything started slowly collapsing around me. There was a rumbling sound and a shaking as the wall on which I was perched folded backwards and down onto itself. I crashed to the ground as the concrete fence posts and panels tumbled down around me. Both my feet and left arm were trapped… I was surrounded by a mountain of concrete slabs and pinned to the ground. My torch was still switched on and shone its beam skywards from within the posts and panels as a cloud of dust lingered in the air.

Three colleagues jogged over to me from their cars, half-laughing.

"You okay, Pork?" asked a voice.

"No," I mumbled back from within my concrete den.

It took several minutes to free me. Everyone looked up in amazement as a cat darted out of the compound through the hole I had made. The creature was no doubt the cause of the noise I had heard,

"Cat burglar!" someone joked.

There was no radiologist on duty when I arrived at the accident unit. They bandaged my badly swollen wrists, arms and both my scraped shins. A sticking plaster was pressed onto the grazes to my forehead. My dented ego was soothed and I was told to come back for X-rays after nine o'clock.

My wife, Gladys, awoke with a start as the bandage-swathed 'mummy' hobbled into the bedroom. A return visit to the hospital later that morning revealed a fractured left wrist. The plaster cast from elbow to knuckles was going to take ten weeks before I was allowed back to work. The broken scaphoid bone is a notoriously difficult one to heal.

I had a long list of jobs to do in our recently purchased house, but effectively only had one arm to work with. I decided to try to dig an inspection pit for the pre-fab garage that I had on order (not easy with one arm). Within a few hours I had mastered one arm digging – *wrap right arm around the shaft of spade and push handle up into my armpit!* It was slow and tiring, but it worked.

At the end of each day's toil the pit was slowly taking shape and nearing the five-feet required depth. My right arm was also altering in size and shape as the daily exertions caused it to take on 'Charles Atlas' proportions. The left, plaster-encased counterpart though, slowly withered away from the lack of use.

After a few weeks on sick leave I was allowed back to work but only on light duties working at the Coroner's office (more Form 12s). I managed the trip down to Cornwall for the holiday I'd been daydreaming about, and at long last the plaster cast was removed for good.

I had to visit a consultant over the claim for my injuries. I removed my shirt as directed and saw the surgeon raise his eyebrows as he surveyed the injured wrist. Both the arm and wrist through weeks of inactivity looked forlorn and stick-like. My right arm, however, looked as though it belonged to another person. The weeks of one-armed pit digging had sculpted it into a bulging muscular device more suited to a Greek statue. The consultant measured both arms at various places from the shoulder down to the wrist and then looked at me with a most concerned expression.

"There has been considerable wastage to your left arm and consequently, this should increase the claim greatly," he said.

I didn't think he'd be interested in my inspection pit, so I left it at that. It wasn't too long before the left arm was almost back to normal and I was able to get back to some proper police work.

The police system for promotion to the rank of sergeant involved a complex three part written exam. Only if you passed could you then apply for an interview board which would be hosted by several senior officers. A constable became eligible to take this annually held exam after completing his first two years' of service. I had applied for the exam at my first opportunity, but had not studied and so failure was inevitable. Those visits to the ballroom at the Trentham Gardens leisure complex where the exam was held had been pretty pointless. I was not alone, as many people seemed to view the outing as an opportunity for a free lunch and a chance to meet up with old colleagues. I again cursed myself for not studying as I came out from the exam after my third try. I knew I now had to knuckle down and get some studying done.

I had been at Stoke five years now and had seen a lot of changes even in that short space of time. Gone were the handsome old Stoke helmets even within the long since, non-existent boundaries of the old Stoke force. In fact, the badge on the helmets had changed a few times as the official title of the force had changed. First it had been 'Staffordshire County Police' and then 'Staffordshire County and Stoke-on-Trent Constabulary'. Finally it had been changed to just 'Staffordshire Police'. A lot of the old Stoke bobbies had said that the official changeover date of 1st April 1974 was 'well chosen'.

So we all had 'buckets' for helmets now and those striking 'closed neck' capes with the brass lion's head clasps were also gone.

Even the old police station in Copeland Street was being demolished to make way for a new road scheme. We now had a purpose-built four-storey nick thoughtfully sited in Boothen Road –

hardly a ten second sprint from Stoke City FC's Victoria Ground. Princess Margaret had officially opened the new police station on Tuesday, 2nd July 1974, and I'd missed it by being off sick with my broken wrist. The new building had every modern convenience including its own garages and petrol pumps. There was a large cell block for both men and women, with a big prisoner exercise yard. There were dozens of offices upstairs, a proper canteen with 'real' canteen staff. A large and well-appointed bar-cum-function room along with a TV room were located on the top floor. There was, however, no snooker room, which seemed to be a feature that was being dropped.

Another change that took place this year was to the flat peaked caps that were part of our uniform and mostly for use when on car patrol. We were all given black and white chequered bands to be fitted around the caps. It was something that the Scottish forces had been using for some time.

We now had only one personal radio to take out on patrol, instead of the two old fashioned ones. The 'Burndept' (shown in photo) was both a transmitter and a receiver. It came with a confusing entanglement of straps to fit it to your chest. Almost all traces of the old Stoke-on-Trent City Police Force had now gone. It had taken years to reach this stage and I suppose that there were still a few ghosts of the old force for many years to come. Once in a while an obsolete Stoke form would turn up with the name of the old force on it. It seemed like a reminder for those who had forgotten or an insight for those who never knew. Funnily enough those old Stoke forms always seemed to have been better thought out than the new counterpart ones.

An amazing computer system came online in February 1974. It was called the Police National Computer (PNC for short). To start with there were just two terminals at HQ and this enabled us to check on vehicles to see if they were stolen.

The Box – the first computer monitor to come into use in Staffordshire.

Over the next eighteen months the records from vehicle licensing authorities were also put on and eventually we could ring headquarters and quickly find out the owner of a car. I expect the motor tax man, who we used to get out of bed all the time, had mixed feelings. He'd get more sleep, but was missing out on all that overtime money.

After a few years each police station had its own terminal, which became known as 'The Box'. It was soon also possible to store and search for the names and records of criminals and wanted people. Ultimately all incidents were logged onto the box, together with the details of staff on duty at any one time. The system was eventually called Command & Control.

In July 1975 my numerous applications were answered when I was temporarily posted to Stoke CID for an official four-month 'CID aide'. This move was par for the course before consideration for a permanent job in the department as a detective constable.

1975 was proving to be a busy year for me. I was interested in drugs work and had been on a drugs course in Hertfordshire shortly before my CID aide. No sooner had I finished my CID stint than I started on an advanced driving course. I particularly wanted this course so that I could become a crime car driver. Most of the other participants had ambitions of becoming Traffic Officers. The Crime Car was a quick response vehicle which attended all major crimes within the division, and so advanced driving skills were necessary.

The other driving courses that I'd taken part in were good, but this was in a different league altogether. We had some of the best, high-speed road cars of the day available to us. The line-up was impressive and included the Ford Cortina 2000e, the Triumph Dolomite Sprint and the Jaguar XJ. We would regularly perform at speeds in excess of 120 mph in an effort to hone the necessary skills.

There were nine of us on the advanced course, along with another eighteen on other courses. The set-up was similar to the intermediate course when I had lost my three friends in that terrible road accident three years before.

Our bedrooms upstairs in the rambling, supposedly haunted Baswich House were dormitory style with bed numbers ranging from two to four per room. Alan Smith and I shared a two-bedded room. The daily intense concentration of high speed driving usually led to instantaneous sleep.

As I settled off one night, I could hear that Alan had already arrived in the land of nod. I don't think I was all that long behind him. I had been asleep an hour or so when I half-woke in a cold sweat, my heart pounding. Disorientated by the darkness of this unfamiliar room, I lashed out at whatever was gripping my feet. I could feel a heavy weight slowly enveloping me from the bottom of the bed. I sat up and violently arched my back against the wall behind me. I let out a blood-curdling shriek and started to kick out at the black writhing mass at the foot of my bed.

"IT'S THERE, IT'S THERE!" I screamed out, pointing in the gloom at the 'THING'.

"WHAT… WHAT… WHAT THE HELL IS IT?" screamed Alan from his darkened corner.

"IT'S THERE, *IT'S THERE!*" I screamed back, leaping from my bed in semi-conscious confusion and fear.

"WHAT IS IT? WHAT THE BLOODY HELL IS IT, FOR GOD'S SAKE?" shrieked back Alan.

"LOOK AT IT… LOOK AT IT… IT'S *THERE!*" I then leapt for safety onto Alan's bed whilst still pointing and shouting at the corner. I was oblivious to the fact that Alan now lay pinned to his bed beneath me and had joined in the screaming.

"WHAT IS IT, FOR GOD'S SAKE? WHAT'S HAPPENING?" shouted Alan's head, the rest of him being completely and tightly sealed in beneath his blankets and my weight.

Suddenly a calm came over me as I realised it was nothing more than a nightmare. Taking a deep sigh of relief I returned to my bed and immediately went back to sleep, leaving my poor colleague wide awake and shaking with fear.

The next day a weary looking Alan proclaimed over breakfast, "Any more nightmares and I'll be asking for a new room-mate." It emerged later in the day that a fellow student in another room had claimed to have been frightened out of his wits in the night. He had seen a shadowy figure walk directly through a wall in his bedroom.

The position of the disappearing figure led straight to the foot of my bed. Many beers were required before I could get off to sleep that night.

The day following 'the ghost' was spent on the specially built driving school skidpan at Hixon near Stafford. It comprised a large smooth-surfaced track with water jets spraying the oil-laden surface. Different lay-outs were made up with cones, and the cars that were used, old Ford Cortinas, had special 'slick' tyres. There was a control room from where instructions were given and assessments made. It was terrific fun and undoubtedly helped us to achieve the necessary high standards.

The Staffordshire Police Skid Pan at Hixon

Ghosts apart, it had been an interesting and exciting five weeks and now with the advanced certificate attained I returned to Stoke as a 'crime car' driver. I only spent a few weeks on this job when I was offered a post with the force Drug Squad. I was delighted, although still a little sad to be leaving my friends at Stoke.

TWENTY TWO

HANLEY police station is an enormous building, which was built as the headquarters of the old Stoke City Force in 1964. Its numerous rooms and offices had all been tailor-made for a specific department, but since the amalgamation of Staffs and Stoke many found a new use. One of these offices now provided the home of the Northern branch of the force Drug Squad. This first floor room was about eight feet wide by fifteen feet long, and was used as a base by up to six of us. As a general rule we worked in pairs and the job involved a lot of undercover work and obs with many late nights spent in pubs and clubs. We were allowed to grow our hair long and dress in whatever clothing was suitable. A lot of our time was spent on search warrants (drugs raids). The department was often used as a source of additional manpower to help out on murder investigations or other major enquiries.

In 1975 a series of arson attacks took place in and around the Longton area of Stoke-on-Trent. The premises were nearly always pottery factories and there seemed to be a large fire almost every week that summer. Many thousands of pounds worth of property was going up in flames. Lives were at risk and jobs affected. Longton CID was stretched to the limit with all their detectives involved on fire enquiries, but still the attacks continued.

The bosses decided to arrange observation teams working nights to try to catch the firebug. More and more officers were drafted in to lurk about and hide in every possible back alley and lonely spot. No consideration was given to the fact that I'd just started my new job on the Drug Squad or that I'd only been a father for a few weeks. I was drafted in to do my bit – a full two weeks' stretch of nights leaving my wife Gladys at home to look after our baby, Adam.

My observation point was in amongst the bushes and gravestones of St James and St John Churchyard half a mile from Longton town centre. This uncomfortable spot gave me a perfect hidey-hole to watch over several pottery plants including the front of the huge Hudson and Middleton factory. I could easily see the large wrought iron gates which formed the main entrance.

Most of the bigger businesses had a security man or a kiln man working through the night, but this had not deterred the arsonist. The first few nights of my duty had been as boring as hell and I relied on the low volume chatter from my police radio to keep me awake. Watching the odd drunk stagger off up the road was my only amusement.

As I was fought to keep my eyelids open the church clock chimed one o'clock and I twitched back into consciousness. I dragged my fingers down my cheeks widening my eyes, trying to shake off the tiredness – and then I spotted something.

I was instantly wide awake and alert. I was sure that I'd seen the slightest of movements from the distant junction with Chelson Street. I shook my head and focussed in on the black silhouettes of the brick bottle kilns of Ashdale Pottery. Just one dimly lit street lamp gave a little perspective to the pitched roofs of factories and lines of terraced houses. I rubbed my eyes again and then – YES! There was DEFINITELY a distant figure peering around the corner.

The outline of the man became clear as he slowly craned his neck around the edge of the wall – a pinprick of glowing red cigarette end visible between the fingers of one hand. He looked left and then right, before stepping out halfway into the street. He took a long drag on his cigarette, dropped it to the pavement and ground it in with his foot. After a second furtive glance around he stealthily made his way across towards the entrance of Hudson and Middleton pulling something from his pocket. It was a pair of GLOVES – he was putting on a pair of gloves! My heart rate started to increase... *This could be the Longton arsonist!*

My eyes were now wide and unblinking as the man went right up against the bars to the eight-foot high gate and peered through. With one last over-the-shoulder look he clambered up, dropped down into the yard and disappeared from view. I pulled my transmitter from my pocket and whispered the situation back to the control room.

"Okay, Pork," came back the radio reply, "stay concealed, keep us updated, I'm getting patrols to close in around the place."

A flurry of urgent broadcasts hissed from my radio as different cars, foot patrols and obs officers were directed in steathily to take up strategic positions around the building. Only glimpses were caught of the shadowy outlines of perhaps a dozen black clad police officers getting ready to pounce.

Suddenly my radio shouted out… "*Go, go, go!*"

Figures appeared from street corners, from alleyways, from behind bins and bushes. Three of the officers ran directly towards the gate and I also broke cover and sprinted over to join in.

Two powerful torch beams shone through into the yard and one constable was already dropping onto the cobblestones on the other side. A large pile of cardboard boxes in a corner erupted into the air and a figure stood up from within it.

"*Police!*" a voice shouted…

"*Police!*" another voice shouted.

The cardboard box figure produced a torch himself and blazed it back.

"*Police!*" he then shouted.

"*What?*" someone else shouted.

"Don't move!" one of the officers said.

"No, *you* don't move," replied the cardboard box man.

"What the hell is going on?" quizzed a different voice

"I'm DC Smith from Stafford," said cardboard box man. "This is my obs point. I was late coming in. I was held up with a job in Stafford, so I came on down and got settled in. The next thing is all you lot appear… frightened the bloody daylights out of me."

I slunk back to my bush.

The arson attacks were never satisfactorily concluded, but the finger of suspicion had pointed towards a local vicar. He was questioned, but due to a lack of evidence had to be released. The suspect went missing shortly after his release and was found dead, having committed suicide by setting fire to himself – then the fires stopped!

After my two weeks working on the fires, I went back to my Drug Squad job and picked up the pieces where I'd left off. It was at this time that the evil crimes of a man who had become known as the Black Panther were constantly in the papers and on the television. The Panther was responsible for the murders of three postmasters. These were offences he had committed during post office robberies in Lancashire and Yorkshire, along with numerous other violent robbery offences.

On 14th January 1975, Lesley Whittle, the seventeen-year-old heiress of a coach travel company, was kidnapped. The young woman was spirited away from her home at Highley, in Shropshire in the dead of night and was then held to ransom. The kidnapper made a telephone demand for £50,000. A complex series of instructions led Lesley's brother, Ronald, under police surveillance, to Bathpool Park, Kidsgrove, within the Staffordshire Police area, to make the drop.

A lot of things had gone wrong, both with the kidnapper's plans and the police operation to catch him. Suddenly there was no more contact, leaving Lesley's mother desperately wondering what had happened to her daughter. The task of investigating the abduction and hopefully finding Lesley alive fell upon West Mercia Police. This force was responsible for Highley, from where the young woman had been taken. The case came to a grinding halt with no clues to where she was or what had happened to the criminal behind the plot.

It was a week later when the West Midlands Police contacted the West Mercia inquiry team. They told them that a shooting had taken place on the same night as the proposed ransom drop. The violent drama had happened along with a suspected robbery attempt at a freight-liner terminal in Dudley. The security guard, Gerald Smith, who had interrupted the robber had been shot five times, but was clinging to life. A car abandoned nearby as well as ballistic evidence had now proved a connection between the post office murders, Lesley Whittle's kidnapping and, of course, Gerald Smith's shooting. A full search of Bathpool Park was ordered, and poor Lesley's body was found hanging sixty feet down inside a drainage shaft.

As the body had been found within the Staffordshire area, the murder inquiry became the responsibility of Staffordshire police to investigate. The colossal inquiry which followed severely sapped the strength of Staffordshire Police. It was conducted from the small police station of Kidsgrove, which was a part of the Newcastle-under-Lyme police area.

A mountain of paperwork was generated by the inquiry. Hundreds of staff, both police and civilians worked on it. There were fears that the upstairs floor of the small police building would not withstand the weight. Structural engineers had to be called in to ensure its safety. CID officers from all over the county had been drafted in to assist, and squads such as the Drug Squad, again, had to supply manpower. Two officers from our squad were already working full-time on the inquiry and, whilst interested in it, I was still trying to get to grips with my new job. I found that because of the manpower shortage I had been thrown in at the deep end.

It was a December evening in 1975 when the Panther was caught. Two uniformed police officers on mobile patrol in Mansfield, Nottinghamshire had seen a man acting suspiciously and decided to check him out. Their suspect was none other than The Black Panther who was on his way to rob a nearby post office. The Panther pulled a sawn-off shotgun from his holdall and turned it on them. He forced them back into their police car and took them hostage. He later admitted that he intended to murder them. After a short drive at gunpoint, a violent struggle ensued, the gun was fired and the three spilled out onto the pavement outside a chip shop. Fortunately the chip shop queue consisted mainly of burly miners who quickly came to the aid of the two constables.

The Black Panther was later identified as Donald Neilson, a jobbing builder from Bradford and the photograph of him shows the violence needed to restrain him. Neilson was transported to Newcastle-under-Lyme Police Station for lengthy interviews and court appearances.

The inquiry was truly monumental in size as it involved so many murders, attempted murders and robberies over such a wide area. It would be many months before the matters were ready to go before the court.

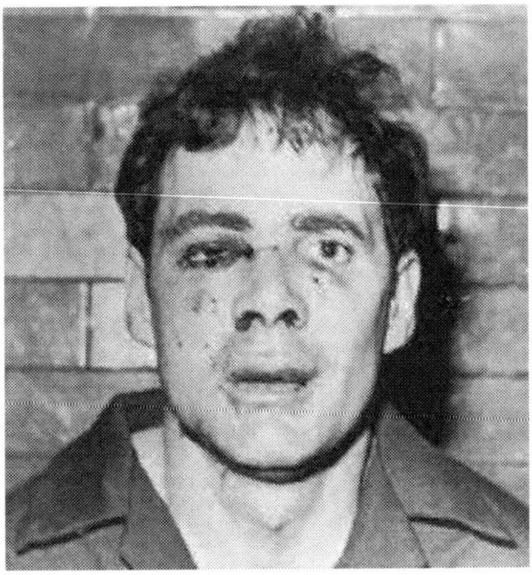

Donald Neilson (The Black Panther).

One Monday morning I took a phone call from the incident room. The task I was given involved a drive to Dudley in the West Midlands. I was to meet with Gerald Smith, the freightliner terminal security guard who had somehow survived being shot five times by

Neilson. He had undergone countless operations, but was reported to be now back home and making a recovery.

It was with some excitement that I knocked on the door of the neat semi-detached house in Dudley. The courageous man I was expecting to meet had looked down the barrel of Neilson's gun, been shot and had survived. Mrs Smith, a slim fiftyish lady with tightly permed blonde hair and a pleasant smile, answered the door. She told me that Gerald had gone back into hospital for further surgery as he still had some bullets in his body which had been too dangerous to remove.

"I have some exhibit labels that he's got to sign, nothing more than that," I said.

"Oh!" she replied in her strong Black Country accent. "Yow'll be all roight, just go and see him at hospeetal."

I drove to Dudley General Hospital and arrived at Gerald's ward, clutching the handful of brown card exhibit labels. "Police," I said to the ward sister, showing my warrant card. "I've come to see Mr Smith… something for him to sign."

"Oh, that's fine," she said, "he's over there, giving out the teas."

She pointed to a tall well-built man wearing a brown dressing gown, who was standing near a tea trolley at the other end of the ward.

I introduced myself to Gerald and explained my task, sympathising that he was back in hospital again.

"Oh, that's okay, nice to meet you. How about a cup of tea whilst we sign?" he said, gesturing over at the tea trolley.

Of course I accepted.

Gerald Smith died two weeks later from surgery complications. I was upset to hear this, I really didn't know the man, but he'd been through so much and seemed perfectly okay and then....

A rarely used piece of law now came into play. The shots fired by Neilson, into Gerald were clearly intended to kill him and did eventually do that. But more than a year and a day had elapsed since the shooting and for that reason Neilson could not be charged with his murder. He could only be charged with his attempted murder. This law has now been changed.

It was July 1976 before Neilson was eventually sentenced to five life terms for his horrendous string of murders and attempted murders. The nineteen armed robberies and many other burglary offences for which he was responsible were another matter. The attempted murder charge in relation to Gerald Smith was ordered 'to lie on file'. The judge added a whole life tariff with no possibility of parole. Neilson died in prison in December 2011 after almost 36 years in custody.

TWENTY THREE

THE 1976 SERGEANTS' exams proved to be another disappointment. This failure was as of nothing when news came through in March of the single terrible road accident which took the lives of another two friends. PCs John Hunt, aged thirty, and Dennis Tunnicliffe, aged twenty-seven were both highly skilled police motorcyclists.

My appointment as detective constable served to lift my spirits only slightly, but the arrival in the Drug Squad office of a new face was very welcome. PC Des Lewis teamed up with me and was soon also appointed as a detective. He would be my partner on the Drug Squad for the next two and a half years. This was a motivating, action-packed part of my service and was made even better as I was working with a man who shared the same sense of humour and passion for the job. We were virtually our own bosses and able to use our own initiative arranging whatever shifts suited our investigations best. We'd work long hours if a case demanded it and a twenty hour day was not unheard of.

It was a regular thing to arrive home at half past one in the morning and get a phone call before you'd even climbed into bed. Call-outs to serious drug related incidents perhaps many miles away were fairly commonplace. It might have been a large drugs seizure, or some youngster who had been found dead with a needle sticking out of his arm.

Search warrants were everyday bread and butter for the Drug Squad. We carried a list of Magistrates' addresses and phone numbers with us. Frequently we'd have to pester one of them in the middle of the night to sign an urgently needed search warrant (usually referred to as a 'ticket'). The signature was needed to make the document legal.

The secret with a Drug Squad search warrant was the element of surprise. Getting in quick was important as it could be easy to throw the drugs on the fire or flush them down the toilet. It wasn't always a good idea simply to try to kick the door down because often drug dealers would have had their doors strengthened purposely. The only thing that you would achieve would be to make a lot of noise, giving the dealer plenty of time to dispose of the evidence. There could also be a vicious dog waiting for you or even small children behind the door. Sometimes cunning and stealth were the best way in.

We were working on a fairly big job involving a Stoke-on-Trent based cannabis dealer. He was selling from his large upstairs flat on the corner of a busy main road. The sturdy wooden door had been strengthened with additional bolts. This door led directly to a flight of stairs, which went straight up into the flat. Trying to kick it down did not seem like a good idea.

We had the ticket ready and some hints about the layout of the flat. We even had an inkling about where he kept his drugs, but we still needed to get in quickly to stop him disposing of the evidence.

Even with our long hair and tatty jeans we were known to most of the local druggies and dealers, so there could be no bluffing our way in. We needed an alternative strategy and decided to enlist the help of a local CID man.

Detective Constable Trevor Clowes was always willing to help out. His immaculate appearance (quite the opposite of ours) was less likely to raise suspicion. His neat hair, jacket, tie, well-creased trousers and highly polished shoes were just what we needed.

Trevor took up his place on the step with the search warrant concealed on an official-looking clipboard as Des and I stood either side of the doorway pinned to the wall out of sight. Trevor gave the door a friendly tap and a short while later the muffled sounds of footsteps descending the stairs could be heard.

"Who is it, what do you want?" a voice shouted from inside.

"Council. It's about your rent, Sir," replied Trevor, in his nicest of tones.

"It's not a council flat," came back the voice.

Trevor looked at me with an anguished wide-eyed expression as the script went out of the window. The letterbox had now opened from the inside and Trevor, thinking on his feet, smiled down at it and cheerfully began to explain. "Yes, I know. We're doing a survey on private landlords, just a few questions. It might be beneficial to you."

"Hold on," replied the letterbox, as I heard the sound of bolts being slid and locks clicking open.

I looked over at Des, who was pressed into the brickwork and quivering like a sprinter in the blocks waiting for the gun.

The door opened just two inches against a sturdy security chain. The pasty, white features and long lank hair of drug dealer, James Ottey, could be seen through the gap, a mistrustful look in his eyes. The features suddenly tightened to one of electrified horror – he had seen us. Trevor was knocked off balance as Des shot out from the corner and shouldered the door hard, ripping the chain off.

"*Drug squad!*" I shouted as the six-foot three-inch, gangling Ottey turned on his heel and set off upwards three stairs at a time closely followed by the two of us. Trevor succumbed to the loss of balance and was sent sprawling across the pavement minus his spectacles and surrounded by flapping papers and clipboard.

Ottey turned left at the top of the stairs into a bathroom. The instantaneous bang of the door was followed by the *clunk* of a heavy bolt. Des ran straight through the closed bolted door, which splintered completely off its hinges.

Ottey stood frozen like a rabbit caught in headlights. His mouth gaped open and his saucer-wide eyes flicked from Des to me before slowly moving downwards. His vision finally settled upon the football sized lump of cannabis resin in his left hand above the toilet pan.

"Need a bigger toilet than that, mate," said Des.

Ottey accepted defeat and handed the bag over.

The haul was later found to contain two full imperial pounds of cannabis resin or 'two weights' to use the druggie vernacular of the day, a pound being a 'weight'. By the standards of the day this was a large seizure and sent a minor shock wave around the drugs community locally.

There were lots of small-time dealers in the area. These were mostly users themselves who made a bit of extra cash on the side to subsidise their own habit. There were a few 'Mr Bigs' that we knew of in Stoke-on-Trent at that time and the main one was known as 'Flake'.

Flake had been a slippery customer who had only been convicted for a minor drugs offence. He was, however, involved in big importation and dealing offences. The latest intelligence suggested that he had a huge stash of cannabis resin and 'bush' (cannabis vegetation). Flake was being brazen enough to deal to selected buyers from his house. We decided to get a search warrant and carry out a raid rather than wait and watch as we had done so many times in the past.

Flake lived in a moderate semi-detached house, together with his wife and two small children. His doors were strengthened and had additional bolts fitted. He had become paranoid about being watched (not without good reason) and was forever looking over his shoulder. When driving he would go around roundabouts two or three times or suddenly pull up to see if anyone was following him. Under the command of Ernie, our Detective Sergeant, and two other detectives we arrived close to Flake's house on a dark, wet winter's evening.

I was armed with nothing more than a soggy search warrant on a clipboard, a pair of spectacles with no lenses and an umbrella. I knocked on the door as the other team members took up various positions around the house. The hall light came on and the familiar outline of the curly-haired bearded Flake came to the door, pressing his face against the glass and squinting through.

The rain was thundering down and I couldn't believe my luck as he started to unlock and open the door to the miserable, rain swept, umbrella-toting figure.

"Hello, what can I do for you?" Flake asked, clearly not seeing through my intricate disguise.

"Good evening," I said, shielding my face beneath the umbrella and holding the clipboard forward. "I've got this for you."

"What is it?" asked Flake in a puzzled tone.

"Search warrant, Flake, DRUG SQUAD," I shouted, pushing my way in before the door could be slammed in my face.

"You bastard, Pye! *You bastard*!"

We swarmed into the house and Flake didn't get chance for a third 'bastard'.

There were the expected shouts of 'police harassment' and adamant claims that there were 'No drugs'. The overused expression, 'I will sue you for every penny' was repeated frequently. Flake also tried a new one, saying he was in the process of bathing the kids and that we surely wouldn't interrupt this family activity. We could get the search done, he suggested, whilst he kept this disruption of his family life away from the children. A look around the bathroom door revealed two small boys splashing about in the bath. Ernie (our DS) suggested that we could be in for criticism if we didn't comply, especially if we didn't find any drugs. After a cursory search of the bathroom it was agreed that he could continue in private whilst we searched the house. Des was given the job of waiting outside the bathroom door, which was to be left ajar.

A few minutes later as I searched through kitchen cupboards with Ernie a tremendous commotion started above our heads. The kitchen ceiling buckled and shook and it was clear that Flake had jumped out of the bathroom window onto the flat roof.

"*Outside*," Des shouted from upstairs.

At the same moment a figure fell past the kitchen window. I darted out through the back door thinking the SAS had arrived as a second figure plummeted into the garden – Des! The side door to the garage hung open. The three of us arrived at the small doorway together and barred Flake's desperate attempt to run off with the evidence – a heavy bulging holdall. He crouched and charged forward in a frantic bid to force his way out – he tried.

The bag contained a massive haul of both bush and cannabis resin. Flake's futile try at running off with it could never have worked. A wrap of cocaine, no doubt dumped from his pocket, was also found floating in the bathwater – so much for his impersonation of a caring father. Flake got twenty-one months in prison. I got a cold.

TWENTY FOUR

DRUG SQUAD searches didn't always go according to plan, as I was about to find out.

With search warrant in pocket it was eight in the morning when we arrived at the rear of a terraced house on the outskirts of Hanley. The occupier was dealing LSD and we'd decided to pay him a house call. The back door looked pretty flimsy and so that was going to be our way in. LSD was easy to flush down the toilet or to throw onto an open fire.

We climbed the wall into the rear yard and with a whispered count of 'one, two, three', kicked the door straight off its hinges. The door lay flat on the kitchen floor and there at the kitchen table sat an elderly gentleman. He was wearing a cloth cap and had a spoonful of cornflakes up to his lips. It was the wrong house! We'd counted one too many and should have been next door. After a quick, but sincere, apology, we did the same again next door where we recovered one measly LSD tablet and a tiny deal of cannabis. We spent the whole afternoon repairing the chap's door then took him to the pub for a couple of pints and heard no more about it.

Another memorable failure came about one summer's evening following a request from the Stafford Drug Squad office. Their information concerned a dealer who was operating from a large house in Burton on Trent. Numerous students lived at the property and there was the potential for many prisoners. A lot of time consuming searching was on the cards.

The entire squad met up at Burton nick, a lovely old building that adjoined the even more impressive magistrates' court. The parade room was full at the briefing. It was a big operation so half a dozen uniformed officers would also be involved. We managed to get into the house without difficulty using the search warrant, but then we had to put up with the expected abuse and swearing. As time went on the attitudes softened – cups of tea appeared, pleasantries were exchanged and first name terms became in vogue as we diligently went through the students' personal belongings.

Some of the uniformed officers were 'rookies', just out of Ryton, and were keenly interested in what was taking place. One of them produced two dead-looking potted plants from the kitchen windowsill, which he thought might be cannabis, but which were pretty obviously tomato plants.

After supervising some of the searching of the house I went out into the enormous back garden which was complete with shed, pergola, greenhouse and a fishpond full of frogs. It was already dark and the torchlights of several uniformed PCs could be seen as they probed bushes, bins, flowerpots and anywhere else that looked likely. The beams of light cut across the garden like a return to the Blitz

I scanned my own torch across the flower borders and spotted something white, poking out from the soil. I knelt down and tugged at the object. As I did so, I was unaware that I was already being closely watched by two of the uniformed officers, who were now standing by my side.

"What's this?" I muttered to myself. It was a fact that many times during searches we had recovered drug stashes buried in plastic bags. "Looks interesting." I said and tugged a little harder at the weighty object.

By this time I was surrounded by a crowd of PCs, plain clothes officers and occupants from the house, all with torches.

"We have found a substance – over," I heard one of the young officers enthusiastically, but prematurely report into his radio, before I could stop him.

"Thank you for that," came back an official sounding voice in reply. "The Superintendent wants a quick report from you as soon as you know what it is – over."

I pulled still harder and could see that it was indeed a white plastic bag and that it contained something heavy several inches beneath the surface.

"It'll be Moroccan cannabis," I heard one exited voice say.

"Must be worth a fortune," said another.

With a little more probing and tugging, I eased the complete bag from the soil. The same voice reported into his radio again: "Yes Sir, it looks like we've got a large haul here – over."

I laid the bag down onto the grass as more rash broadcasts were made by the same voice. "I think we should consider the police photographer to take pictures of the item in situ – over."

It was solid, quite heavy and about fourteen inches long, but the light of so many torches from different angles made it difficult to get a proper perspective. I unrolled the bag and opened the top. The 'thing' was jammed sideways into the bottom. Complete silence now enveloped the whole scene as I carefully put my hand inside to free it. I grasped a slimy solid tubular object and the word 'ERRRR' involuntarily came from my mouth. My mind raced back through the years... What was that word that was always cropping up? NO, this was not excrement. It was a maggot-infested pet cat that had departed this world some three months earlier.

The word 'ERRRR' was closely followed by several different voices, some copying my phrase and others showing their own distaste with much worse expletives along with howls of laughter. We never did find any drugs, the tomato plants were tomato plants and 'The Voice' was given the job of telling the Superintendent what had really happened.

We debriefed in the Coopers Arms until the early hours. Funny how no one wanted to share my crisps!

Bingley Hall is the main building within Staffordshire's County Showground and is situated a few miles outside Stafford. This enormous structure featured regularly in my life during those Drug

Squad years. One reason was that it had taken over from Trentham Gardens as the preferred venue to hold the police promotion exams. I'd actually studied hard for the sergeant's exam this year. Nearly all of my spare time had been spent at my mum and dad's in the quiet with my books out and it had paid off – I'd passed.

The other reason for the repeated visits to Bingley Hall was because it was one of the country's main venues for pop concerts. The Drug Squad had to attend most of these gigs. Yes I know it sounds harsh – being paid to watch some of the world's greatest music stars – but there you go! It was a certainly a perk as we'd all get in free and were allowed to go backstage and pretty well anywhere we wanted. I saw Queen, Bob Marley, Cat Stevens, David Bowie, Genesis along with Pink Floyd and many others. Seldom did we get 'interrupted' with the need to arrest someone for possession or dealing.

I was now eligible for promotion to sergeant, but was also entitled to sit the only other exam in the police promotion procedure – the inspector's exam. I enrolled for this immediately and within a few months of passing the sergeant's exam was back at Bingley with my pen, pencil and ruler. It paid off – I passed and so had both exams out of the way.

Des and I were authorised firearms officers, although the need to carry weapons was rare in those days. The most enjoyable thing about it was that once a month we'd have a full day of weapons training.

Swynnerton Army Camp outside the town of Stone was one facility which allowed for police weapons training. Whittington Army Barracks at Lichfield was another which also catered for this. Both of these military bases had up to date indoor and outside firing ranges. In later years the force acquired its own shooting range near Uttoxeter. We often spent a whole day practising on the outdoor ranges with various different firearms, including .38 revolvers and pump action shotguns along with .22 revolvers on the indoor ranges.

There was a special indoor range at Swynnerton, which was housed inside a large building and was constructed in the manner of a street with shops and houses. There was even a Reliant Robin car parked in the street and a pub at the end of the road with the corny name of *The Skillat Arms.* The range had been built to train troops going out on duty in Northern Ireland. There was a control room at the other end of the street, with bulletproof glass. The lighting could be altered to make it day or night and mechanical targets popped up from different locations. If you hit the target it would automatically fall down. You had to be careful, as a false target could suddenly pop up in one of the windows. It might be a man holding a Black and Decker or a woman holding a baby. If you shot one of these you'd never hear the last of it.

The control room staff could introduce simulated crowd noise and even make the car suddenly flash its lights. Small controlled explosions were used to catch you unawares and unnerve you. The facility had been used for the filming of one of the episodes of the hit TV series *The Avengers.*

There was also an indoor range at Whittington which used a different system. A cine film of a supposed armed robbery would be projected onto a large screen. When one of the robbers in the film posed a threat by pointing his gun at you, you'd fire at the figure. The noise from the shot would automatically make the film freeze and then shine a light through the back of the screen. This would show where, or if, you'd hit the gunman. These days out were a welcome change, but we'd have to continue with our normal drugs work after we'd finished.

LSD (lysergic acid diethylamide, to give it its full name) kept cropping up and always went hand in hand with cannabis; wherever you found LSD you would always find cannabis. In 1977 an operation took place in North Wales where, after months of surveillance and undercover work, the Drug Squad had uncovered the largest LSD factory ever known. The drugs raid on the property, a remote farmhouse, recovered enough LSD for thirty million doses. This illegal drugs laboratory was responsible for the majority of the LSD that was turning up throughout the globe. The tablets produced there were known to the druggies as 'Pyramid' due to their shape, and came in different colours. So much LSD had been produced by the gang that Pyramid still kept turning up for a long while after the operation.

During my drugs course at the Hertfordshire Police HQ back in 1975 I met Detective Inspector Dick Lee. DI Lee was one of the leading lights in the operation which was entitled 'Operation Julie'. The success of Operation Julie was so profound that LSD virtually vanished from the drugs scene for a long time.

TWENTY FIVE

DES AND I had managed a productive year with plenty of good busts, a few cock-ups and plenty of excitement. All of this changed when another major inquiry hit Staffordshire on the 20th September 1978. The terrible, ruthless murder of young paper boy, Carl Bridgewater, at Yew Tree Farm near Stourbridge, hit the headlines.

Thirteen-year-old Carl had been delivering his newspapers on his routine round which took in the isolated farm. The building was just within the boundary of Staffordshire Police and not far from the town of Wombourne. It appears that Carl disturbed a team of burglars stealing antiques from the farm during the temporary absence of the owners. One of the burglars shot the poor boy in the head at close range with a twelve-bore shotgun, killing him instantly. This turned into a huge and lengthy inquiry involving scores of Staffordshire detectives.

The fact that we lived almost at the other end of the county was no bar. Within a few days of the crime Des and I were both drafted in to work full-time on the inquiry. Our day would begin at seven o'clock each morning with a forty mile drive to Wombourne Police Station. This went on every day, seven days a week for several months and it could be midnight or later before we'd get back home.

I was now a dad with two young children and a third one imminent. Eldest, Adam, aged three, and Julie, aged two, seemed increasingly puzzled at the strange face that would occasionally appear – the one called 'Dad'. I had only been working on the Carl Bridgewater murder for a few weeks when our third child, David, was born. I was allowed four days off.

I would usually take the Drug Squad van home overnight and pick Des up from his digs in the morning. He lodged at the single police officer's accommodation above the Magistrates' Court in

Water Street, Newcastle. Part of this building had originally been built as the old County Police Station in the days when there was a separate Newcastle Borough Police Force. There were around half a dozen single policemen living there, although the rooms they occupied on the first floor had probably been originally built as offices. The Newcastle Police Club and snooker room took up some of the ground floor along with a canteen. The rest of the building was still used as the Magistrates' Court.

The police station at Wombourne was built to the same plan as the one at Kidsgrove. It was going to be subjected to the same sort of extra stresses as Kidsgrove throughout the Black Panther Inquiry. The place was simply groaning under the weight of all these overweight detectives, filing cabinets and all the other paraphernalia that went along with the inquiry.

Our job was to track down and interview certain suspects. These people were earmarked as suspicious through all manner of permutations and possibilities. We needed to investigate how well their descriptions fitted men seen near the scene of the crime. The list included the owners of blue estate cars similar to one seen driving away from the farm. Shotgun certificate holders lengthened the list as well as crooks suspected of having illegal guns. Even criminals with old convictions for farmhouse burglaries or antique thefts had to be eliminated.

Each team of two detectives had reams of 'actions' to deal with. Action forms gave the details of the type of inquiry which had to be completed. Our job mostly involved tracking down particular suspects and we could find ourselves travelling all over the country with the aim of finding these people. Many of them were vicious hardened criminals who hated coppers. We needed to know their whereabouts on the day in question, together with a full description, fingerprints and an alibi.

The list of suspects being churned out was endless. There were many teams like ours, all with similar workloads. To make things worse we were working mostly in and around the Black Country in the West Midlands and infrequently in Staffordshire itself. It was all new territory to us and the strong accent took some understanding.

After a while we came to know our way around places like Cradley Heath, Bromsgrove, Walsall, Dudley, Wolverhampton, Brierley Hill, Gornal and Lower Gornal. We soon perfected our own version of the Black Country accent. This requires the mouth to be set turned down, with the top lip straight (you're doing it, now aren't you?). The bottom lip had to slightly protrude with a half-inch bit of open mouth showing. This, we called, 'Brierley Mouth', and it was all that was required to set you off on a near perfect Black Country accent.

In among the scores of 'no-hope' suspects we did come across some who had a chance. But of course each one had to be treated with the same suspicion. One suspect whose name arrived on an action form was Leslie Gaiter. Gaiter had a lot of convictions for house burglaries involving antiques. It also came to light that he had a blue estate car like the one spotted at the murder scene and he looked similar to a man seen nearby. More to the point was the fact that Gaiter had most definitely been responsible for a nasty and expensive burglary at a farmhouse in Shropshire two years before. Antiques had been taken during this crime and Gaiter had been arrested and interviewed, but the police had never been able to prove a case against him. Gaiter lived in the suburbs of Liverpool in a nice semi-detached house with his wife and teenage children.

We showed the details to our detective inspector and it was decided that we would take a team over to Gaiter's house in Liverpool with a search warrant. We would arrest him on suspicion of murder then take him back to Wombourne for interview. Nothing could be more simple. Famous last words.

With meticulous planning and background enquiries completed we arrived at Gaiter's house on a Wednesday lunchtime. Having discovered that he'd taken the day off from work we expected this to be easy. Our team included a detective inspector, a detective sergeant, Des, myself and three local DCs. We were both armed and had the benefit of the Liverpool Police firearms team with us as well as a police dog, Black Maria and a SOCO – the works!

Gaiter Junior greeted us at the door. "Oh, Dad's gone to the match at White Hart Lane in London… Tottenham versus Liverpool, he went this morning."

This was a blow. It meant that we'd still have to get on with the house search, looking for evidence connected to the murder, but it was even more important to arrest Gaiter before he was tipped off. A flurry of phone calls took place between Staffordshire, Liverpool and the Metropolitan Police, whilst the team got on with the search.

Later that evening a call came back from the Met. "We have your man; he is detained at Shepherds Bush Police Station."

Gaiter had been in the crowd waiting for the match to begin when he was surprised to hear the PA system announce his name. 'Will Mr Leslie Gaiter from Liverpool please report to the security office'.

Amazed and worried as to what catastrophe had happened at home, and well before the days of mobile telephones, he had gone straight to the security office. He was greeted by a Met Superintendent who knocked the wind out of his sails with, "Mr Leslie Gaiter, I arrest you for murder."

It was ten o'clock that evening before the DI, Des and I arrived at Shepherds Bush. We were taken straight to the cell where Gaiter was detained.

He stood up from his bench with a worried expression as we walked in. "What the f***'s going on?" he said, with a quavering Scouse accent. "I come down here to see the match. Been in the ground twenty minutes. Hear me name called out in front of me mates and thirty thousand other bastards. Then there's this giant 'bizzy' (Scouse for policeman), who tells me he's arresting me for *muuurder.* I mean *f***ing muuurder.* Then I get chucked in here and that's f***ing that for the next six hours. I've been straight for two years and then *muuurder*, what's going on?"

After an hour and a half of questioning we decided to keep Les in custody and then take him back to Wombourne for more interviews the following day. He was bedded down for a sleepless night in his cell and the three of us were directed to the police accommodation block. This was an old Victorian building used as lodgings for single police officers and to cater for stopovers like this.

We were each given a small room, complete with a washbasin and, yes, I could hardly believe my eyes – khaki-coloured lino. We dumped our belongings, which consisted of nothing more than a briefcase each. I washed my hands and face, and tried my best to clean my teeth by rubbing them with my fingers. We then all bolted for the nearest pub.

It was well after closing time already, but the licensee, Mick, a dumpy little Irishman, had been warned of our arrival. Our hosts, the local CID, who were also his best customers, had told him to look out for us. The pub was full and the doors were locked.

At 2 a.m. we all retired to bed for a few hours. Not much was said in the Staffordshire Police Ford Cortina on the way back to Wombourne. After a couple of hours of interviews and all the form filling and fingerprinting it was decided that Les was not our man. This was not the end of it for him though.

Whilst under the pressure of a murder arrest, Les tried to impress us with his honesty. He fully admitted to the antique farm burglary in Shropshire that he'd been suspected of two years before. Detectives from the town of Wem were delighted at the news and came over to Wombourne to lengthen Les's day a little more.

It was many months later before the inquiry closed with the arrest and charging of a group of men. A lot of long days and late nights had passed and hundreds of miles had been travelled. Scores of interviews and statements had led to dozens of suspects and prisoners. The murder detective's diet of bags of chips, bacon sandwiches, curry and beer had taken its unhealthy toll and we were overdue for a return to a more sensible lifestyle. A lot of the teams were sent back to their divisions to resume their regular jobs. A few of us had to stick it out for a little while longer to clear up some of the outstanding enquiries that still needed to be done.

At this time a well-known BBC TV newscaster, Reginald Bosanquet, was going through a difficult time in his life. Reg often appeared reading the news whilst tipsy and sometimes even downright drunk. We'd do our level best to get back into the nick in time for the news, and typically ended up howling with laughter at Reg's latest gaffe. As a result of this the nickname of 'Reg' was born into the Staffordshire Police and would spread to some other forces as well. Both Des and I were now known as 'Reg', in addition to any other nicknames we possessed. It was found that the name could acceptably be used as a nickname for just about anyone. It effectively took on the usefulness of the term 'mate', especially in police circles.

TWENTY SIX

SO I EVENTUALLY returned to Hanley and back to Drug Squad work with the hope that the slightly shorter working days would allow a little more normality back into my life. With my inspector's exam passed and the law books pushed back into the cupboard perhaps I could devote more time to my family.

Illegal drug abuse was rife at this time. The Northern Soul music scene was still active and was used by a lot of dealers to feed the habits of unfortunates. These youngsters were gullible and naive enough to gamble with their lives so that they could keep awake and dancing through the all-night discos. They would travel many miles for a chance to be part of the scene. Northern Soul was great music, but its association with drugs gave it a bad name. A lot of people went on to become serious addicts when their experimentation led them to try other more harmful substances.

Chemist shops were burgled on most nights of the week and the DDA (Dangerous Drugs Act) cabinets were forced open, or ripped from the wall. Everything stored in the cabinets was used or sold on by the druggies, from diamorphine (heroin) right down to barbiturates (downers). Amphetamine (speed) was the most popular drug with the Northern Soul music scene and the biggest target for theft from chemist shops. It had many legitimate uses, the most popular being as a slimming aid.

A detective sergeant at our Stafford office had the job of going around the county examining the DDA cabinets in all the chemists' shops. He would come across all manner of strange drugs and potions that had lain there for many years. Arsenic and even cyanide would occasionally crop up. The odd bottle of something called 'tincture of cannabis' dating back to before the Second World War would sometimes come to light.

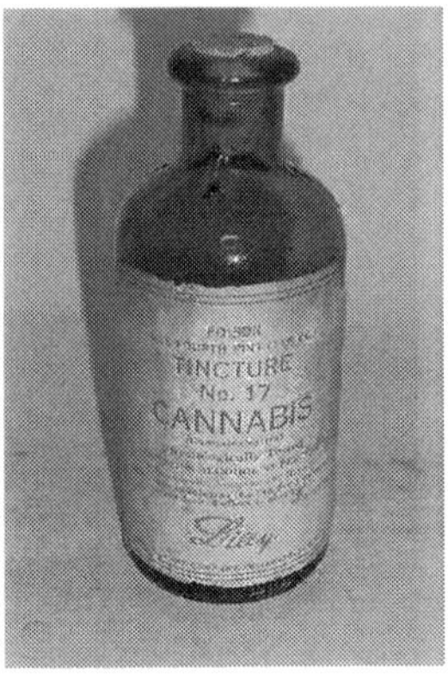

It was used as a form of 'cure-all' with all kinds of claims written on the label. The druggies would dip their cigarettes into it and smoke it if they got their hands on it.

The Wigan based 'Casino Club' was the main Northern Soul club in the country at this time. Most of the speed stolen in chemist shop burglaries locally would ultimately end up there. The remaining stolen drugs would be 'cut', watered down or generally unhealthily messed about with before being sold on. The aim of this was to increase the measurable quantity and therefore enlarge the eventual profit. Local pubs and clubs would serve as the outlet for these even more dangerous drugs which would change hands for exorbitant sums.

The flood of illicit drugs that became available led to many overdoses and deaths. They came in clusters whenever a strong uncut substance got into the hands of dealers and users who were unaware of its strength or what it really was. These terrible facts were demonstrated precisely by a series of events which started with an early Sunday morning phone call. The story which led to my 3 a.m. visit to a flat in Norton Stoke-on-Trent was a tragic one. The twenty three year old man who lay dead on the floor was known to me; I had arrested him several times and had tried to talk sense into him on a number of occasions.

It proved to be a long and even more harrowing day as more phone calls followed with similar messages. The distressing scene was repeated twice more with my visits to another two very young and very dead men. News from the hospital added another six dangerously ill overdose victims to the list. Fortunately they survived.

All the victims (both dead and living) were known to me because of their involvement in drugs. It was established that they had underestimated the strength of the street drug which was doing the rounds. It turned out to be a very pure and powerful version of Crystal Meth (Methamphetamine).

One of these deaths resulted in the arrest of one of the overdose survivors. It was discovered that he had injected his late friend with the drug that had killed him. Some weeks later I charged him with manslaughter. I spent several weeks on the inquiry, which was headed by Detective Chief Inspector Keith Houlston, a pleasant, humorous man and a good friend in years to come.

As the case was so serious it had to be heard by a high court judge and consequently, Shrewsbury Crown Court was the eventual venue. The court hearing lasted almost two weeks and when I look back, despite the drama and sadness of the events, some humour came from it. During the fairly boring journeys between Stoke and Shrewsbury, Keith and I used to play a game he'd invented to play with his kids whilst going on holiday. Every time you passed by a pub on your side of the road that had a creature within its title name you'd get points for how many legs it had. Examples would be 'The Red Lion' – four legs – four points. 'The King's Head' – only two points. How I wished we could go past the Shropshire Fly for some bonus points, but there were only so many ways you could get to Shrewsbury.

Keith was always very professional and meticulous and this was apparent throughout the hearing. It was inevitable that my mind would wander back to one of our journeys – *'right, Porky, White Horse, that's another four for me'*. I wondered what the judge would have made of it. The accused was found guilty and received a lengthy term in prison.

The druggies would try anything for a 'buzz', but without exception each one, even the pill heads of the Northern Soul scene, all started out on cannabis. The theory that cannabis is not a gateway to other substance abuse and that it is a harmless recreational drug seems to be popular. Trendy people and politicians try to be everyone's friend by promoting this idea. Having seen at close quarters the damage and destruction caused by cannabis I know this is not the case.

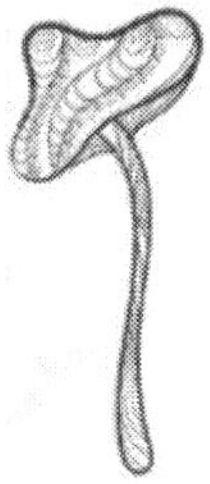

The use of magic mushrooms was a seasonal thing. They would make their appearance at the end of summer or early autumn. These tiny, beige fungi with pointed caps grow wild in patches, sprouting up following a wet spell. Their real name is *Psilocibe Semilanceata* and when eaten they produce LSD-style hallucinations. Most weekends at the right time of year would result in a handful of youngsters being examined at the local hospital by a puzzled doctor. The wide-eyed, arm-waving hallucinations could take a while to diagnose.

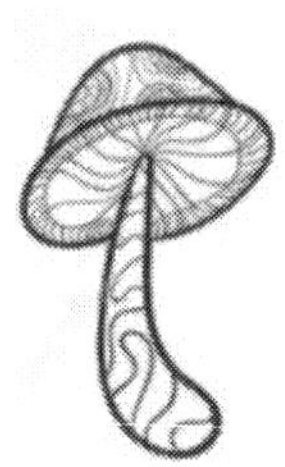

One of the more peculiar substances the druggies found they could get a high from was a perfectly legal herbal cigarette. It could be purchased over the counter and claimed to help asthma suffers. It was found that if the cigarette was broken open and the leafy contents sprinkled into a hot drink, the resulting beverage would produce hallucinations and weird behaviour. The concoction became known as 'goon dust'. My first encounter with it was when I was called down from the Drug Squad office and asked for my opinion on a young man who had been brought in. He had been found riding a bicycle through the town centre whilst wearing nothing other than a woman's flowery dress. As he had no underpants on, and the bicycle was a racer with drop handlebars, it must have been quite a sight. For some reason he was also armed with an aerosol tin of fly spray that was fitted into the drinks holder between the handlebars. He had been using this to give any onlookers the occasional squirt. He had consumed two large mugs of goon dust tea. The manufacturers soon took the asthma cigarettes off the market.

Towards the end of my Drug Squad time, Des and I, together with another colleague, DC Bernie Pearce, had been investigating a drugs ring in the Potteries town of Longton. We had good information that cannabis was being sold from a particular house and that the dealer was also receiving stolen property as payment for drugs. We had been watching the house using the force observations van on and off for the best part of a week.

The obs van was a tatty-looking, green Commer Spacevan, which had been made to look like a tradesman's vehicle. It had a partition between the driving compartment and the rear, with a little door which allowed us to climb into the back. We could then covertly take up our places without getting outside and being spotted by anyone. There was a spyhole through the partition, to look through the windscreen from the back. The one-way glass in the rear windows stopped people seeing us, but allowed us to look out. There were also tiny spyholes in the sides and a flap in the partition on the driver's side, so you could reach through and flick the ignition key on to wipe the windscreen. This was useful if it had been raining and was arranged to work without switching on the engine. It did, however, mean that the ignition keys had to be left in.

We had been watching the house on and off for three days. The neighbours seemed to be getting annoyed that this tatty van was frequently left in the street for hours on end. Often right after we had parked, a resident would appear from one of the houses looking annoyed and puzzled as to how they never caught anyone leaving the empty van. On one occasion an inquisitive neighbour pushed his face right up to the one-way glass. The glass wasn't one hundred percent one-way and so we lay on the floor hoping he couldn't see us.

We had to park opposite the gates of a haulage firm to get a good view of the target house. It was in the middle of a red-hot summer, we were sweltering and had to strip to our underpants when the heat became too much. A bottle of beer each would help to keep us cool and as there was no toilet in the van we used our initiative (and the empties) when the call of nature arrived.

Early one evening, as the hot spell continued a large lorry appeared and parked some way up the road from us.

"What's he doing?" whispered Bernie.

"That's a lorry from the haulage firm," Des said. "He's not going to be able to get into the yard because of how we've parked."

The driver jumped down from his cab and stood looking over at our van with an annoyed expression. Shaking his head, he walked over to the haulage yard and started to undo the gates.

We held our breath as he turned and made a bee-line for the van. He peered in through the front window before wandering around and putting his face up against the so-called one-way glass in the back doors. We crouched out of sight and had still not taken a breath when he went back to the driver's side window. Upon seeing the keys dangling from the ignition, he pulled open the door and we felt the van settle down as he climbed into the driving seat.

In our hidey-hole a matter of feet away from him, the three of us sat on the floor, glistening with sweat, wearing nothing but our underpants and trainers. We heard the engine start, and all shared the same anguished expression as we quietly took hold of our individual urine-filled beer bottles to prevent any further catastrophes.

The driver crunched the van into first gear and then, not being familiar with the clutch, kangarooed it off up the road as we held on tight and kept quiet. After about thirty yards we were thrown up against the partition in a jumble of arms and legs as the brakes were angrily stamped on.

The thought struck me: *Here I was wearing nothing other than my underpants and trainers. I was covered from head to foot in sweat and entwined with my two sweating male colleagues. They too were similarly scantily clad and each of us was holding a bottle of urine. Should the driver find the viewing flap and peer through there would be no acceptable explanation.*

After yanking on the handbrake and banging the door as hard as possible our chauffeur stormed off back to his lorry, annoyed that he had been inconvenienced. The three of us looked at each other in disbelief.

"We've just been taken and driven away!" I quietly exclaimed.

The next day we returned to the plot and were a little more careful about where we parked. Our information now added that the drug dealer had swapped some of his drugs for a number valuable stolen paintings. A Magistrate had signed us a search warrant earlier in the day and so were ready to go in when the time looked right.

We discussed the best way to go about the raid. We were worried that even though we had watched for many hours, we had not seen any sign of paintings being taken in. We looked on with interest as we saw the dealer and his girlfriend leave the house by the front door and drive off in their car.

Des and I decided to do a recce – we needed to see if anything was obvious through the back window of the house. We took a two-way radio that operated between us and Bernie in the van and casually wandered down the street towards the house (fully dressed). When we were sure that no one was watching we dodged into the alleyway running along the backs of the row of two-up, two-down terraces.

Peering over the locked gate into the backyard, I whispered into my radio to Bernie. "Okay, we're going over the wall."

"Righto!" came back Bernie's voice.

We clambered up and dropped down into the small backyard, confident that as the dealer had only just left we were in no danger. I peered in through the kitchen window as Des looked into the living room.

"See anything?"

"Not sure," replied Des. "There's a picture hanging on the wall, but with these net curtains I can't make anything out."

In the kitchen window a piece of cardboard was stuck into one of the small mullioned panes, which had obviously been broken some time before.

"How about this, Reg?" I suggested.

Des took a quick look. "Why not… we've got a warrant and there's no reason for them to know we'd already been for a look around."

I poked the cardboard inside and opened the window. We climbed through into the kitchen. The door to the lounge was closed and the family cat, which had been locked in the kitchen hissed, fur on end and tail erect at the intrusion. As we opened the door through to the lounge the cat followed us in, giving its imitation of what a cat on hot bricks probably looks like.

We checked the room. *Bingo*! There were paintings everywhere; at least a dozen standing against the walls – definitely the stolen ones. Two luxuriant cannabis plants flourished in pots in the corner and a set of brass scales was on the table. Alongside the scales were several small chunky objects wrapped in silver paper.

The two way radio crackled into life with Bernie's frantic voice. "They're back! They're outside now!"

"What?" I shouted back as I headed for the kitchen.

"He's getting something out of the boot," Bernie said. "She's standing by the door getting her keys out."

"The cat," Des said. "If it's not in the kitchen they might suspect something." He turned back into the living room. The animal had become a little more at ease with the intruders and was lying peacefully on the arm of the sofa.

Bernie's voice, although on low volume was shrill and anxious.

"She's put the key in the door."

Des grabbed the cat by the scruff of its neck and released it into the kitchen. But not before it had dug its claws into his thumb. "Bloody hell!" he muttered.

I was now outside and as soon as Des had followed suit I pressed the cardboard window pane back in place.

Bernie's voice piped up again. "She's in and he's right behind her."

We both scrambled over the gate and into the alleyway as Bernie's frantic tones repeated: "Speak to me for God's sake."

We quickly followed up the recce with an official search and the arrest of the owner. The haul of recovered property included a lot of cannabis, some LSD, the plants, scales and a several stolen paintings.

The paintings were returned to their owner and at a later court case the dealer received a prison sentence for the various drugs offences and for the crime of handling stolen property.

TWENTY SEVEN

I KNEW THAT my time on the Drug Squad was nearing its end when an offer came through for a CID course. A force policy recommended that no one should serve in one department for too long. I took heed of the warning sign and jumped at the chance of the course at the West Midlands Detective Training School.

Some long-awaited good news arrived along with the course invitation. The high-level inquiry and report into police pay and conditions, which had been undertaken by Lord Edmund Davies, had been published. We would be getting a substantial pay increase and other benefits, including overtime payment. The extra money might mean that I would be able to upgrade my tatty Hillman Avenger Estate car.

I'm sure that the thought of all that extra money went through my mind when I parked the said 'heap' on the car park of the training centre on Birmingham's busy Pershore Road. The building was named 'Tally Ho' and resembled a 1950's high-rise block of flats. As well as CID subjects it was also a centre for all manner of other police instruction.

With my case in one hand and a suit draped over an arm, I walked past the statue of Sir Robert Peel, the father of modern policing, and into the foyer. A uniformed PC slid the glass widow hatch to one side and gave me the key to room 305.

"You've to be in classroom number seven at 11 a.m."

My room on the third floor looked out over the main road and was to be home for the next ten weeks. Some memories flooded back as I looked around; wardrobe, bed, sink, mirror, mat and oh, *green* vinyl lino tiles – different.

Down in classroom number seven, the twenty-one desks were filling up with moustachioed look-alike detectives. In those days it was the fashion to sport a drooping 'tash'. I think that the only person in the class without one was the lone woman detective on the course.

Most of the other detectives in the class had short police-style haircuts, apart from one or two of us who had been working on Crime Squads or Drug Squads. All of us, however, wore suits, and I knew that if I did get a CID posting I too would have to revert to a neat trim. Most of the suits would disappear after the first week of 'making a good impression'. They would be replaced with the CID dress of the day – leather jackets, but always a collar and tie.

Sitting behind me on that first day in the classroom was a man who would become my friend until well into our retirement. Graham Timson from Kettering in Northamptonshire had an infectious laugh and the same bizarre, childish and stupid sense of humour as my own.

Our class instructor introduced himself. "Detective Sergeant Jim Evans… Nice to meet you all. Lots of work to do over the next ten weeks and I'm sure we'll have a few laughs along the way. We'll be starting some proper work shortly, but on an important note, do we have any wholesalers amongst us, anything to sell?"

By this, Jim was referring to the fact that as we had come from all over the country many of us would have contacts for all manner of cheap goods. Courses such as this were the ideal market place. It was accepted that we would sell the goods at a little more than we bought them and everybody was happy.

Jim continued, "Graham Timson, you're our Northampton representative, any shoes?" (Northamptonshire was one of the country's foremost areas for shoe manufacture).

"Yes, Sarge, got a bedroom full, all good prices."

"Okay then… John Pye, our Stoke-on-Trent rep, any pots to sell?"

"Yes, Sarge," I said, "a car load… dinner services, tea sets, mugs, you name it, plenty of bargains."

I had been tipped off about this nice little earner by other course-goers and so had visited Beresford's pottery in Longton. Beresford's would let police officers going on courses have whatever they wanted on sale or return.

Various other wares were also on offer, including suit lengths (material for suits), and someone was able to get all manner of saucepans and other kitchen equipment.

"Okay," said Jim, "we'll have a sale after tea tomorrow night in this classroom. I'll make sure all the other classes get to know, along with the cleaners and kitchen staff."

Jim then nodded over at the one empty desk in the classroom. "You'll note that we have someone missing. David Downwood from the Royal Ulster Constabulary, Northern Ireland, is stuck on a court case, but hopes to be with us for Wednesday."

Law notes and legal books were handed out before we were invited to give a cameo picture of ourselves to our fellow students. It was a good way of getting to know everyone. The Tuesday sale went well. The classroom was filled with all the promised plunder every item a bargain. Dozens of staff and students attended, and could not believe the cheap prices. Both Graham and I boosted our beer money and took orders throughout the entire course.

By Wednesday our RUC colleague David, had arrived. Much of his recent service had been spent working on crimes involving the IRA. The course was probably a bit of an overdue holiday for him. He had been working on the most awful, sickening and horrible IRA atrocities. He was a star, but had clearly had a difficult and stressful time. Many of the RUC officers who had been involved in this type of work were completely worn out mentally. David was used to wearing a gun virtually twenty-four hours a day, and admitted to feeling undressed and uneasy without it.

The course got into its stride and we developed a routine as we were bombarded with copious amounts of criminal law, legal practice, police procedure and practical exercises. We delved into every possible aspect of the differing categories of crime and investigation. We even studied in detail exactly how an ID parade *should* be performed!

There were piles of homework every evening and every weekend. Our day would start at 7.30 a.m. and finish around 9 p.m. In this time we would fit in meal breaks and perhaps a game of volleyball between lectures. After 9 p.m. we would escape for a few hours, to one of the local pubs or to the bar.

We took David out for a curry one night; it was the first time he'd been able to relax properly for a long time. He was utterly drunk as we sat around the table with various steaming curries. His first mouthful of vindaloo resulted in a coughing fit and spluttering cry of, '*Tooo hot*' as he poured a jug of water over the offending dish. We had to compensate the waiter for the mess by having a whip-round.

Occasionally we'd collect a takeaway curry or a Chinese from one of the nearby restaurants on Pershore Road. This was okay, but led to everyone borrowing plates from my crockery stock and I'd wake up next morning to a sink full of dirty dishes.

In keeping with the responsible and sober attitude that is synonymous with being police officers, some of us had visited a joke shop in Birmingham. The police buzzword of the day was 'proactive'. One particular purchase was made with nothing more than a quick laugh in mind. We were certainly not thinking proactively, but what transpired made those exploding cigarette pellets a fortuitous buy.

We had a full afternoon lecture one day from the army bomb disposal unit. The Captain and his chain smoking corporal who went by the nickname of 'Ziggy' kept us enthralled with interesting demonstrations and detail. They took us out onto the rugby field and detonated some Semtex explosive whilst we watched from a considerable distance. We were astonished that the tiny amount could produce such a tremendous blast. Even from a good distance away I felt my trousers flap in the shock wave.

We trooped back into the lecture theatre and I was suspicious of a couple of pieces of cardboard lying about. A torch and briefcase also looked out of place and caused a few furrowed brows. One detective bowled into the class without a care in the world and plonked his foot squarely on one of the pieces of card. A tremendous explosion echoed around the room and everyone dived for cover. This was, of course, Ziggy's little trick, a way of showing us how simple it could be to plant and conceal explosives and how easily they could be disguised. It wasn't long before we had endured several more bangs from the innocent-looking items. We were left nervously twitching as we lurched, hands over heads, down to the canteen for a half-time tea break.

It was time to get our own back on Ziggy and although many people's cigarettes had already been detonated since the Joke Shop visit, there were still three pellets left. God was smiling on us when it was realised that the Corporal's fags had been left on the lecture dais! It was a simple matter to nip back into the room and seed his packet. We kept our fingers crossed that he would pick a live one before they had finished for the day.

The lecture continued after the break with Ziggy and the captain playing their well-rehearsed parts. We were all a little distracted each time the corporal lit up another as we waited with squinting eyes for the inevitable. Graham was quietly laying bets as to which numbered cigarette would explode. It was number four!

Ziggy casually pinged his Zippo lighter and drew in, eyes closed as he filled his lungs.

Bang!

He dived beneath the dais, his papers tumbling to the floor. The captain fell backwards against the table and the whole room let out an ear-splitting cheer. Choking on his half-consumed lung full of smoke, Ziggy looked up from floor level and coughed.

He shook his head before admitting, "I've never been caught out before."

Another daft prank especially suited to the lecture theatre was that of making small paper hats. These would then be ever so carefully placed onto the head of the person sitting in front of you. As the room was tiered down, the head in front was at the optimum height for covert hat placing. On one occasion we had a line of eight detectives sitting attentively listening to a lecture all unknowingly wearing a neat little hat. The giveaway would come when a hat wearer raised a finger to make a point. It was asking a bit much of the lecturer for him not burst into laughter. The situation of a grown man making a considered contribution to the conversation, whilst wearing a small paper hat was only ever going to go one way. The other offshoot of this was that everyone then became paper hat paranoid. Any new lecturers would be puzzled as to why everyone in the room kept patting the tops of their heads. It's a wonder that we actually learned anything.

There was a group of four open showers on each floor of the residential block. A transparent plastic shower curtain was all that afforded the occupant a degree of privacy. On the wall of each corridor was fixed a large, sturdy, red steel fire hose reel complete with many yards of thick, red rubber heavy-duty piping. The reel was mounted on a giant metal hinge, so that it could swing out away from the wall whilst in use. A large chromium tap was fitted to the business end and the water pressure was immense.

When the reel was swung outwards it automatically engaged the water pressure. It was then a simple matter of turning on the tap to achieve a tremendously powerful blast of water. This most useful tool of torture was used on fellow students as they were in the middle of a soothing, hangover-relieving, steaming hot shower. Suddenly the plastic shower curtain would be blasted to the ceiling by the full force of the ice-cold jet of water, which threatened to remove skin. People were seen, towel under arm, sneaking off to another floor for a safe shower.

So fierce was the pressure that if the hose got dropped it would thrash about like an electrified snake. During one of these crazy moments I received the heavy metal nozzle sharply on my foot, sending me hopping away in excruciating pain. As RUC man David turned off the nozzle tap a hissing and tearing sound signalled the arrival of a serious problem. This was followed by an explosion of water as the hosepipe ripped open, sending gallons spraying into the air. Everyone ran for cover, David crashed to the floor cracking his head open on the window ledge. Graham, who had a sprained ankle from an earlier sporting injury, bravely grappled with the writhing hose whilst hopping on his good leg.

Several minutes of high-pressure water went by, before we discovered that we only had to swing the reel back to the wall to cut off the supply. The damage, however, was done. The fourth floor was several inches deep in water which was cascading down the stairs. David's head was badly cut, with blood dripping into the torrent. My big toe was like a balloon and Graham winced with pain as he splashed about to retrieve his walking stick, which was in danger of being swept away. All three of us went to hospital. David had six stitches, I had an X-ray on my badly bruised toe and Graham was found to have an even more sprained ankle than before.

When we returned later that evening we feared the worst. We were expecting to see the fire brigade, plumbers' vans and probably a Superintendent ready to send us back home. It was as though nothing had happened… just a few damp patches on the floor.

"Did we dream it?" I said to the other two.

"Nightmare, more like," said Graham, leaning on to his walking stick.

We settled down to a small tot of David's poteen (moonshine Irish spirit). It would be a celebration, as we didn't appear to be in trouble – and then all the lights in the entire building went out.

"SHIT" said the three voices in the darkness in unison.

Apparently an inspector in a room below had come in after an evening at the bar, switched on his light and *bang*. Water was running through the ceiling rose in his bedroom, cascading down his light shade and onto his bed. Two feet of water had filled into the bottom of the lift shaft, and someone had mentioned our names 'in dispatches'.

At nine o'clock next morning the three of us were lined up in front of the desk of the course commandant, Detective Chief Inspector Ray Dyde. Alongside the boss stood the poker-faced Detective Sergeant Jim Evans.

David had an egg-sized black lump on his forehead with the stitches holding together a nasty gash. I stood to attention in my best suit. I would have looked smart had it not been for the size twelve white Plimsoll which was fitted to my injured left foot. This had been borrowed from Graham and was not a good match for my own brown shoe on the other foot. Graham stood next to me, bent over as he leaned more than usual on to his buckling walking stick.

DCI Dyde kept his gaze fixed down on his desk as he spoke to us.

"What the hell have you three been playing at? All the lights are out on the second and third floors. The lift is out of action and we might have to get the police bloody frogman out to fix it. We've got an Assistant Chief Constable staying over tonight and I've got to try to find some way of keeping this from him… Just look at the state of the three of you."

He lifted his head and set us with a stare over his half-moon glasses, pressing his lips ever more tightly together as his self-control battled to keep the humour at bay. He looked back down at his desk.

Jim Evans' grim expression was also slowly cracking as he kept his vision firmly on a mark on the ceiling.

"Get out, and consider yourselves lucky."

The three of us Right-Turned and hobbled out. No sooner had we closed the door behind us than we could hear the two of them roaring with laughter. Nothing more was said of the hosepipe incident. The bonus that came from it was that anyone could take a shower in uninterrupted peace whenever they wished.

Yes, there had been a lot of fooling about and a lot of laughs, but there had also been a lot of hard work. The accumulation of the detailed practical and theoretical knowledge would help us all in the years to come. The end of the course culminated in a week of exams, practical tests and presentations.

We all had a comprehensive record of achievements throughout the course to take back to our respective forces. Fortunately there was no mention of hosepipes and other such misdemeanours. The friendship and camaraderie that had developed would stand us in good stead many times in the years ahead. Many of us would make contact during investigations which crossed borders. An end of course celebration was held in the nearby Selly Oak pub.

On the Friday lunchtime we said our goodbyes, hefted suitcases, boxes, bags, books and stocks of unsold goods into our respective tatty cars and left Tally Ho to return to the real world.

TWENTY EIGHT

IT WAS NOT long after my return to the Drug Squad that my CID posting came through – Hanley. My actual physical move was only a matter of yards down the corridor from the office that I had worked from for the past three years.

Hanley CID was a large and busy department and I knew that some things would be similar – strange shifts, long hours and not much time off. I arrived on my first day, complete with the first smart haircut I'd had in three years and wearing a suit – no more jeans and trainers.

I was given a desk, complete with the usual in-tray already piled high. There was a phone on each desk, and most of them seemed to be ringing constantly. The sheer quantity of jobs that kept coming in was ridiculous. Of course, much of it was the same minor stuff that I'd had a taste of whilst doing my CID stint at Stoke – petty theft and minor assaults. But each day also bought with it a constant stream of burglaries, car thefts, serious assaults, expensive criminal damage, con tricks, major frauds and sexual offences. All these crimes had to be investigated.

An everyday priority was to deal with prisoners who had been arrested in the night. There could be further enquiries, interviews and possible court appearances. This often took up a most of the day, leaving all your other investigations and paperwork to mount up.

The detective whose turn it was to do nights for a week was run ragged from the moment he arrived at ten o'clock each night. He'd have to go from one job to another between the towns of Hanley, Burslem and Tunstall throughout his entire shift. His tour of duty was supposed to finish at six o'clock, but he would often still be typing up his report at nine.

Due to the hectic workload, Hanley CID office had the luxury of an office detective sergeant in addition to the existing operational detectives. Ken Lawton, otherwise known as 'Lawt' was a wise and cunning man who would take the mickey out of you before guiding you along the best path. Lawt's sidekick and assistant was the office DC – Charlie Edwards. Charlie's job was to classify the various crimes and see that the daily paperwork found its way to the correct destination.

Every burglary back then had to be attended by a detective and my morning, when not dealing with overnight prisoners, always involved visits to these crimes. The same old villains' names would crop up time and again. Many were people I knew only too well from my Drug Squad days – druggies burgling to fund their habit. A lot of time was also spent giving evidence at both at the Magistrates' and the Crown Courts.

One morning a young constable arrived in the office. His new Burton's suit was the give-away – he was starting his four-month CID aide. Young Geoff White had predictably been nicknamed Chalky, but already answered to the name of Reg as well. Chalky was a rarity for a police officer, possessing both common sense and intelligence (it was usually one or the other). He spoke with a slow nasal drawl and could make a joke or a funny story out of nothing. He also had a liking for beer and a dislike for criminals, shirkers, skivers and thugs. We got on well.

Chalky had worked as a patrol constable in Hanley town centre for most of his two and a half years of service and was already well acquainted with the local villains. I met him one Saturday morning as I came in through the front doorway of Hanley nick. He was the 8 a.m. early CID man and was heading down towards the cells with a bundle of papers in his hand.

"Loads of prisoners in, Reg," he drawled, "could do with a hand."

It was well after midday by the time we'd sorted out all the prisoners. It had been a manic day with all the other detectives busy with overnight burglaries. After catching a bite of lunch, we found that there was still an outstanding burglary that hadn't been visited. The break-in at Newbold Optician's in the town centre had been reported earlier that morning but still awaited the attendance of a detective.

I parked the van around the corner from the optician's shop and we both made our way in through the front door.

"CID," I said to the manager, Mr Thomas, "sorry for the delay, we've been up to our necks."

"No problem, your fingerprint man came around earlier, but the whole thing has messed us up."

"What's been taken, Mr Thomas?" Chalky asked.

The manager frowned as he looked at us. "Two hundred pairs of spectacle frames… and a clock."

"What? Just the frames, no glass in them?"

"That's right," said the bemused manager. "They're valuable in total, but absolutely no use to anyone other than an optician, and the clock was only worth about fifteen quid."

Chalky glanced at me concealing a grin and the thought passed between us, *what the hell would anyone want with two hundred pairs of spectacle frames?*

We checked the shop and found that the offender had broken in through a back window. Drawers and cupboards and been searched and some additional petty cash also stolen. It was all fairly standard stuff. Chalky took a statement from Mr Thomas and we made our way back to the office to try to get on with all the other work we hadn't even touched.

A couple of days later two newcomers to the area were suggested as being the culprits. The drinks we'd bought for the right local crooks had delivered to us the identity of two Scotsmen.

We had never heard of Duncan Adams and Tommy McPhee before. They were indeed recent arrivals to the large council estate of Abbey Hulton, which was about one mile out of town. It was a rough area and we'd frequently find ourselves there, kicking in someone's door, or dealing with a serious domestic assault.

The word was out that these two had amassed a stash of spectacle frames which they were trying to offload in local pubs in return for pints of beer or whiskies. The information seemed justified when we visited the home of the unsuspecting Tommy McPhee. He had yet to become acquainted with the local CID and so our arrival at that particular moment was unfortunate for him. As he opened the door it was clear that he was in the middle of a party-piece with his family. The 'prop' he was using to create his Dame Edna Everidge impression somewhat gave away the game. A tear of laughter rolled down his cheek and it was clear that there were no lenses in the frames of the elaborately stylised pink and diamante studded spectacles.

"Good evening… gentlemen," he said, his smile beginning to recede as the penny was dropping that Stoke-on-Trent coppers look a lot like those in Scotland. "What can I do for you…?"

"CID, Mr McPhee." I announced.

"We've got a search warrant," said Chalky. "Nice glasses."

It was pretty obvious that we'd got our man, or at least one of them, but Tommy insisted that he had bought the spectacles from a man in a pub. He went on to add that the same man had also supplied another pair which we found Sellotaped onto the pet dog's head. A later search of Duncan's house (the Scottish accomplice) turned up an additional three pairs. After a night of 'reflection' in the cells, the pair agreed to get all the frames back by the following night. True to their word they met us in the Corner Cupboard pub and handed over two Tesco bags brimming over with the missing specs.

Hanley CID office was an enormous space. It was normal for there to be as many as thirty people sitting at desks, answering telephones and standing in groups discussing operations. It was amusing the following morning when two detectives from another force arrived to discuss a cross-border case. The bewilderment on their faces was clear as they scanned around puzzling as to why every single person – civilian staff, cadets, typists and detectives – were wearing some form of spectacles. These ranged from John Lennon style to horn-rimmed or blue butterfly-winged.

Our own disbelief would come later in the month when we were told that both Tommy and Duncan were going to plead 'not guilty' at Crown Court. This was in spite of all the evidence which included their admissions.

Crown Court was always a bit of a nail-biting affair. Even when sure of your ground there could be some smart-arsed barrister trying to score points in an effort to discredit you. In a 'not guilty' case witnesses cannot go into the court room until they are called. They are not allowed to speak to people who have already given evidence and so have no idea what's going on or what has already been said.

Chalky was called to give evidence first, and even though I knew we'd done everything by the book, I still sat outside fidgeting pensively. I wished I could hear what was going on. What nit-picking thing that had nothing to do with the case was the defence probing into in an effort to throw up a smokescreen?

"DETECTIVE CONSTABLE PYE!" shouted out the court usher.

Straighten tie, deep intake of breath, notebook in hand and enter courtroom.

I was familiar with Hanley Crown Court by this time, but it never made any difference. The dark Victorian wood panelling and lofty carved plasterwork ceilings intensified the severity the mood. The acoustics of the room were flavoured with a haunting echo which always made my pulse race.

The prosecuting barrister led me through my evidence and I was allowed to use my pocket notebook, but not before the stock questions.

"And these are your original notes, are they, Officer?" he asked.

"Yes, Sir," I replied.

"Made as soon as possible after each event?"

"Yes, Sir."

Everything seemed to have gone ok, and then it came to the defence's turn.

The barrister gave me an arrogant stare. "Original notes then Officer? Made… you say… as soon as possible?"

"Yes… Yes, Sir"

"So, Mr. Pye…" droned the defence barrister, "you and DC White had been in this public house with Mr Adams and Mr McPhee. You have stated that the alleged handover of the spectacle frames had taken place at this time. Did you and Mr White then religiously make up your pocketbooks together… did you… as soon as possible?"

"Y-yes. Y-yes, Sir," I stammered, wondering why he was dwelling on this point and what exactly Chalky had said.

A trickle of sweat meandered down my temple.

"How long, Officer?" demanded the barrister.

"What, w-what? Pardon, p-pardon, Sir."

"How long after the pub meeting, Officer, did you and Mr White make up your pocketbooks?"

"Well, Sir, erm…"

My mind went into overdrive… *Did we get called to another job, or did we go back to the nick?*

"I'm waiting, Officer", demanded the barrister.

"Erm, er… about forty-five minutes, I should think, Sir. Yes, about forty-five minutes," I finally managed to say.

"Thank you, Officer," said the barrister. "No further questions, you may sit down."

With a slight tremble I walked from the witness box and headed towards where Chalky was sitting on one of the chairs reserved for police. He fixed me with an emotionless tight-lipped stare.

"How was that?" I whispered, as I sat down next to him.

"Crap!" was Chalky's corner-of-the-mouth reply. "You've dropped us in it."

"Why, what did you say?"

"Three quarters of an hour!"

The Scottish burglars were convicted and sentenced to a short term in prison. The office joke went around that they'd been framed!

One afternoon we visited the home of a well-known crook on the Abbey Hulton estate. The off-licence had been screwed – again! The management were so fed up about the number of times the place had been burgled that they were considering closing the branch down. This time someone had helped themselves to a few hundred cigarettes and taken the safe away.

By knocking on doors we'd found a neighbour who had looked from his window in the dead of night to see two men walking along the street. One was pushing a wheelbarrow that contained a safe. The question came to mind: *Well, why didn't you ring the police?* But perhaps wheelbarrow safe-pushing had become a regular pastime.

The witness had identified the man who was walking with the wheelbarrow-pusher and now we stood at his front door awaiting a reply to our heavy handed knocking. It was a house we'd visited many times.

"Oh! It's you bloody pair again, is it," he said as he opened up. "Come in, do what you like, I'm watching the racing." He then slumped down in his chair in front of the TV.

I told him some of the story.

"Oh! That youth with the safe, the other night, the one in the wheelbarrow?" he said, without removing his stare from the screen.

"Well," I sarcastically said, "how many different safes were being shifted about that night?"

"I only saw the one," was the humourless reply. "I don't know who he was. I just got talking to him. I was on my way back from the club."

Chalky looked over at me and I knew that we both had the same vivid picture in our minds. It entailed various groups of people walking around the estate of a balmy evening, each pushing a wheelbarrow loaded with a safe.

The house was a tip – stuff everywhere, from dirty dishes and old takeaway cartons to dog muck in the hall. A nauseating smell permeated the entire house. We unenthusiastically started the search in the living room, wandering back and forth, passing the man as he sat glued to the television.

The smell grew stronger as I approached the settee.

"What the hell is that stink?" I said.

The man looked up briefly from his chair.

"Yes, I noticed that the other day, it's horrible, nearly put me off me takeaway last night."

As I pulled back the settee I was startled at the sight of a large brown dog lying outstretched on the carpet. "Bloody hell!" I exclaimed, expecting to be savaged, but the dog made no movement.

Chalky came over and with a bigger frown than normal, drawled… "It's dead, Reg."

The man continued to watch the TV, gripping the arm of his chair as his horse came up on the rails with a chance of being in the frame.

"There's a dead dog behind your settee," I shouted, trying to overcome the sound of the TV commentary.

"YES!" shouted the man, jubilant that his each-way bet had come in at number three. "What's that you say, youth?" he finally added.

"I said there's a dead dog behind your settee."

The man lifted himself from his armchair and peered over,

"So that's where he is. I was only wondering the other day where he'd got to."

"The dog's dead, mate," shouted Chalky. "Didn't you think to look for him? When did you last see him?"

"Oh! It must be a week, it's a shame, but he was getting on."

"So, you've been living in this house for a week with a dead dog behind the settee then?" I said.

"Yes, it's a shame, but he's had a good life."

The wheelbarrow safe-pincher was eventually traced and charged with burglary. He made a full admission about how he had spent a full two days chiselling open the back of the safe. His labours had been eventually rewarded with the retrieval of the entire contents – a small bottle of Baby Bio plant food.

TWENTY NINE

ALAN (GROWLER) HOWELL had been our detective sergeant for some time. He was a little eccentric but dedicated and passionate about the job. Growler was an old-style detective, who could become enraged at the slightest problem (hence the nickname), but took pride in always getting his man. His everyday smart turnout would put a Burton's shop window manikin to shame – a suit, or blue blazer with brass buttons and highly polished shoes. Growler had frequent tantrums whenever he saw or heard of something not to his liking. He would go off into a rant describing some vile torture he would like to inflict on certain criminals. Police officers, who in his mind had not carried out their duty correctly, would also be on his list for similar punishment. His arm waving illustrations regularly took place in front of a captive audience of hysterical detectives.

With the spread of the universal nickname of 'Reg', confusion was inevitable. One morning the office was its expected manic hubbub, with upwards of twenty people, including detectives, uniformed officers and civilian staff. Telephones were ringing and there was the customary bustle.

Growler sat at his desk by the window engrossed in his paperwork and as the telephone on his desk made the slightest of pings, he grabbed it. The bellowed response he gave into the mouthpiece was his natural telephone manner. "CEEE EYE DEEE, SERGEANT HOWWWOOL SPEEEKING."

A short conversation ensued, following which he looked over at the rest of the office in general and spoke in a loud voice.

"Phone call for *Reg*."

Twenty people stopped what they were doing and started towards Growler's desk... Growler returned to the caller.

"Everyone's called bloody Reg around here," he said, and promptly replaced the receiver.

One summer's evening a report of a robbery at a Chinese takeaway came via a 999 call. It was a nasty job, the Chinese lady owner and her husband had been bundled into the back room and tied up. They had then been taken upstairs where a mattress was placed over them, pinning them down and nearly suffocating the lady. The couple's children had shouted for help from a bedroom window and this had raised the alarm. A lot of violence had been used, and the owners, who did not speak good English, were clearly petrified. Cash had been taken, and other members of the public had seen the offenders make off at high speed in a car. Someone had taken down the registration number and oddly it was noted that the offenders were Chinese themselves.

We contacted our local Chinese interpreter, who we had used several times before. He was a pleasant man who had lived in Britain for many years and had adopted the name 'Frank' in preference to his Chinese name. Frank joined us in the interview room where we were sitting with the owners of the take-away. Frank's English was excellent but he always found difficulty with some pronunciation.

"Hiya, Mr Plye, you okay?" Frank said.

"Yes thanks, Frank. Can you ask them what's gone on tonight, sounds nasty."

Frank chatted away in his native tongue to the couple for a while. A heated exchange developed and the couple became more frantic with every phrase they uttered. Frank's mouth was by now wide open and he had stopped talking. He seemed speechless. Gone was his broad grin as he turned to us.

"This was the work of Triads," he said, with real fear in his eyes. "These people are so frightened I don't even know if they'll give you statements."

"Triads, Frank?" said Chalky. "How can they be sure? I mean, here in Hanley?"

"Oh, yes, Mr Chalky," said Frank. "There's a big Triad organisation in this country. These people know they were Triads all right, and they'll stop at nothing; they're vicious evil men."

The parents admitted being too frightened to alert the police themselves and it was only because of the screams of the terrified children that we came to know about the incident. With a lot of reassurance the couple eventually made statements.

Shortly afterwards the car used by the Chinese gang was traced to a chef at a Chinese restaurant in Chester. The car was seized and the owner, Cho Sang Lee, arrested and taken to Hanley police cells.

The scale of the Triad organisation was soon revealed and details of many similar robberies at Chinese businesses throughout the country came to light. The usual theme was that the Chinese owners would be so terrified that they would fail to report the matters to the police. It seemed a certainty that the crimes that the police knew about were just the tip of the iceberg. There had been murders involving the Triads and reports of victims of crime having fingers chopped off to create terror in the community.

A search of the car involved in our robbery revealed few clues, but one was a page of foolscap paper upon which was some Chinese handwriting.

Although clearly petrified at the involvement of Triads, Frank was interested and keen to help. He was visibly shaken when he examined the paper.

"The man you have arrested is an important and dangerous man. He is a member of the 14k, the worst of Triads. He is a *Red Stick*, a high-ranking member."

Frank went on to explain that the document also gave a list of other Chinese businesses that may be potential or past victims.

Any dealings with our prisoner, Lee, were difficult. He would feign ignorance of English or stare blankly at the wall throughout an entire interview. Due to the language barrier (whether real or not) it was necessary to have Frank present to interpret. Although trying to be helpful, Frank was frightened for his life, and so did not want Lee to see his face. We decided to position Lee with a large cine-projection screen on the table between him and Frank. Chalky and myself each sat either side, and so could see both men.

It became hilarious, as Frank additionally did not want Lee to get to know his name. In a moment of private humour we decided to temporarily rename Frank as 'Reg'. It was a name that Frank could only pronounce as 'Ledge'. As the interrogation took its course the inevitable slip-up happened with one of us automatically calling him 'Frank'.

"No, no,' Frank insisted, "I am… *Ledge*."

Our enquiries took us to many different parts of the country, including Liverpool and Blackpool. At Blackpool Police Station we met a young police constable who, having being brought up in Hong Kong, could speak Chinese fluently. The bearded, completely British-looking officer's expertise was in great demand throughout the country due to the mounting numbers of Triad crimes. It was useful to have him secretly listen in on Chinese conversations for us.

Growler, being our supervisor, took a lot of interest in this unusual case, and would occasionally come with us on enquiries. We'd planned a trip to Chester Police Headquarters the following day and Growler had invited himself along. This was in spite of the fact that he had been suffering terribly with gout for a few days.

As I came into the office at eight o'clock the next day I could see Growler standing at the far end. He was resplendent in an immaculate blue blazer with brass buttons, crisply ironed white shirt, red tie and razor-edged grey slacks. I was puzzled as I caught sight of Chalky sitting at his desk shaking his head. He pointed a finger towards Growler.

I moved a little closer to Growler who was busily talking into the telephone and writing with his free hand. My mouth dropped open as I spotted his feet. He was wearing a pair of blue velvet carpet slippers! I looked back over at Chalky and, wide eyed with disbelief mouthed the word, "Chester?"

Chalky nodded.

The entire day over at Chester seemed to be taken up with different reactions from various people. It included members of the public, uniformed officers, detectives and some high-ranking Chester officers. They were all interested and puzzled by the sight of this extremely smart detective sergeant from Stoke who was wandering around their headquarters wearing carpet slippers.

One of the turning points of the inquiry would be through the inevitable use of one of my pet hates, an ID parade. My mind would always go back to my first hopeless attempt, but the thought of trying to arrange an ID parade for a Chinese man was daunting. Where on earth were we going to find another dozen or so Chinese men, let alone ones who resembled our suspect? However, after many futile attempts to find even one who was willing to help, because of the Triad connection, someone came up with an idea.

Ten miles from the city, near to the town of Stone, was an establishment that was looking after and housing a large number of Vietnamese Boat People. These were refugees who had fled their country to escape persecution. Although the skin colour was slightly darker, they did have similar oriental features to our Chinese man, their language was, however, totally different.

An approach was made to them and the response was overwhelming. Everyone wanted to be involved. Two police personnel carriers were dispatched to make a good selection and bring the chosen ones back to Hanley. It was decided to hold the parade in the police Station's Assembly Hall. The room was originally designed as a ballroom and still (at that time) used as such for dinner dances and other entertainment.

The boat people arrived and were settled for the time being in the adjoining bar-room, whilst the other arrangements were organised. The room was busy with uniformed and plain clothes officers, police photographers and solicitors. Frank was also there to help with the translation. The clamour of unintelligible voices coming from the bar-room, where the boat people were waiting, grew by the minute as they excitedly chattered away.

I turned to Frank and told him that it was time to bring the suspect up from the cells.

"Okay, but he must not be able to see me," was Frank's worried reply.

"How the hell are we going to get around this?" I said to the inspector in charge.

Eventually we came to a solution which required nothing more than a pair of scissors, a brown Manila folder and some *Blue Peter* skills. Frank followed us down to the cell block, together with a solicitor to collect the suspect. He rigidly kept his folder, into which two eyeholes had been cut, in front of his face as he interpreted from behind. We arrived back in the Hall with Frank whispering a reminder: "To call him 'Ledge' at all times."

Growler limped about the room, sporting an expensive charcoal grey suit along with colour-co-ordinated bright red slippers. The afternoon's proceedings and the day's hard work proved fruitless, as neither of the Chinese witnesses picked out the man.

Our volunteers all had a super day out and were thrilled when they were paid the regulation fee of £3. It had increased a little since the days of the Salvation Army ID parade. Their delight was increased when they were allowed to spend it in our bar and they turned it into quite a party. The case culminated at Stafford Crown Court with Lee being found not guilty. You can't win 'em all!

THIRTY

Another busy weekday passed and it was half past six when Chalky put down his pen and announced that he was off home. A muttered, "See you tomorrow," was returned by several colleagues as he disappeared through the door. It wasn't many minutes later before we were all called over to the window.

"Looks like someone's been hurt," said Lawt.

We peered down to see a small gathering of people clustered around a prone figure on the pavement.

"It's Chalky!" exclaimed Charlie Edwards.

"Is he pissed?" asked a frowning Lawt.

"No, Sarge," I chipped in. "He's been in court all day, looks like he's done his ankle in again."

Chalky, a naturally clumsy man, had badly damaged his right ankle several years before. This injury coupled with his compulsion to play sport whenever possible and a need to get all tasks done at double speed, presented the possibility of an ankle-catastrophe at any moment. The gammy foot joint was always lurking – waiting, ready to be sprained.

I darted downstairs and after establishing that this was indeed the case, helped my ashen-faced colleague to limp painfully back upstairs to the CID office.

"Done it this time, Reg, good and proper," he droned with a pained expression and slumped down into a chair. His right foot was at a strange angle, his ankle swelling by the second.

"Right, Charlie," commanded Lawt. "First aid manual."

Charlie promptly produced a force-issue first aid book, and the comedy continued as he flipped through the index looking for *ankle*.

Lawt then took the book and read from it in a loud voice.

"Make a triangular bandage."

Chalky gasped in pain as someone removed his shoe, whilst Charlie scrabbled about in a drawer for a first aid kit. Upon finding the manky looking plastic container, Charlie pulled a dirty-looking small paper package from it marked BANDAGE. Ripping it open he pulled out an off-white square of gauze cloth, placed it onto the desk and folded it corner to corner, making a tatty-looking triangle.

"Done," said Charlie, looking up and clearly pleased with his achievement.

Lawt continued to read, whilst occasionally glancing at the patient's foot. A slight swivelling of the book allowed him to keep the diagram in sync with the injury. "Place the top point of the bandage beneath the ankle so that it points up towards the back of the knee." More book swivelling followed as Lawt prepared to offer the next instruction.

Chalky's gasp of pain as Charlie lifted his now melon-sized ankle upwards to slip the dirty crumpled rag beneath it stopped the fiasco. His ashen pallor had now taken on a dark greenish grey.

"Reg," he said, "take me to the hospital. This triangular bandage thing's not going to work."

We arrived at the North Staffs Royal Infirmary Accident Unit some fifteen minutes later in the CID van and commandeered a large red leather wheelchair. I trundled my forlorn- looking friend through to the reception desk. After going through the necessary details we settled down to await our turn. I took up a grey plastic chair whilst Chalky was parked alongside still in his wheelchair. I looked around at the multitude of variously injured folk and resigned myself to a long wait. We talked for a while about different cases we were working on to try to keep off the subject of the painful ankle and then suddenly Chalky went strangely quiet.

After several minutes of deep thought, he spoke pensively.

"Reg…"

"What?"

"Reg… do you think I'll have to take my trousers off?"

"Yes, bound to, they'll have to X-ray it and all that. You might have to have it in plaster, why?"

There was a long pause before he looked at me, swallowed, and said "Reg… I've got no pants on."

I tried to visualise Chalky sitting waiting after his X-ray naked from the waist down, with other people sitting either side of him reading magazines. After these visual images all I could muster was… "Oh dear!"

"Reg," said Chalky, quite firmly now, "Reg, can I borrow your pants?"

Well, the things you do for mates!

We were getting near to the front of the queue and I knew that there was not much time left. I dashed off to the gents and in record time removed my underpants and restored my appearance back to normal. I set off down the corridor hoping that no one would know that I now had my underpants crushed into a ball in my right hand. With my arm outstretched like a relay runner and ready to pass on the baton I broke into a sprint. As I turned the corner, all I could see were the grey plastic chairs and a gap where the red wheelchair had been. He'd gone; he'd been taken, possibly by a beautiful young nurse. I caught up with him at the X-ray department, as a giggling nurse was in the process of slicing through his grey flannels with a pair of scissors. My ashen faced chum announced: "Too late, Reg, I've had to own up."

The loft, the roof-space, the attic – call it what you will. It's that small area between the bedroom ceiling and the tiles in a house with a pitched roof. Back in the day, and certainly during my time as both a uniformed and detective constable, loft searches were a regular part of the job.

For some reason thieves, drug dealers and fugitives looked upon the loft as a place of sanctuary. A hiding place for stolen goods or even for themselves if arrest was imminent.

The vast majority of housing around Stoke-on-Trent consisted of two-up, two-down terraces, with a small back yard and an outside toilet or bathroom extension.

The stairs were invariably steep enough to practise mountain rescue and only wide enough for one slender person at a time.

The loft hatch would often be at the top of the stairs or in one of the bedrooms. Access into the loft itself was never for the faint-hearted or for the overweight.

The idea of a sliding ladder fitted inside the loft was unheard of in those days. Folding steps were in equally short supply and this often brought daring and initiative to the fore. A dressing table or chair would be dragged into place and one or the other of the police volunteers would be ordered upwards.

Quivering wrists would attempt to funnel the usual oversized police backside through the tiny square and would be aided by several helping hands from beneath. Once inside the loft extreme caution had to be taken. The building standards and ideas of the modern day would take decades to arrive in Stoke-on-Trent. There would be no lighting and there were no floorboards. The actual floor of the loft was non-existent and made up of the three inch by two inch wooden rafters forming the ceiling of the floor below. The fourteen inch gap between the rafters was to be avoided at all costs. The standard, unwieldy six foot, fourteen stone PC along with his size eleven feet was not best suited to this activity. Tottering by torchlight upon a two inch wide piece of timber with head brushing against the underside of the roof tiles was always an accident waiting to happen.

A stumble, and a giant police boot even placed softly down between the rafters would be a catastrophe. The ceiling of the room below was weakly constructed via a Victorian process known as 'Lath and Plaster' – one inch wide by one quarter of an inch lengths of brittle wood tacked to the bedroom side of the rafters and then plastered over.

These tiny homes had been erected one hundred or more years before for pottery workers and their families. That preceding one hundred years had been time enough for the accumulation of several inches of dense black dust and dried mortar which had fallen down from the roof tiles and was known as 'bodging' in the building trade.

The lath and plaster spaces between the rafters could take no weight at all and would snap or burst through to the room below in the blink of an eye.

It was usual for a search of the bedroom to continue whilst the loft search also took place. Bearing in mind the frailty of the slender rafters, and to a much greater degree the lath and plaster, the thought of a huge copper blundering about in the dark above your head increased the trepidation of those in the bedroom.

The occasional muffled "Whoa," or "Christ" from above would always stall the bedroom search and produce worried upwards glances.

Such was the case during one particular CID search. The loft volunteer, a detective resplendent in smart brown suit, had disappeared upwards via a dressing table, helped on his way with pushes, nudges and numerous derogatory remarks about his weight, size and what he may have stepped into earlier. The search of the bedroom beneath was being conducted by a detective sergeant and two constables. This continued smoothly apart from the occasional worried upward glance which was prompted by the creaking of tortured rafters.

A sudden violent jolting of the central lampshade came at the same time as the beginnings of a muffled "Whoa."

Heads swivelled and eyes fixed onto the ceiling as the sound elongated and raised an octave.

The ceiling burst open. Black dust, tile bodging, plaster and laths exploded downward as the soles of two huge feet plummeted through with a detective attached.

In the midst of a thick choking cloud the officer landed perfectly on his toes with his arms above his head directly in front of the startled DS. He drew his arms down to his sides and came to attention in the manner of a Romanian gymnast awaiting the score card. He then bent slightly forward, brushed his trousers and jacket down with the flat of a hand and said, "No, nothing up there, Sarge.'

At half past eight one morning I arrived in the office. I would have been earlier but for the full ten minutes I'd spent scraping ice from my car windows. The winter of 1981/82 was one of the coldest on record with temperatures plummeting down as low as minus 13 degrees. Chalky, the early man was sitting at his desk, phone pressed to ear. He continued to talk into it at the same time as gesturing me over with a roll of the eyes and slow tilt of the head. He tapped his pen down onto the lines of his distinctive scrawl which were etched onto a notepad: *Naked man found dead on wasteland, side of Carmount Inn.*

Within ten minutes we had made it to the scene.

The Carmount Inn was a big old public house on the Abbey Hulton council estate. At the side of the building was a large area of partially fenced off wasteland. It was littered with rubbish – old sofas, bottles, bits of cars and other stuff that people had dumped.

Everywhere was covered in a thick white crusty frost. A couple of panda cars had already arrived and closed the scene off from the public. The pub licensee, Clive, was standing holding a tray of steaming cups. He'd spotted the body and reported it with a 999 call before taking on the important duty of tea-making.

We picked our way through the ice coated junk and arrived alongside the Scenes of Crime Officer (SOCO) who was busily making notes. This was the strangest of scenes. The body, a middle aged man, lay on the ground curled up in the foetal position with his head resting on his clasped hands – stark naked! Had he not been in the middle of a field of rubbish and covered in frost you would have thought he was in bed at home and fast asleep. His jacket, trousers and underwear were all folded and piled up neatly near his feet, along with his shoes, each one of which contained a sock. It didn't take long to establish the man's identity; his dole card was in his trouser pocket. He turned out to be a fifty-nine-year-old alcoholic who lived alone only about three hundred yards away.

A lengthy day of enquiries revealed nothing particularly odd or suspicious and the cause of death and answer to the strange circumstances was in fact hypothermia. The man had wandered off from the pub the night before, very drunk and had collapsed unseen by anyone. Being only lightly clothed in what was desperately cold weather it hadn't been long before the onset of hypothermia. In the delirious state bought on by the condition, the body loses heat at such a rapid rate that the person starts to feel unbearably hot. The body temperature quickly plummets to a fatal level.

We later learned that removing the clothes and folding them tidily is a classic example found in hypothermia cases. The disorientated mind tries to make some order of the situation to relieve the unbearable heat.

THIRTY ONE

WITH MY EXAMS out of the way it was now time for a stab at promotion. After attending a promotion board at headquarters I was suddenly back in uniform and on shifts as an acting sergeant at Hanley. This didn't seem much like promotion.

After two months of this I was summoned to see the Chief Constable, Mr Charles Kelly. Our Welsh Chief, Arthur Morgan Rees, had retired in 1977.

Mr Kelly told me he was promoting me to uniformed sergeant and sending me to – BIDDULPH. This was a bit like offering me a nice sweet and then pouring bleach all over it!

Biddulph was a market town in the Leek division. It was quite a distance to travel every day and the work was going to be completely different from anything I had known before. How long was I going to be at this place? Would I ever get back to normality? Why the hell had I bothered to pass my exams?

I arrived at my new workplace on Monday, 17th May 1982. The Falklands War was in full swing and it was in the news that a twenty-eight-year-old naval petty officer from Biddulph had become the first local casualty. Fortunately he was only injured, but it put my minor discomfort into perspective.

My new shift consisted of six male constables at the small but fairly newly built police station on the outskirts of the town. Our territory covered a large area of mostly farming communities and had more than its fair share of eccentrics, sex offenders and extremely violent men (oh, and women!). It was, however, pretty quiet compared with Hanley.

My new teammates were a mixed bunch – an old-ish chap, who was near retirement, two fairly young constables and three of a similar age to me. I had intended using the 'smartness and punctuality' speech that had been drummed into me over the years. I stopped in my tracks at the sight of one scruffy young constable with baggy flapping trousers, filthy boots and unkempt hair. I sent him home with the warning not to come back until he looked like he used to do at Ryton.

I disliked my first taste of having to discipline someone like this, especially on my first day. I always felt that I could get the best out of people with good humour and self-respect, but realised there would always be exceptions.

The lads on the shift were a decent bunch, apart from sadly, the same constable I had to send home. He turned out to be a sex fiend and was arrested off duty, up to no good on the fire escape of the local squash club. He was peering into the ladies' changing rooms through the extractor fan. He, of course, got the sack.

There was a distinct lack of entertainment in the town. Biddulph weekends for the locals tended to be boredom personified. Consequently, if a diversion of some kind had been arranged, the locals tended to go over the top.

One Saturday evening a large fancy dress party at the Town Hall was drawing to a close. We were short-staffed due to illness when John Caddy, one of the shift PCs turned up for duty. This was despite his bandaged hand following an injury at home. I was more than pleased to see him.

John was on town centre patrol near the town hall at 1 a.m., as some of the revellers were turning out. He shook his head as he spotted a German SS Officer urinating against the wall. The disgusting behaviour was in full view of a party of milk maids, a lady in a crinoline dress and Dr Who. Aware of being outnumbered, and thinking of his disability, John decided to tick off the SS Officer and send him on his way.

"Sorry, mein Führer," came the reply, as the officer clicked together his heels with his willy still hanging out and thrust up a Hitler salute.

John was still intent on sending the miscreant on his way. "Just go… *now*!" he ordered, but was surprised to feel someone tightly grip his arm from behind.

He spun around to see his attacker swaying like an inebriated skittle. It was none other, than the local troublemaker and busy-body who went by the odd nickname of 'Bunty'.

"Leave him alone you… leave him alone, bloody copper, he's not hurting you," shouted the tottering lout.

"Keep out of it, Bunty, it's nothing to do with you." John ordered.

At that Bunty launched himself and tried to pull the constable to the ground. The struggle between the two men continued for a few seconds with John attempting to radio for help. Suddenly Bunty loosened his grip and stopped… he had spotted John's bandaged hand.

"What you done to your hand?" he spluttered.

"Burned it on the iron," was John's reply.

"Is it okay?" enquired Bunty.

"Yes, not too bad," gasped John.

With that, Bunty got back into the attack, tightening his grip and trying to take John off balance. After a few seconds more, he stopped again.

"Hand okay?"

"Yes, it's okay."

More struggling… stop… struggling…

"You're sure now?"

"Yes, I'm still okay."

This ridiculous scene continued until I arrived to help out. Bunty was arrested and driven back to the police station. We passed by the SS Officer, who was happily, but unsteadily, marching back home minding his own business. His willy was now safely tucked away.

En-route to the nick Bunty continually asked as to the state of John's hand. The situation reached a bizarre climax in the custody office of the police station. Bunty removed his false teeth and threw them at the cell block wall smashing them on a radiator pipe… I'll never know why.

Many odd duties were the responsibility of the police in those days. Shops which sold fireworks for Guy Fawkes celebrations had to possess a licence and these had to be examined before November 5th. We also had to carry out what were called 'Aliens enquires'. NO, these were not little green men. They were foreigners living in the country in certain uncommon circumstances. Diseases of animals legislation was another time consuming duty which seemed as far away from cops and robbers as you could get. Of course I already knew about the role of the police in these things, but until my move out into the countryside none of it had affected me much. Now I was finding myself visiting farms to witness sheep dipping and issuing pig licences to farmers!

I longed to get back to CID work, but tried to make the best of my lot. Things were never consistently busy, but did once in a while come in waves and catch you unaware. How true this was one summer Sunday afternoon as I strolled down to the town centre with the inspector who had come over from Leek. We were chatting and I mentioned light-heartedly that I was a bit cheesed off and hoped to get back to CID. "Nothing much happens at Biddulph." The words had hardly left my mouth when we heard the unmistakable sound of a shotgun. The inspector narrowed his eyes as he looked at me. He was about to make a comment when right in front of us a car, with tyres screeching, smashed into the rear of a van. The driver had pulled up rather abruptly at a pedestrian crossing. A wheel trim flew off and skimmed between the two of us, as a motorcycle ploughed into the back of the car sending the rider flying up onto its roof.

The radio crackled into life.

"Report of a shotgun being fired in Diamond Close. Any patrol to attend."

I raised my radio to my mouth, intent on reporting the accident and mentioning that we had heard the shotgun as a man dressed in running shorts appeared in front of me.

"There's a bloke down here in the garden," he gasped. "I think he's dead, looks like he's been electrocuted by his lawnmower."

The inspector looked at me.

"Not much happening?"

This proved to be a long day.

One morning PC Kenny Harper, came into my office. "Seen this, Sarge?" he asked as he placed a glossy covered hardback book down in front of me. The book was entitled *The Hamlyn Book of Horror* and depicted a demonic-looking Dracula figure with a wooden stake embedded in his chest.

"What the hell's this, Ken?"

"It belongs to my lad, he's pointed out to me that *you* are in it."

Kenny flicked through the pages and opened the book at an article entitled 'The Man in Stoke-on-Trent'. It was a complete short story about my vampire encounter some ten years before. The article even included a black and white drawing of a policeman entering a bedroom with torch in hand to the sight of a body lying on the bed.

"And this is me, then?" I said, pointing at the picture.

"Guess so, Sarge. Will you autograph the inside cover for the lad?"

Fame at last!

A well-dressed man came into the enquiry office one afternoon with a large brown cardboard box, which he placed on the counter.

"Good evening, Sir, and how can I help you?" I said with my most welcoming of Biddulph smiles.

"I'd like you to have a look at this please, Sergeant," he said, gesturing towards the box.

I stepped forward, but was almost sure I had seen the box move slightly under its own power.

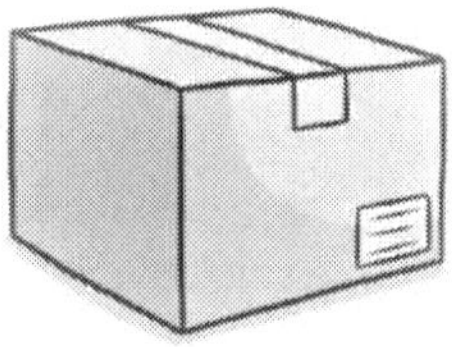

The man opened the lid and as I peered inside a gigantic snake rose up from within, right in front of my face. I staggered backwards, knocking the nuclear attack early warning box from the shelf and ending up sitting on the floor against the table.

"Why the hell have you bought it in here?" I shouted… my welcoming Biddulph smile now replaced with a look of total disbelief.

"Well, we found it in the fields at Knypersley and thought you'd know what to do."

The man was ordered to return the three-foot long grass snake, to where he had found it.

Two weeks later a quiet summer evening presented the opportunity to get through some paperwork. Daydreams filled my head as my thoughts drifted back to my drug squad and CID days. But those thoughts were soon interrupted.

"Sarge, there's a strange woman at the counter, says she wants to speak to the person in charge. She's got a box with her and she won't speak to anyone else."

"I hope it's not another bloody snake," I said making my way into the enquiry office.

Through the sliding glass window I could see a petite woman in her mid-thirties with her back to me. She was clutching a shoebox to her chest as she looked out through the glass front doors.

"Hello," I said adopting the 'grass snake' defensive position.

The woman spun around.

"You in charge?" she demanded.

"Yes, at the moment, what's the problem?"

"And you're a sergeant, are you?" she quizzed.

"Well, yes," I said, puzzled as I checked to see that no one had torn the stripes from my sleeves.

"How do I know that you're a real police sergeant?"

"Well, I'm here in a police station wearing a blue uniform with stripes on my arms, is that not good enough?" I replied, with a degree of sarcastic annoyance.

"No, it's not… this is serious, I shall have to see your identification," the woman demanded wide-eyed and holding the box ever more tightly to herself.

What the hell could be in the box? Somebody's head perhaps?

"Very well, madam," I patronised as I pulled out my warrant card and held it forward.

She scrutinised the ID for a few seconds then opened the box and pulled from it… a gun… a silver, heavy-looking revolver. She pointed it directly at me through the open sliding window. I dropped to the floor beneath the counter thinking that this deranged woman must have heard voices commanding her to go and kill a police sergeant.

"This gun," she said, slamming it down onto the counter, "is my husband's and he's a stinking bastard."

Realising that the gun no longer presented a problem, I picked it up and checked it for safety – the bullet chamber was empty.

"What's this all about?" I said, now realising that I was not the intended victim of some Biddulph-based, police sergeant slaying cult.

It turned out that her husband, who was an accomplished engineer, had actually made the gun as a training project many years before. It was exquisitely crafted, but highly illegal, as it worked perfectly with .22 ammunition. After years of mental health problems and domestics, the woman had taken this path as a way of getting her husband into trouble. He had to make a court appearance over the unlicensed gun, received a fine and the gun was destroyed.

I had now become highly suspicious of people entering the police station carrying cardboard boxes, and so when an elderly lady carefully tiptoed in through the front doors one morning my pulse rate increased. She was holding yet another cardboard box… this one was out at arm's length. I was undecided whether to drop to the floor as a matter of course or run off. The lady's trembling hands slowly placed the box down onto the counter with agonising care.

"I think you should take a look at this, my dear," she said.

I cautiously moved closer as the lady produced a copy of the *Daily Express* from her pocket.

"Read this first, young man," she said, pushing the newspaper over to me. The paper was folded over at an article entitled, *Exploding Treacle Tins*. A photograph accompanied the piece, showing a tin of Lyle's Black Treacle, which had somehow become distorted into an almost perfect spherical shape. The article described how, in recent weeks, several similar old tins had blown up with considerable force in people's pantries. The fermentation, created by the hot summer and the considerable age, had generated such pressure that some of the tins had eventually swelled up and burst. I carefully lifted the lid of the box to reveal an almost completely round tin of black treacle. The wording and colouring of the tin gave it an obvious pre-war appearance. It seemed astonishing that the lid had not eventually popped open on its own.

With even the slightest movement of the box, the tin rolled from one corner to another as there was now no flat side for it to rest upon. The pressure inside must have been immense. I carefully carried the box out into the backyard of the police station and set it down by the wall. If it were to explode the flimsy cardboard box would offer no protection at all.

After hearing about the incident the detective sergeant appeared from his upstairs office. He offered his military and bomb disposal experience to us by throwing the tin as hard as he could at the garage wall. The tin exploded with a dull thump leaving a two feet wide, black treacle splatter on the garage wall and several dollops on one of the panda cars. Beware of people carrying boxes!

Things always seemed to happen on Sunday afternoons. I had been on patrol in a panda car with PC Ken Harper when a radio call directed us to the compound at the back of a motorcycle spares' garage in the town centre. Someone had been spotted in suspicious circumstances.

Of course the property was closed for the day, and as we were close by it took only seconds to get there. We heard a powerful motorbike revving up as we arrived and I ran around into an alleyway leading to the rear of the garage with Kenny in hot pursuit. I saw a figure astride a large red motorbike facing towards me and about twenty yards away. Upon seeing me the rider opened the throttle with a roar, the front of the bike lifted and he drove straight at me.

The alleyway in which I stood was narrow, and littered with equipment and other rubbish. As the motor bike raced towards me I instinctively pressed myself into the brick wall on my left. The front mudguard of the bike caught me a sickening blow to the right leg as the handlebars hit me in the ribs. I grabbed the rider around his helmeted head and clung on as the bike charged forwards, dragging me along with it. The engine note changed as the rider started to lose control with the added weight of Kenny, who by now was somehow perched on the handlebars. The machine and the three of us were all flung violently in different directions as it smashed into a pile of wooden pallets. The engine roared at full revs and the rear wheel spun dangerously as it lay on its side. Kenny and I struggled violently with this madman who'd nearly killed us.

We overpowered him and turned off the engine. He had been stealing motorcycle parts, and a later search of his home and garage revealed an Aladdin's cave of stolen motorbikes and parts. I ended up with bruised ribs, a badly gashed shin and a commendation from the judge at the later Crown Court hearing. I also lived in hope that the incident might spark a memory in the mind of a distant senior detective in some faraway HQ office that the name 'Pye' once featured in the CID.

I put together an escape plan when the news came through that there was a vacancy for a detective sergeant on the Special Branch and so I sent in my application. It later came to mind that my title would have been 'DS Pye'. It was an unfortunate quirk of fate that this sounded more like 'DS Spy'. I accepted that this could create a few problems in the role of a Special Branch officer and certainly a few jokes. I didn't get the job which was perhaps just as well.

I was, however, soon on the move when, after twenty-two months at Biddulph I received a call from the CID boss, Detective Chief Superintendent Malcolm Bevington, who said, "Do you fancy being a detective sergeant at Stone CID?"

Silly question!

THIRTY TWO

I STARTED AT STONE in early 1984. It was an old, characterful building with stairs and corridors leading everywhere... and yes they were covered in khaki-coloured lino! Part of the building had originally been the magistrates' court and the CID office was the old courtroom itself.

Stone police station covered a vast sub-division encompassing a third of the entire county. Its CID office comprised of a detective inspector, a detective sergeant (me) and eight DCs. We had other 'satellite' police stations at Great Haywood, Gnosall and Madeley and the latter even had its own little CID office with two of our detectives working from there.

We had more than our fair share of crime to deal with. High value house burglaries were a particular problem because it was such a big area with a lot of isolated expensive houses. These attracted the attention of travelling crooks and the patch was a major target for burglars from Liverpool. They would come down the M6 and pop off from Junction 15 to see which pads were worth screwing. We seemed to be forever travelling back and forth to Merseyside to search houses and arrest villains.

Later in 1984 I started an advanced CID course at Wakefield in West Yorkshire. It was six weeks, very intense and with a similar theme to my Birmingham course several years before. There were twenty-six of us from all over the country, including two RUC officers.

Britain was in the middle of the Miners' strike at this time and West Yorkshire Police used the Wakefield centre as a locus for their policing of the picketing. We would get woken up most mornings at five o'clock by the noise of dozens of police personnel carriers laden down with hundreds of uniformed officers starting out for picket duty. I managed to sell a bit more pottery, but there wasn't so much fooling around – perhaps we were getting old!

I had not been back at Stone long when I lost another two friends who were both killed when their police vehicle was involved in a high-speed accident, whilst answering an emergency call on the A500 near the city centre. I had served with PCs Bob Owen and Graham Whitehurst and remember them as friends.

Stone CID had its fair share of characters. Peter Rowley was a detective who should have been on the stage – a born comedian with an ever-ready joke to relieve the stress or anguish of a disturbing incident. His brilliant renditions of Dame Edna Everage were heard at the most appropriate and inappropriate of moments. His very 'in your face' builders bottom would be unwittingly on display at even more unexpected occasions. Many times I have, with some embarrassment, had to shield Peter's rear from the astonished gaze of a member of the public. Peter's enthusiasm to bend and pick up a clue frequently diverted the anguish of a crime victim even if only temporarily.

Patrick (Nult) McNulty was another member of the team and another character. The word 'smart' was not sufficient for Nult – 'dapper' would be more fitting. With his expensive suits and two-tone leather shoes he set the standards high for the rest of us. If some annoying or amusing incident happened (which was most days), in no time at all, Nult would have composed a suitable poem encapsulating the incident and lifting spirits.

One grey, miserable and wet autumn afternoon, Nult and I were returning to the office in the CID car. As we passed through the village of Yarnfield we spotted a young man who was wanted for several burglaries around the town centre. Nult was his regular immaculate self with a light grey suit, white shirt, dark blue tie and expensive-looking light and dark grey leather shoes.

The villain, Darren Hulse, spotted us and was immediately away like a rabbit around the side of a vehicle repair garage. I flung the car onto the forecourt and my eager colleague was out from the passenger door and after him. The puzzled garage employees dashed outside to see what was going on as I escaped my seat belt and leapt out to join in the pursuit. The fit young burglar vaulted straight over a farm gate at the side of the garage and was soon doing his best to make progress across the muddiest, most unpleasant-looking ploughed field I had ever seen.

Undeterred, Nult, in all his finest regalia, but not being up to vaulting, quickly climbed the gate. He splashed down into the field and set off after the rapidly diminishing figure. He had gone only a few yards when his beautiful footwear became so heavily laden with mud that he could hardly pick up his feet. With another struggling step his right foot came up minus the shoe. The forward momentum continued to propel him onwards, arms waving wildly, as his left foot remained firmly gripped by the suction of the ankle deep mire. His body quivered momentarily and then shot forwards as the foot came out of the shoe. He stumbled on for several yards shoeless, arms flailing about for balance and churned into the mire face down like a human plough.

I had only made it to the gate, before my cunning sergeant's instinct gave me the realisation that this was a futile pursuit. The uselessness of the chase coupled with the fact that this had been turned into such a wonderful spectacle additionally halted me from joining in. I could not contain my laughter as I radioed in with the direction in which Hulse had been seen heading. I then realised that I had been joined at the gate by all the staff of the garage, who were laughing hysterically. The amusement increased as Nult turned around, his front plastered from head to foot with thick black sludge and corn stalks. He tentatively tiptoed forwards a few steps, losing a sock but finding a shoe. He pulled with all his might to release it from the suction, falling on his backside as he did so. On finding another shoe, he managed to release it only to discover it was one of Hulse's trainers. Now tarred and feathered, both back and front, Nult looked skywards. He shook a clenched fist upwards and shouted "You Bastard," before hurling the trainer an amazing distance into a nearby stream.

With both shoes recovered and car seat protected by plastic bags, I drove Nult back to his home at Stafford for a shower and change. I wanted to take him back to the nick first, so everyone else could have a look, but he wasn't having any. Strangely he never did compose a poem about this one.

John (Punchy) Cowan, another team member was a muscular, strong man who vaguely resembled film star Charles Bronson. John was a gentle, inoffensive man, but was capable of sorting out even the most violent of criminals when pushed to the limit.

One Saturday afternoon a report came in that burglars had been disturbed at the isolated home of a wealthy jeweller in the village of Butterton, six miles out of Stone. John and I attended and discovered that two offenders had broken into the house whilst the elderly owner was out. The eighty year old arrived back as the burglars were in the middle of deciding what to take. They fled the scene without harming him and made their getaway in a car they'd cheekily parked in the driveway. The sprightly old gent had managed to take down the registration number of the car and thought that one of the crooks was a young woman. A lot of jewellery and ornaments had been taken, along with a yellow candlewick bedspread that had no doubt been used to carry the stolen property. The thieves had also hauled a heavy safe out of the house onto the veranda, where it remained perched on top of a creaking wicker chair. Had it not been for the owner's arrival, this would probably have been lumped into the boot of the car.

The MO fitted closely with other burglaries on our patch and could have been the answer to a lot of crime. The possibility of a starting point with the car registration number turned out to be a something of a let-down. We came to a dead end after finding that it had been bought from a Manchester car auction by a man named Mr

Smith, with a false address. All was not lost though, when a later computer check revealed that the car had been towed away after being parked illegally in Manchester City Centre three weeks before. It had been collected from the police pound by a Mrs Michelle Waylan from Middleton.

A call to the Middleton CID came up trumps as Michelle Waylan was the wife of well-known burglar – Shaun Waylan – who specialised in stealing jewellery. A quick eyeball on the Waylan house by the local CID annoyingly showed no sign of the burglar's car. But a white van parked outside the front door was checked and found to have been circulated as wanted by Derbyshire Police. It had been spotted near to another burglary in the Peak District. A strikingly similar MO had been used and jewellery along with two expensive fur coats had been taken. Interestingly this van had also been purchased by Mr Smith.

Middleton CID needed no prompting and raided Waylan's house, arresting him and finding piles of valuable jewellery and other property beneath his floorboards. John and I met with Middleton CID the next day and soon identified some of Waylan's floorboard cache as being from our Butterton burglary. Additionally we spotted further valuables taken during other raids on our patch. A rent card for a lock-up garage was recovered from Waylan's house and once again the cleverly thought-out name of 'Mr Smith' had been used. A search of the garage, which was close by, revealed the yellow candlewick bedspread from our burglary. It was all coming together nicely.

Waylan was trying to keep his wife out of it, whilst also admitting to nothing himself. Michelle actually worked as a cashier for a well-known bank in Manchester and appeared, to the untrained eye, to be a perfectly innocent and honest person.

In with the jewels recovered from beneath the floorboards was a jewellery valuation certificate made out to a name and address in Blackpool. We quickly discovered that this house had been another target for Waylan. The jewels it described had been stolen along with a cheque book in the owner's name. The stolen cheques had been used to purchase property from stores in Leeds a week after the burglary. We now had a lengthy list of household goods to look for as well as untold amounts of jewellery, and the 'fur coat' list was also on the increase.

Another search of Waylan's house resulted in the recovery of even more property – curtains, ornaments, rugs, lights and expensive ladies clothing. These tasteful additions to the family home had all been purchased with the stolen cheques. The pair had superbly fitted out their entire house with the proceeds of various crimes. Even a stolen camera was found to contain photographs of a gloating Waylan standing next to a pile of obviously recently stolen booty. For some reason he was pictured with his willy hanging out. Why?

The net was closing in on Michelle too, as she was clearly in it up to her neck. It was only a matter of time before the evidence came to the surface. Shaun had now been connected to dozens of high-value burglaries. The property recovered from beneath the floorboards was nothing compared with what was still missing. We then found that Michelle had a safety deposit box kept at the branch of the bank where she worked and we were eager to check the contents.

I visited a magistrate and applied for a search warrant on the actual bank. You can imagine the disbelief on the Magistrate's face. However, he signed, and away I went. The bank manager's jaw dropped as John and I stood in his office and related the story. A pensive-looking Michelle stood in the corridor outside the office fully aware of what the 'hated two Johns' were up to.

The box was brought into the manager's office and, with several other senior members of staff present, the security ties were removed and the lid opened. An air of disappointment went around the room as the contents were shaken out onto the manager's table. Not a single item of jewellery, just a few scraps of paper with writing on. A closer inspection showed the writing to be lists of cash adding up to many thousands of pounds.

"These look like account numbers," said one member of staff, pointing to the numbers written above some of the lists. "Probably a building society, the Leeds at a guess."

Michelle spent her first night suspended from her job and in the cells back at Stone Police Station. Enquiries about the numbers on the scraps of paper revealed that three building society accounts had been set up – Mr Smith had been busy again! We were even provided with CCTV photos of Mr Smith at the counters of the building society, opening the accounts. Mr Smith was, of course, none other than Shaun Waylan. It began to look increasingly likely that Michelle had actually been on some of the burglaries with her husband, including the Butterton job, but proof in this direction was lacking.

My most loathed piece of police procedure loomed again – an identification parade. We hoped that this one would prove that Shaun and Michelle were the man and woman described by a Scottish lady witness who owned an expensive ladies' outfitters in Leeds. The lady had been duped by the couple, who had purchased several hundred pounds worth of expensive ladies' clothing from her store using cheques from the stolen chequebook.

We had searched the Waylan house again and had found every item of the clothing in Michelle's drawers and wardrobe. The irate shop owner inspired me with confidence when I interviewed her. "I'd bloody well know those two thieving gits anytime, even in a hundred years I'd spot them," she said in her strong accent.

Could there be the possibility of a successful ID parade?

Two parades were organised – one for Shaun, and one for Michelle. Everything was arranged impeccably and my fingers were crossed tightly behind my back as our fiery Scottish witness was invited into the room to view the first parade. She walked in, took one glance at the line-up of similarly dressed, petite and attractive young women and her eyes widened with anger as she spied Michelle.

"That's the little bastard," she shouted as she marched straight across to Michelle and invaded her space. "Number bloody seven." Her finger was pointing and about an inch from Michelle's flickering eye lids. "Thought you'd got away with that one then, you little cow," she shouted over her shoulder as she was directed out.

The lady managed a repeat performance on the next parade for Shaun, with even more expletives. Afterwards, as I took a statement from her about the two parades, she confessed to having enjoyed every minute. Me too.

The case was strengthened even more with the discovery of yet another car bought by 'Mr Smith' and connected to Waylan. This vehicle had been issued with a parking ticket in Leeds on the day of all the cheque cashing. I had never had a case where so many clues had been left and where everything fitted so well into place. It was therefore a blow when I was telephoned at home on a rare day off. The caller told me that Waylan had escaped from Newcastle Police Station whilst on one of his weekly court appearance remand sessions. He had been slippery throughout and someone had dropped their guard – he'd gone.

Things carried on; there were still a lot of other enquiries that had to be completed, not to mention all the other everyday stuff that was always coming in.

The words of my old Chief Constable, Arthur Rees, were proved correct when I appeared on the telly. *Granada Reports* did a feature for us in an attempt to find the owners of some of the little mountain of unidentified jewellery. I was interviewed, showing and describing the jewels in the hope that we might prove where they had come from and so detect a few more cases. My kids were loaning out the video of 'Dad on Telly' to their school friends. Mum and dad, even after all those years were waiting for their turn to show their friends in the pub. I cringed as I waited to see the recording for the first time. Had I subconsciously slipped in a few robotic police phrases? No, it wasn't too bad.

One morning a few months later, as I trawled through the pile of tele-printer messages that had come in over the weekend my eyes landed on the description 'FUR COATS'. I was reading through the various crimes that had been committed in other parts of the country.

I was looking at a national tele-printer broadcast about a burglary at the isolated home of a racehorse trainer in Exeter. It had Waylan's MO all over it and, as well as jewellery, two valuable fur coats had been taken. Waylan was the only burglar I had ever known who had an eye for fur coats. He clearly knew how to get the right money for them, as we had never recovered any of them. I was on the phone to Exeter CID within minutes. I told the detective the story and gave him the issue number of the *Police Gazette* showing Waylan's photo. Two days later the same DC rang me back with some interesting news. A burglar had been interrupted at the home of a wealthy landowner and a high speed car chase had followed. After driving through fences and across parkland he had been arrested. The man was refusing to give his name, but despite a few lumps and bumps he fitted the photo of Waylan.

Punchy and I collected our paperwork together and headed down to Exeter. The overnight stay included a few celebratory pints and Waylan became our handcuffed passenger for the journey back to Stone. He eventually received a lengthy sentence, as did Michelle for her part in these crimes.

It was remarkable how the silly mistake by Waylan's wife of collecting the car from the police pound had given the breakthrough to all of this. It was equally as curious how the strangest of things could end up solving another case, even such an innocuous item as a tent.

Ashley is a village almost off the edge of the Staffordshire map. The morning visit I made together with DC 'Simpo' Simpson was in answer to an overnight burglary report. The building society branch office had been broken into and a heavy safe containing a few hundred pounds completely removed. The thieves had left behind several two-feet long, hollow metal tubes and from the marks on the floor these had been used to roll the safe out through the door.

Within an hour we received a second report that a car had been abandoned in a field half a mile away. Upon arrival we found that the car, a small tatty saloon, had been driven off the road and down a steep grassy embankment into a field. It had been raining all week and the bank side was a slippery, muddy mess.

The doors to the car hung open, papers were strewn everywhere and partially embedded in the mud, was the safe. Its door had been chiselled from the hinges and lay alongside, together with bankbooks and documents.

Inside the car were more of the same metal tubes that we'd found at the building society office. There were deep furrows in the mud where the thieves had been trying to drive the car back up the embankment. They clearly never stood any chance. They had obviously driven the car down there so that no one could hear the noise as they chiselled away for hours. The fact that they never considered that they would not be able to get back onto the road gave a clue to what boneheads they were.

Enquiries about the car came back with the expected blank – it had been purchased in a false name. But then it was discovered that a 'police interest marker' had been placed on its PNC file. This was a very useful piece of 'criminal intelligence' – a shrewd move by an observant Preston based police officer who had spotted two local, criminal yobs in that car a couple of weeks before. He had taken the time to register what he had seen so that every police officer in the country could connect that car to these men should it be used in crime. My phone call to Preston CID made it clear to me just what a thorn in their side these two well known, arrogant, thieving brothers were and so, armed with a search warrant, we made a joint house call.

The reception was the routine unpleasant, rowdy shouting-match with swearing and threats. Most of this turned to silence at the sound of my clear and loudly voiced jubilation. To the inexperienced eye I had found nothing more incriminating than a tent with no poles! Other evidence, however, supported the case. A perfect imprint was found of one of the brother's trainers in mud inside the building society and also on a map inside the car.

At the Crown Court case, months later, the judge watched the display arranged by the prosecution with interest. The executive from the tent makers, together with the help of Simpo, swiftly erected the tent at the front of the court. This added to the mounting evidence that the poles were of their manufacture and designed only for this model of tent.

The judge, of course, was not aware that only a few days prior to the case I nearly had my evidence jeopardised by none other than a fellow colleague. The uniformed inspector at the police station had undertaken a spring clean of the property store. Without much thought he had deposited 'Exhibit A' (one metal safe door) at the local scrapyard. Finding out in time, I managed to retrieve the door. The brothers went to prison, and as it was too far to join up for a celebration with Preston CID, both offices separately enjoyed a few beers.

THIRTY THREE

IN NOVEMBER 1986, yet another friend and colleague was killed on duty. Twenty-six-year-old PC John Taylor died when he fell through a window from the fifth floor of a block of high-rise flats in Honeywall, Stoke. He had been struggling to arrest a burglar. The burglar survived. A commemorative stone for John now stands in Kingsway near Stoke Town Hall.

In June 1987 I was detailed to perform armed protection duty for two days for members of the Royal Family. They were to take part in a televised charity performance along with dozens of other celebrities. The format followed that of the television show *It's a Knockout*. It was to be hosted by the – many years later discredited – British television presenter Stuart Hall and was conceived and organised by Prince Edward.

The *Royal It's a Knockout* featured Prince Edward, Princess Anne and the Duke and Duchess of York as team captains. As well as Stuart Hall, it was also hosted by comedian, Les Dawson, and the comedy actress Sue Pollard.

I was ferried up to Alton Towers on the first day along with a large contingent of other CID and uniformed officers. It was half past six in the morning and the weather was simply appalling. It was a near constant cloudburst as we ran from the police bus into a small flapping marquee for cover. The tent had been pitched on the side of a slight incline. Why were all the tents I have ever been in always on a slope?

Our second-hand or possibly borrowed tent looked pretty shabby against the fire service's magnificent inflatable and heated accommodation. This was positioned some distance away on a level piece of ground. Even the short run into the tent had soaked us. There were dozens of plain clothes officers, but only eight of us were armed. We were all handed shoulder holsters, which we fitted according to our own comfort beneath our jackets. We then had to sign for our Smith and Wesson .38 revolvers. The smaller version we were using for this duty carried five bullets, and we also had to sign for the bullets and some spare ammunition.

Considering this was June, it was not only wet, it was also cold. We were told that we all had to be inside the 'big-top' style circus tent for our eight o'clock. briefing. This was a good quarter of a mile from where we were waiting in our own shabby marquee. Time was getting on and so a few of us started to ask a pertinent question. How were we to get to the big-top in view of the now unrelenting torrential downpour? It dawned on us that the bosses had made no provision for this. The police bus had gone and we were expected to walk. We stuck it out as long as we could, but eventually some senior officer ordered us all to make our way.

I was already slightly damp from my first run from the bus. I was wearing my best suit with my camel Crombie overcoat. None of us had an umbrella. I guess it would have been rather in the way if we had to draw our guns and take aim with an umbrella in the other hand. With every step forward everyone took on another half-gallon of rainwater. The gun strapped to my left breast was now becoming heavy and I was feeling ever more uncomfortable.

Eventually we all slopped into the big-top and took up our seats for the briefing as rivulets of water streamed away from our feet. I was so wet now that I feared that should I have to shoot anyone, my rusting gun would not fire.

After the briefing had finished I went and found a new-looking gents toilet and tried to dry myself out a little. I took off my socks and shoes and fitted the socks over the nozzle of the hand drier causing the sock to billow out as it dried. The shoes took longer and were so wet that they started to curl up at the toes like a clown's shoes. Perhaps I should go back to the big-top!

When I had done my best at drying out, I took up my place in one of the tents. Various celebrities, including John Travolta, Christopher Reeve, Michael Palin, John Cleese and Rowan Atkinson, wandered in and out taking little notice of the dripping detective. I was unconcerned as a figure strolled past me with a casual, but precise, 'Morning', which was clearly directed at me. Being more concerned with the wetness of my trousers and underpants, I instinctively replied, "Ha do, mate", looking up I discovered that I had *'Ha do mated'* Prince Edward himself! The prince looked back at me with a puzzled expression, possibly thinking that I was a foreigner or the local lunatic, and then carried on with his business.

I was never so pleased to get home and into a hot bath at the end of a long and wet day. We were allowed to take our empty holsters home with us so that we could save time and fit them as we got dressed the following day. The kids were full of it that evening, with the two boys each taking turns at trying on the holster. Daughter Julie wanted to know which film stars I'd seen.

Early the next morning I was dried out and spruced up again, complete with shoulder holster and suit number two. It was a good job it was only two days! My Crombie coat had spent all night on the radiator.

As I joined the other firearms officers in the still flapping, but not so wet, police tent, I was handed my revolver with its chamber open and empty. I signed for both the gun and the ammo as I had done the day before.

For safety, we had been taught to go down on one knee whilst loading, making sure the safety catch was on, and then holstering the gun. I went through the procedure then pushed the barrel of the gun down into the holster for a nice snug fit. The gun didn't want to go down, something was stopping it and so I carefully removed it and felt down inside my holster. My fingers gripped the unknown object and pulled it free. It was the pink plastic toy gun that I had seen the kids playing with the night before at home. Swiftly, before anyone saw, I thrust the toy into my Crombie pocket. I sniggered as I imagined what could have happened had I been called upon to draw my weapon. The scenario crossed my mind of a maniac assassin screaming towards one of the Royal Family. I would have had my chance of becoming a highly decorated national hero whilst clasping a pink plastic water pistol and shouting, 'FREEZE ASSHOLE.'

It was another wet day and nothing much happened. One or two princes and princesses, together with dozens of film stars and TV personalities rolled around in the mud, dressed up as giant vegetables, but no one was shot.

Throughout my time at Stone there was plenty to keep us all busy. There were many interesting and extraordinary jobs. Some cases were terrible and sickening along with several bizarre deaths. Each one had to be investigated to find out what the cause had been and if there had been any criminal involvement.

There were lots of suicides; it was that kind of patch, for some reason. Our area was vast and covered thousands of acres of farming land and many of the residents were legal shotgun owners. Often, the preferred method of ending one's life would be the handy family shotgun and of course these scenes were particularly harrowing.

Cannock Chase is a designated area of natural beauty, made up of many square miles of thickly wooded and dense forest. A sizeable portion of the area came under the jurisdiction of Stone police station. Over the years it has been the scene of numerous murders and suicides. Bodies could lie undiscovered for months or even decades.

I once had to deal with the discovery of a man's body in a car on one of the Cannock Chase car parks. The rear passenger side window had been wound down an inch and a Hoover-type pipe connected to the exhaust and threaded in. The man lay dead in the driving seat – another suicide – simple! No – not simple – the engine had been switched off, ignition keys pulled out and placed in the driver's door compartment. Both the driver's seat and the passenger seat were halfway in the reclined position. The slightly open back window had been forcibly pulled out of its guides leaving just enough space to put an arm through from the outside.

It turned out that the man had died from poisoning by the exhaust fumes, but he had a secret which none of his close family or workmates knew about. He was a family man living with his wife and children in a neat semi near Lichfield. But he had been involved in a gay relationship with a young man from Birmingham for some time. This man was traced and found to be a rent boy. It had been a fairly long-running affair, but the young man didn't seem to care in the slightest that his lover was now dead. There was never a suspicion that the rent boy had killed the man, but the strong possibility of a suicide pact, which IS a criminal offence, did enter the inquiry. Why was the passenger seat down, who had turned off the engine and who had put the keys in the door compartment?

I found that the pipe would fit comfortably over the passenger seat only when it was reclined, and the rent boy had a sound alibi – he was with another man.

The weather had been hot for weeks and the car, which had been driven regularly throughout, was covered in a film of dust. As a result recent finger-marks clearly showed on three particular areas of the paintwork, albeit that they were insufficient to lift any fingerprints. The area around the driver's door handle was one, but this was to be expected as the driver (now dead) had obviously used that door. Strangely another place was the front of the bonnet. It showed a wild pattern of scrabbling smudges which almost shouted the word 'PANIC'. Someone had been more than anxious to try and pull up the bonnet, but had been defeated by the lock. A third display of smears in the dust was evident all around where the rear window glass had been pulled out. Again 'PANIC' had been at work; the glass and paintwork were criss-crossed with a wild arrangement of streaks. These must have happened before the window came free from the runners allowing access to the car.

My guess was that someone had stumbled across the car – engine ticking over – doors locked and driver unconscious. The vain attempt to lift the bonnet was perhaps in an effort to stop the engine by pulling off the spark plug leads. The eventual forceful act in pulling out the window had given access to the inside. But the switching off of the engine had come too late – the man was dead.

The victim clearly intended to kill himself as the PM showed that he had also taken a large quantity of paracetamol and drunk a bottle of sherry. The theory was eventually arrived at that a courting couple, probably having an illicit affair, had stumbled across the scene. If this was the case, they had done everything possible to try to help before realising that it was too late.

Press appeals promised to keep their identity safe. No one came forward, but to this day someone knows.

One summer evening I was called to a report of a burnt out car at the isolated beauty spot of Hanchurch Woods. The report said that there was a body in the car. I arrived at about six o'clock to find several police and SOCO vehicles along with the fire brigade were already there.

The still-smoking remains of a family saloon stood in the corner of a secluded car park. The nearby trees were badly scorched, and the stones and earth had been burned to create a surrounding circle of fine grey ash. The intense heat had lifted every scrap of paint from the contorted shell. All the glass had melted and the tyres and number plates were completely burnt away. The entire inside of the car was gutted, leaving only the metal framework of the seats and the cores of the wiring.

On the wire frame remains of the rear seat was a large, black smouldering mass. Perched precariously on top of this was the unmistakable shape of a human skull – scorched and wafer-thin due to the heat. Like something from a horror movie, two wisps of smoke trailed upwards from the eye sockets. Blackened stumps of bone protruded from the mass where arms and legs had been.

On the ground, far enough away to still be relatively intact lay two empty cans of Tennent's extra strong lager. Inside the car in the back with the body lay the fragmentary remains of another two beer cans and what was left of two metal oil-type cans. The distinctive smell of petrol was still apparent, even after the intense fire was out.

The barely legible vehicle identification plate eventually showed the car to be a Ford Sierra, owned by a Stoke-on-Trent based firm. The case had initially looked suspicious with the body being discovered in the back seat. But it soon emerged that the corpse was that of a sales rep of the firm, who had been disillusioned with his job and was being treated for depression.

The problem of positive identification could only be overcome by using dental records. It wasn't until the following day that I managed to track down a dentist who had treated the man several years before.

He turned out to be a rather irritating, arrogant man who initially declined to assist until he was warned that his actions were obstructing the Coroner. His attitude changed as I led him through into the mortuary examination room where the charred remains lay in pieces on a white porcelain slab. After regaining his composure he was in no doubt, from the dental chart, that it was the sales rep.

There were many more similar tragic episodes, including one where a jealous boyfriend lay in wait for his vivacious young girlfriend in the village of Madeley. He viciously attacked her with an axe. She survived after months of surgery and intensive care, but was destined thereafter to a life of disability and disfigurement. He served a few years in prison – so unfair.

In the village of Baldwin's Gate a shotgun incident almost involved another death. A local woman suffering from depression tried to kill herself by jumping from a motorway bridge. She made a 'supposed' full recovery, but then went on to use her husband's shotgun to blow off part of his leg whilst he lay sleeping in bed. The bedroom was a dreadful sight and it was amazing that he survived.

Another was the discovery of the putrefied body of a new-born child in the bedroom of a schoolgirl in the small market town of Eccleshall. The thirteen-year-old girl had become pregnant by her fifteen-year-old boyfriend, but had not realised until the baby was born one evening whilst she did her homework. She insisted that the child had been born dead, and the condition of the body prevented any other opinion being proved. She had tried to carry on with her life for six months before the body was discovered in a plastic bag in her bedroom by her horrified mother.

With the main West Coast railway line running through our patch, we had several horrific death scenes to attend. The tragic sight of the body of a thirteen-year-old boy lying at the side of the track has always lived with me. The train had arrived at the station with its door hanging open. The boy's father alerted the authorities; he had been waiting to collect his son from the station and quickly became worried. Other witnesses testified that the boy had been fooling about by opening the door and hanging out of the window. The father's grief was so disturbing.

On another occasion I had to visit a terrible scene where a middle-aged man, who had been diagnosed with terminal cancer, had committed suicide. He had thrown himself in front of a train as it passed through the hamlet of Stableford, near to Stone. The man had parked his car on the nearby roadside and climbed down onto a concrete parapet at the side of the track. His jacket, trilby hat and cigarettes were left together with a suicide note, on the parapet before he had launched himself in front the express train. He was smashed into a thousand pieces, the largest piece I found being half of his head.

As I walked along the track dictating the scene into my portable Dictaphone, I heard a familiar voice shout to me from the nearby bridge.

"Hey up, Reg!"

It was Glyn, a detective I had served with at Hanley and who lived close to this vile scene.

"Hiya, Reg," I replied.

"Looks like you've got a bit of a job on," shouted Glyn, all too aware of such atrocities from his own experience.

There then continued a short exchange of pleasantries between old friends who hadn't seen each other in a while, including, 'You going away this year?' and such like.

I continued my dictation.

"Left hand lying on railway sleeper, portion of intestines hanging from bushes."

I went over the day's events later and my thoughts strayed back to the conversation with my friend. Had fifteen years of police work changed me so much from that silly nervous boy who sat waiting for his cadet's entrance exam and was it a good thing?

THIRTY FOUR

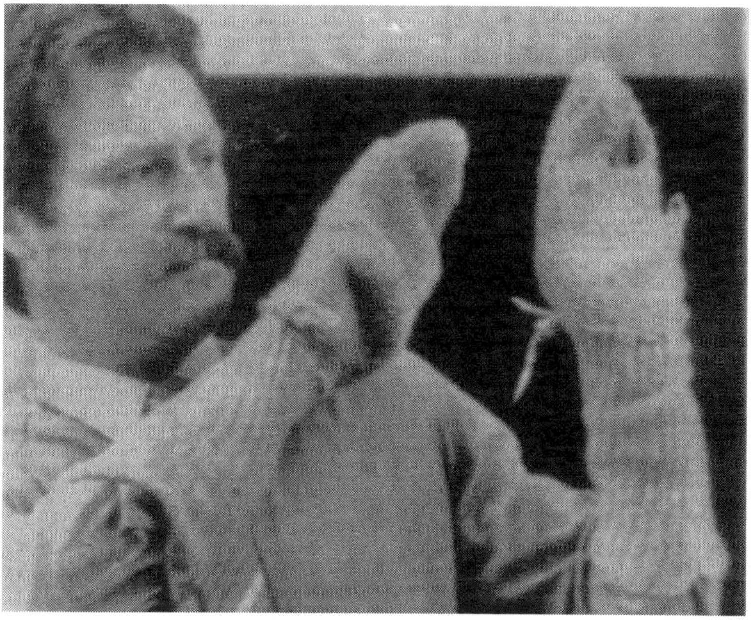

'Sock Man' (photograph courtesy Sentinel News & Media)

THE REGULAR association with tragedy was undoubtedly lessened by the fooling around, mickey-taking and practical jokes. This camaraderie surely helped to keep one's sanity intact.

I had visited the scene of a nasty burglary out in the village of Woodseaves near Stafford. It was the second time in a month that the frail eighty-five-year-old lady had fallen victim to thieves. The raiders had broken down her back door and pushed her out of the way as they stole one hundred pounds – her pension money for two weeks. One of the men had worn a pair of tatty hand knitted socks on his hands to stop fingerprints being left and had dumped the socks in the garden.

The local newspaper published a story on the incident in which they included a photo of me wearing the socks on my hands.

It wasn't long before photocopies of the sock-clad DS were published on every police noticeboard between Newcastle and Stafford. Suggested titles included: *Reg examines the wife's handiwork* and *No, Porky, on your feet.*

We had several different detective inspectors in charge of Stone CID during my time there. They were all nice guys, although 'Harry' was a boss who often let his enthusiasm get the better of him before he got his brain into gear.

We were working flat out on a rape report which had allegedly taken place at Hanchurch Woods. The investigation was coming to an end with no sign of an offender on the horizon. When someone suggested that we should put the case on *Police 5,* it seemed like a reasonable call.

Police 5 was a five-minute television programme presented by Shaw Taylor. It gave the details of serious cases, and requested witnesses to come forward. The programme was a forerunner to the later, highly successful *Crimewatch* series. Shaw would finish off each programme with his catchphrase of 'Keep Em' Peeled' as he pointed a finger towards his eyes.

Shaw arrived with his film crew at our CID office in the morning and we went through the case with him. He made notes and decided on the best way to get the message over. It was not his first visit to Stone. He had 'helped us with our enquiries' a couple of times before and would usually buy us a beer afterwards.

Some filming and interviews were completed, and we were pretty well out of ideas when Harry rose from his chair with a 'Eureka!' look on his face. "I'll tell you what we could do…" he said.

Under normal circumstances such an enthusiastic opening would have attracted the interested and undivided attention of the audience. We however, were all used to Harry's madcap schemes, which had led to countless wasted hours, wrongful arrests, complaints and reams of unnecessary reports.

We listened impassively as he continued with his facial-beaming now set at maximum. "We could get the police helicopter. They could take one of the film crew up and it would give the public a proper look at the area whilst Shaw gave his commentary over the film."

Harry's enthusiasm seemed to win Shaw over and so, still full of enthusiasm for his good idea, he grabbed the nearest phone and telephoned the Air Support Group. The helicopter was shared between nearby forces and in no time Harry was through to a sergeant in their control room. We all sat listening to the phone conversation as he explained the situation and what we required.

"Oh, so our force would have to pay then because it's not a standard job… Yes, I see… So how much would it be? Right… Is that all? Two seventy-five an hour… Oh, plus VAT. Well, that's nothing, I'll pay that myself," enthused Harry.

We all exchanged corner of the eye glances, as we started to comprehend Harry's thoughts. Did he really think that he was going to get the services of a three-quarters of a million pounds helicopter for £2.75p… plus VAT?

Harry made a few more arrangements before replacing the telephone handset and looking up with a still beaming face. "Sorted," he said, adding a confident nod to the bemused and disbelieving group that surrounded him.

"You do realise, do you, Boss," said Nult, with his customary deadpan expression. "…That he was telling you it's going to cost the force *two hundred and seventy-five pounds* an hour plus VAT?"

The colour drained from Harry's face as the reality dawned.

Some big changes in the law were introduced around this time and these came with the new Police and Criminal Evidence Act (PACE). The legislation set out substantial alterations to prisoner's rights, police powers and procedure. It was important that every officer in the force got to know and understand the new law and so it inevitably led to – yes you've guessed – ANOTHER COURSE!

The 'course syndrome' didn't end there for me as my PACE course was quickly followed up with a month's course to learn all about a new major crime computer system. This had been introduced following the headaches occurring on big murder inquiries such as the Yorkshire Ripper and the Black Panther. The system was a national one and was called HOLMES, which stood for Home Office Large Major Enquiry System. It was all new to me, as the nearest I'd ever been to a computer before this was 'The Box'. The course was intensive and complex, but I got through it okay.

In September 1989, I had to go and help out at Newcastle CID with a murder investigation. All major enquiries for the north of the county were operated from the old Magistrates' Court building in Water Street, Newcastle. The single men's bedrooms that used to be on the first floor had been given over for the use of major investigations and now contained desks, computers and filing trays. The Newcastle Police Club, with its bar and function room, were still in use downstairs. The court had been operating from a new building in the town centre for some time.

I'd had enough of deaths and murders over the past few years. I had already helped at Newcastle on a different murder. A young Asian man had been beaten to death and his body dumped in a stream. The only good thing about this latest inquiry would be that I would be back working with my old friend Chalky again. Geoff White had done well since the days of Hanley CID. We'd kept in touch over the years and I wasn't surprised, when I heard he had been appointed as detective inspector in charge of Newcastle CID.

I was having problems with my back as a result of an old injury and so it seemed ironic when I arrived at the murder room that my job title was to be 'ACTION MAN'. I would have preferred to go out and do some proper enquiries, but I guess I wasn't up to it as I was soon to undergo an operation.

Chalky showed me to my office on the first floor. "Here you are, Reg," he said, "tastefully furnished."

The old, pale blue four-panelled door swung open to reveal a small simple room with a high ceiling, which would be my workplace.

"But, Reg," I said, (yes I know this Reg lark gets confusing) "...this was Des's bedroom."

He shook his head as he looked around, "an historical room," he said and wandered away down the corridor.

The room had changed since the days when I'd pick up a bleary-eyed Des Lewis for Drug Squad shifts and duty on the Carl Bridgewater murder. It had been split in half to make two rooms and a large old-fashioned cupboard was in place behind my chair.

This particular murder was not a run-of-the-mill affair. The victim, a housewife lived in an area known as May Bank, about half a mile outside Newcastle. The lady had not been seen for some time and neighbours started to become suspicious. Someone then remembered the husband had been seen digging the back garden and laying a new lawn!

One thing had led to another before the police decided it was time to offer a helping hand with the gardening. The lady's body was discovered buried under the new lawn, and eventually the husband admitted to being responsible for the death, but claimed severe provocation.

Whilst Chalky was in direct charge of the investigation, other more senior detectives had a hand in it and would frequently show their faces to supervise and offer suggestions. Geoff White was still blessed with his bizarre sense of humour and regularly played crazy tricks on me. My desk faced the door and occasionally as I sat working I would realise that the door was ever so slightly, slowly creaking open. There was no one to be seen and no hand on the door. I had to ease myself up in the chair and look down to floor level where I would see a prone Chalky lying flat on the corridor floor. His head poking around the gap and looking up at me like a mad person. Such idiocy helped us both get through the long days.

Once in a while we would get a visit from the CID top boss. Detective Chief Superintendent Malcolm 'Malc the Talc', or 'Bev', Bevington was a suave, good-looking man (hence the nickname). He knew his job, he liked a laugh, but you always had to remember that he was 'The Boss'.

I arrived at my office one morning at about eight. and rummaged through my in tray. We had pretty well wound everything up and the court file was nearly ready. I settled my aching back down into the chair and started to sort out the day's work. I looked up from my desk as the office door swung open. It was Bev – grey pinstriped suit, dark well-groomed hair – ultra suave – as per normal.

"Morning, Mr Pye," he said, looking down at me.

"Morning, Sir," I replied, as I eased up out of my chair.

"Anything new in, or are we all systems go?"

"I think everything's on track now, Boss." I replied.

"Good… have you seen Mr White yet?"

"No, not yet, Boss, but his coat's hanging up, so he's about somewhere," I replied, hoping that Chalky was in.

"Right, I'll go and find him," he said as he turned and walked off down the corridor.

I settled back down into my seat as the clicking of Bev's heels disappeared away down the corridor towards the main office. I rubbed my chin as I pondered over the reply written on a returned action form.

Suddenly, startled by a noise from behind, I flinched and jolted halfway across the desk knocking wire trays and paperwork to the floor.

"What the bloody hell?" I exclaimed as I swivelled, still halfway across the desk.

The two doors to the cupboard both opened and Chalky peered out from the gloom… eyes wide.

"Shh!" he hissed. "Has he gone? My whole job flashed before me. I've been hiding in here waiting to jump out on you. I climbed in when I heard you coming up the stairs. I was on the verge of bursting out when I heard him come in. I was praying that you didn't want to get anything out whilst he was still here."

All that sitting in my computer chair at Water Street pretty well finished my back off. I could hardly walk and soon after this I underwent an operation to remove part of the offending disc. I was off work for a while, but the operation had been successful. I wasn't back at Stone for long before I was summoned to see the Chief Constable.

I had applied for promotion to Inspector some time before and I'd been on the selection boards. With a few stints of acting uniformed and acting detective inspector under my belt I guessed this was a promotion call. I knew that it would be as uniformed inspector rather than detective. It was a case of – *where was he going to send me?*

Visits to the Chief's office were pretty rare (for me anyway). My only other ones had been over the vampire affair to see Mr Rees back in 1973 and then for my promotion to sergeant in 1982.

Mr Kelly looked across his desk at me… "I'm promoting you to uniformed inspector and sending you to…."

The wait seemed interminable. *Biddulph* flashed through my mind.

"Hanley," was his eventual announcement.

Great, I thought, *back home at last, even though it is uniform.*

It was certainly time to move on as I'd been at Stone for six years now, including all those courses and times away helping out on murders and bits of acting inspector here and there. I'd loved Stone, and, despite all the deaths there had been some interesting enquiries and good results.

THIRTY FIVE

IT WAS TIME for another trip over to the uniform stores at headquarters. The ageless Mr Ryan was still there; he measured me up for my new inspector's uniform – white shirts! All the old blue ones that I had left over from my sergeant's outfit could now be used for gardening and mending the car. I was now getting a smart, flat, peaked cap with its black material strip across the peak and a pair of brown leather gloves rather than black ones. I'd also be getting yet another of Mr Ryan's famous envelopes. This one was full of chromium plated 'Bath Stars', (also known as 'pips') which were to go on my shoulder epaulettes. Some things clearly hadn't changed… I'd still have to bodge holes to fix them on.

I seemed to have more pips than I actually needed. I wondered if anyone might notice if I put three on each shoulder, giving me the rank of chief inspector. I decided it probably wasn't worth the risk and made do with being an inspector.

I was told that the shift I was taking over was made up of two sergeants and fifteen constables, including four WPCs. I headed toward the parade room for my first stint – an early (6 a.m.) shift. It was a strange, unnerving feeling as I walked down the familiar corridor on the ground floor from the inspector's office.

I welcomed the fact that I had an old friend with me, John Bowers, who had joined the cadets with me all those years ago. John had been a sergeant on my new shift for some time and was able to tell me how low morale was. He opened the parade room door for me and I took a deep intake of breath as I stepped inside. The rumbling scraping sound of fifteen or so chairs being pushed backwards filled the air as everyone rose to their feet.

How strange this was. Could it be that almost twenty-one years had passed by from when I was the one standing to attention and saying, 'Yes, Sir, no, Sir?'

I was aware that I was being scanned by a multitude of eyes. These were mostly young men and women of a similar age to me when I was at Stoke in the early seventies. No doubt they were all thinking similar thoughts. What is this boss going to be like? Is he going to make our lives hell? Is he just going to be trying to make a name for himself?

In the short few seconds that it took to walk over to the central chair at the end of the table, I thought back to my first few years. My ambitions had been to help people and use my wits and intuition to win every time against crooks, violence and antisocial thugs and, if possible, to have some fun along the way.

So that was what I suggested and for good measure threw in that I expected: *smartness, punctuality and that the public should be treated with courtesy and good manners… and that if they didn't know, they had to 'ask'.* It wasn't until they'd all left the room that I realised I'd reiterated the words that were said to me by Chief Inspector Phillips, as a cadet back in 1967. They were, of course, similar words that had also been spoken to me as a nineteen-year-old constable by Inspector 'Wild Bill' Holdcroft in 1969.

The shift members were all real individuals. Several had been in the services or in a trade before becoming police officers. One new arrival on the shift was Simon, an ex-sailor with bags of enthusiasm, but little in the way of luck. Every inquiry he took on went wrong and turned into a paperwork nightmare. He had been lumbered with a strange theft investigation. Someone had stolen hundreds of old Victorian blue bricks by uprooting them from the pavement in a street near to the town centre. The blue brick inquiry seemed destined to follow him for the rest of his life.

I had a meeting with the Superintendent one morning and he had expressed his concern saying: "What about young Simon on your shift? Seems a nice lad, but can't shift his paperwork."

"Yes, Boss," I replied, finding it difficult to refrain from the CID vernacular. "He's got the 'Midas Touch' in reverse – everything he touches turns to shit."

"That sums it up nicely," replied the Superintendent, nearly choking on his tea.

After Simon's blue bricks was finally resolved he became a new man, although the reverse Midas touch was not completely gone.

My time at Hanley was like a breath of fresh air. I'd loved CID work, but maybe I had become out of touch with all the other things that were going on. This was an opportunity to get involved at grass roots level again. There was, of course, a mountain of paperwork each day, but I wasn't going to let it stop me getting involved. I'd missed going on patrol as I used to all those years ago and so took every opportunity to get out, either walking the town centre beats or driving to show my face at different incidents.

The morale on the shift was boosted – maybe it was my imagination, but the long faces were replaced by smiles, camaraderie, pranks and good humour. With the increase in morale came the bonus of a higher standard of work and a much bigger input. We arranged a curry club and would all chip in to pay for the ingredients. The feast would be cooked one night a week, whilst on nights, by the shift curry officer, PC Pete (Nico) Nixon. The tantalising, spicy aromas would start to waft through the building from about 5 a.m. and we would tuck in after finishing duty at 6 a.m. We always had to put some of the food to one side for anyone who had to work over on an incident. We would take it in turns to do the dishes (me included). It must have been a puzzle to the members of early shift following us on duty, when they realised that we were eating curry at 6 a.m.

PC Phill (Digger) Barnes was an old friend. We had joined the cadets together and also served alongside each other as constables at Stoke. Phill was a member of my new shift and worked in our control room (the nerve centre). Back then there would be a control room at each sub-divisional police station. Hanley's was in a big first floor room which was separate from the action of the cell block and the enquiry desk at the entrance.

There was a large foyer at Hanley Police Station where people would wait to be attended to at the enquiry desk. One busy Friday evening Phill answered a call in the control room:

THERE'S A BIG FIGHT GOING ON IN THE FOYER.

Ever protective of his younger colleagues, Phill had presumed that the fight involved his fellow shift members. He pulled out his phone plug and raced off downstairs. He burst into the foyer with his telephone headset and mouth piece still fitted onto his balding pate. 'What's going on?' he bellowed.

An elderly gent was standing at the counter in the otherwise empty foyer waiting to produce his driving licence. The startled man spun around to see the wide-eyed uniformed constable standing with sleeves rolled and fists clenched. His headset wires lashed from side to side in keeping with his confused head movements as he tried to make sense of the lack of fighting.

Phill quietly closed the door and disappeared back upstairs as quickly as he had arrived. The call had been from the *Foyer Nightclub* in the town centre.

The sheer volume of jobs coming in through Hanley's Control Room was enormous. We could have as many as over one hundred 'open incidents' (incidents being dealt with/not finalised). If we had whittled this down to thirty by the time we handed over to the following shift, we had done well. There would be occasions when everyone on the shift was committed on one or more jobs and I would attend and deal with incidents myself.

The variety of different incidents was phenomenal. As always throughout my police service, there were sudden deaths (still called Form 12s) and as shift inspector I had to visit each one.

During one night shift I went out to a house on the Bentilee council estate. A telephone caller had reported a horrible smell and swarm of flies coming from a downstairs flat. It had the hallmark of a Form 12 of the worst kind.

A constable had broken into the flat and been immediately overwhelmed by the flies. He directed me through to the downstairs toilet. Both of us were now wearing gloves, raincoats and a towel around our heads as fly protection. The smell was vomit-inducing and the barely recognisable, rotting liquefied corpse of the tenant of the flat was lying on the floor. Obviously the man had been dead for a long time. It seemed cruel that living so close to other people, it had taken such a long time before anyone became concerned. The remains of the body could actually be seen to be moving, caused by the writhing of the thousands of maggots.

On arriving home that morning, my clothes smelled so strongly that I had to remove almost everything and dump it all outside the back door. Fortunately the neighbours hadn't got up and didn't manage to catch a glimpse of me stripping off. I even emptied several flies out from my pockets.

The most heart-breaking of incidents that I ever had to attend were those that we have all come to know as 'cot deaths'. It didn't matter how hardened you had become through years of police work. The sight of a tiny lifeless baby would always be something that would live in your memory.

Of course such deaths were, and still are, the subject of intensive debate, and many people have dedicated their lives to uncovering some factor that could be a primary cause. A lot of care and detail always went into the investigation of cot deaths. These would entail a routine sending of mattress, bedding and any other everyday items away to the forensic science laboratory. The hope was to find something that might reveal a cause. The one component which always seemed to be present in every home cot death that I attended was that there were smokers living in the house.

Hanley still covered some of the same deprived areas that it had done when I worked on the CID back in the early 1980s. There were several large council estates where alcoholism and drug abuse were rife. When I had first joined, many of the deaths resulted from industrial diseases caused by the pottery or mining industries. This had now been overtaken by alcohol and drug-related deaths.

I had other duties that I had to see to, apart from the running of the shift. I was the appointed Diseases of Animals officer for Hanley. Maybe they gave me this job when they discovered I had been at Biddulph. Fortunately at Hanley this was one task that, for a change, never seemed to create any extra work for me.

As an inspector, I was occasionally called upon to be in charge of an identification parade for the CID. It seemed fortunate that no one had heard of my past experience in this particular field. Everything was done precisely and properly with specially printed booklets. It looked easy, but then again my role as inspector *was* easy. I just had to appear at the last minute expecting everything to be done. All that hard work trudging around and ringing up to get the stooges – that was where the work still was.

I realised that the shift morale was now good when I came on for night duty one evening. I discovered that on almost every door inside the station was pinned a photocopy of a photograph of me. The photograph in question was one that had been taken back in 1978 when I was on the Drug Squad. It had been included in my personal file for staff appraisal purposes.

The picture was truly hilarious and showed me with shoulder length hair and a Mexican style moustache. I was wearing a jacket and tie, and my shirt tastefully included a facsimile of human faces. I had purchased two such shirts from a local drug dealer, who must have had a side-line in shirts.

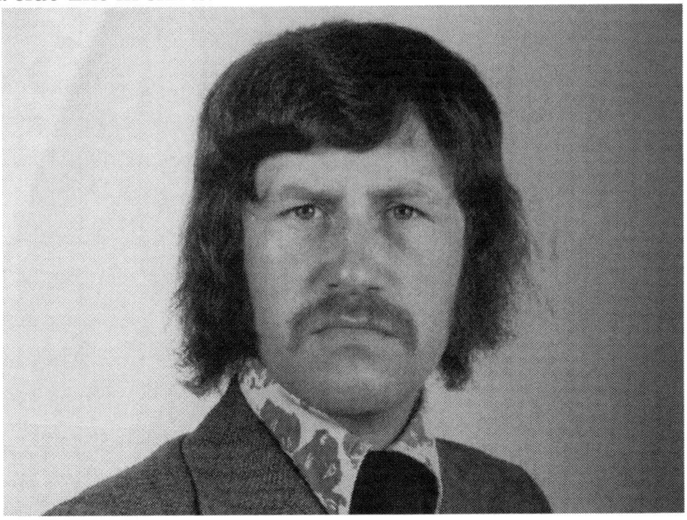

The Drug Squad photo (dig that shirt!)

The station was in uproar at the sight of these photos and I even found one hanging in the toilets. Enquiries pointed towards 'Blue Brick' Simon, who had been given the photo when the police photographic studio was having a clear-out.

It was whilst I was on duty one evening that the tale of the vampire came back to haunt me yet again. Twenty years had passed since the event, but the ATV studios had tracked me down. Their phone call researcher asked me to appear on the *Friday Night Live* programme that they had planned to run. The theme centred on Dracula and vampires. The lady told me that they had got together a lot of people from all walks of life who believed in vampires. Some of these nutters even professed to be vampires themselves or claimed to have been attacked by one. The producer had found out about my case and wanted me as a guest to talk about the incident.

Old Chief Constable Arthur Rees was no longer there to point me in the right direction. Headquarters decided that I could appear on the show if I wished. I took the careful option and decided that the TV appearance would simply not be worth the mickey-taking that would follow. I declined, but watched the transmission a few months later and was relieved that I had made a good decision. It consisted of several people dressed in black capes, a couple of self-professed witches and one man who claimed to have had to drive a stake through someone's heart. I felt that I had had a lucky escape.

There were many hair-raising car chases during my time at Hanley. One of these involved a particularly nasty drug-dealing burglar, who I had arrested years before on the Drug Squad. A report came in at two o'clock one morning, that along with two others, he had burgled a house in the nearby town of Leek. The trio were using a stolen car which had been seen on the road from Leek to Hanley.

I knew that the man had a girlfriend in a flat just out of town and went for a look. As I drove towards the house I saw that the hunch had proved right. There was the car with its lights on and engine running. On seeing me, the driver rammed the car into gear and sped off. There then followed a manic piece of driving as he careered back and forth up various side streets and back alleys, which were barely wide enough to get a car through. He smashed dustbins out of the way and ran over a parked moped as the crazy journey continued.

I kept pace with him from a safe distance and could clearly see the two other heads in the back of the car being flung about as the car bounced from one wall to another. In an act of desperation he tried to shake me off by careering at high speed into an alleyway that was too narrow for the car. Sparks flew and door handles and wing mirrors were ripped off as he tore along. I took a different route as he disappeared into the gap, but knew that he would have to emerge into the road that I had taken.

As I pulled out into the street, there he was in front of me, but not heading away from me, heading towards me and clearly intent on ramming my police car. Parked cars lined each side of the narrow street and I could hear my radio telling me that other patrols were on their way. I jammed the car into reverse and set off backwards as the stolen car nosed right up to my front bumper. My car whined as the revs increased the speed to around 30 mph in reverse.

I was running out of road and decided that I would have to brace for the impact, but as I slowed down, so did he. With nowhere else to go I came to a halt. He gave my front bumper a frustrated nudge then sped off backwards, as though to show me – *I can do that as well.*

It was now roles reversed in the truest sense, but he hadn't mastered high-speed reversing and corrected his steering a little too much. He smashed the already battered vehicle into two parked cars, jamming it firmly up against a house. After scrambling through a window he was on his toes, leaving his two partners in crime trapped in the back awaiting arrest. We later found him hiding under the floorboards in his girlfriend's flat. The car contained the stolen property taken during the earlier burglary.

In 1991 I became eligible for the Police Long Service and Good Conduct Medal. It was certainly true that I had managed the twenty-two years as a regular officer that counted as the long service. As for the good conduct part – well sometimes.

I received my medal along with several other good friends who had joined the force with me as cadets, including my old school friend, Ian. We had started out on our careers on the same day back in the winter of 1966. Also there was my buddy from Ryton, Eric Cartwright, and my other two Ryton chums, Graham Woodward and Terry (Cherry Blossom) Lockett. I proudly accepted my medal from the Deputy Chief Constable, together with the blue and white tunic ribbon to be worn on my uniform. It was identical to the one I had spotted on Sergeant Haywood's uniform twenty-five years before on the day of my cadet's entrance examination. Where the hell had all those years gone?

THIRTY SIX

STOKE-ON-TRENT is a huge urban sprawl being made up of the six original towns of Burslem, Tunstall, Fenton, Longton, Hanley and Stoke.

All these busy town centres are completely joined up by residential and industrial regions. To the uninitiated the whole area appears to be one concrete jungle rather than separate places. The nearby town of Newcastle is also joined seamlessly into this mass, making the entire district appear as one gigantic city.

Hanley is the City Centre and the busiest of the towns which make up Stoke-on-Trent. It has always been regarded as *the* shopping centre of North Staffordshire and boasts a lot of the prestige stores. Shoplifting in Hanley has, in consequence, forever been a major headache. Like all other busy police areas, we were unfortunate enough to possess our own home-grown professional shoplifters, who would be 'bang at it' every day. It was a fact of life that as a habitual shoplifter became more well-known he would also find it difficult to make a living on his own turf. A day trip to somewhere farther afield was a good solution, giving the necessary anonymity. The chances of being recognized as a thief by police officers or store detectives were reduced significantly.

Reg Lownes was Stoke-on-Trent's biggest shop lifting problem and certainly deserved more than one small Christian name (albeit a good one!). Unless Reg was having a day out pinching elsewhere, he would be brazenly thieving on a large scale in Hanley. Frequently he would be arrested and always charged if there was enough evidence. He was a slippery customer who had developed a street-wise knowledge of the system which he used to advantage.

When he suspected he was under surveillance his squirrel-like tactics were deployed by hiding stolen property in any number of secret town centre locations. After enduring arrest and hours of 'No Comment' interviews he would return maybe even days later to collect the booty.

Confusion could reign if the police radio announced: 'Reg is on the town'. To any new recruits, who were trying to come to terms with their newly acquired police lingo, this could have meant anyone!

Shoplifters came from all different walks of life from High Court judges to down and out vagrants, or from professional thieves like Reg, to the elderly and absent-minded.

As shift inspector I would have to spend a part of my day down in the custody suite, which adjoined the cell block. It was my duty to supervise what was going on with the prisoners. I had to check that the paperwork was okay and that the prisoners were being treated correctly (whether they deserved it or not).

I would regularly be present when a prisoner was brought in by an arresting officer to be booked in.

As Hanley had such a shoplifting problem it had one entire shift of officers (known as shift five) whose job it was, theoretically, to deal only with shoplifters.

One afternoon a fairly elderly lady was bought in whilst I was down in the custody suite. She had been arrested for shoplifting. The poor soul was bemused by the situation and obviously needed looking after rather than putting before a court. She had stolen a packet of Jaffa Cakes from Woolworths, which had a value of a few pence.

Sadly, before any kind of help could be offered to her, the legal niceties needed to be complied with. This entailed searching her and listing, to the last penny, her money and any other valuables in her possession. Identity checks had to be completed and all the same rigmarole that would have gone along with the arrest of a serious bank robber.

The lady was bewildered by the events and was strangely adamant that she would not allow us to search her tatty and decaying-looking string shopping bag. However, at the custody sergeant's insistence, the contents were eventually removed and placed on the counter for listing. A silence overtook the room as the young PC, who had arrested the lady, removed fifteen brown envelopes from the bag. A look of complete disbelief took over his face as he opened each one to reveal its contents of one thousand pounds. In total she had £15,350 with her.

A sad story of turmoil and depression lay behind the events and it transpired that the cash was the proceeds of the sale of her house. She had kept the money with her rather than trust it to the safe keeping of a bank. She was released into care without charge, but not until a bank account had been opened and the money deposited there for her.

Black police humour followed the arrest, with someone trying to work out how many packets of Jaffa Cakes you could purchase for £15,350.

Another 'non-standard' shoplifter was a young black chap who was a drug addict. He was a travelling shoplifter from Wolverhampton and trying to steal something worthwhile to get money for his heroin. The nineteen year old had gone into one of the exclusive jewellery shops on the town. Somehow he had managed to get hold of a valuable, heavy, chunky gent's gold bracelet. He had come under suspicion early in the game and the police had been secretly called.

Before he knew what was happening, eager young PC Ian Crutchley arrived in the shop and with the description that had been given, made a beeline for the offender. The panicking shoplifter discreetly pulled the bracelet from his pocket and stuffed it into his mouth.

As the constable closed in the young thief's panic level increased so much that he swallowed the bracelet. He admitted afterwards that he didn't know how he had managed it, as the bracelet was enormous. He choked as he got it past his throat and could feel it slowly moving down his gullet into his stomach.

The lad was moved about between police station, court and hospital. A close watch was kept on him over the next few days in the hope that he might pass the bracelet out naturally. The thought of it still brings tears to my eyes (those sharp chunky bits, ooh!).

The bracelet had decided to stay put in his stomach. The hospital doctor was confident from the X-rays that it would never make its own way out. For the young man's safety it was decided that it would have to be removed by surgical operation. This was carried out successfully and the bracelet was returned to the shop after a clean and polish.

The lad in question turned out to be a likeable young man, whose life had been ruined by drugs. The case was a feature on the TV news and in the national newspapers at the time. I often wondered who eventually purchased the bracelet and if they got to know of its travels.

The first Gulf War was now in full swing and some recently retired members of the military forces were being recalled to duty. They had to report to the police station with their paperwork for processing before being issued with a Travel Warrant giving them free rail journeys to their military base. There weren't that many, but I had a plan and so I told the enquiry office staff that I would deal with the first 'recall' that came in.

I didn't have to wait long before I found myself at the counter filling in the necessary paperwork for a former sailor. After making out the travel warrant I photocopied the entire bundle and handed over the sailor's originals. I later Tipp-exed out all his details from my copies and photocopied them once again. I now had a pristine and unused set of Recall to Duty papers.

As the news started to grow about the imminent hostilities, young Simon, the ex-navy PC of blue brick fame became interested. He made a joking comment hoping that his services would NOT be required.

Simon's details were carefully and authentically typed on to the blank form and a discrete enquiry to the personnel department provided me with his old service number.

A recorded delivery envelope addressed to *The Officer in Charge, Hanley Police Station* was faked, together with an accompanying note from the Superintendent. This was the same boss who had found the 'Reverse Midas Touch' so amusing. At the 6 a.m. duty parade the next morning, the room was packed. Everyone except Simon knew about the impending hoax. Sergeant John Bowers and I went through the morning's paperwork and dished out various jobs to be done and handed out mail.

The moment arrived. "Oh, one for you here, Simon," I said. "It's come from the War Office straight to the Super, he's put a note on saying he wants to see you as soon as he gets in."

I handed the bundle on and it was passed down the table to Simon, who was already a picture of puzzlement. Everyone else in the room was talking to each other and shuffling paperwork about, trying to look uninterested. Simon suddenly stood up from his chair, holding the papers in his right hand and pointing towards them with his left. His mouth was wide open, but no noise could be heard. Everyone carried on with what they were doing as though Simon didn't exist.

Eventually Simon managed some speech: "But, but, but, but…"

"Someone started a moped up?" said John Bowers as he puffed on his cigarette.

"I've been called…" Simon gasped.

"Call PC Dudman!" said someone, and a titter went around the room.

"Whatever is the matter, Simon?" I quizzed.

"They've called me back to duty for the Gulf War," Simon finally managed to blurt out.

"Oh, dear, that's annoying," I said, "I hope they give us someone to replace you. Right! Parade's finished now everyone. See you all later on."

There was a hint of stifled laughter, which rose slightly over the rumble of the chairs as the shift stood and went off to their patrols and other duties.

"You stay in and get on with your reports this morning, Simon," I said. "You'll need to get rid of all that paperwork before you go. Don't forget that you've got to see the Super."

"But, Inspector, but, but…"

I left the room feeling a little guilty.

"You can't leave him too long like that, Sir," said young policewoman, Vicky, "he might string himself up."

"I know, Vicky. The Super wanted to be in on it, so we'll try to keep him alive until he arrives."

Fortunately the Super was early that morning and was all ears to see how the call-up had gone. He had difficulty keeping a straight face as I related the moped impression.

"Right, get him to come up then, before he tops himself. It wouldn't look good at headquarters if he did and they knew I was in on it."

"Okay, Sir," I said and hurried off to get Simon, who I found in almost the same position still clutching the papers in his right hand.

"Right, Simon, the Super's ready for you," I said.

I knocked on the Boss's door and walked in, closely followed by a shell-shocked Simon. I knew that other shift members were lurking in the corridor.

"Right then, Simon," greeted the Super. "What's all this recall to duty business?"

Simon stretched out his right hand holding the bundle of paperwork and with a gaping mouth could yet again only utter… "But, but…"

A shuffling was heard outside the door, as the Super spoke, "do I take it then, Simon that you don't want to go?"

"No, Sir," came back Simon's first intelligible sentence for some time.

"Well, I'll tell you what, don't bother; you stay here at Hanley, but no more blue brick enquiries."

"Sir, if you can sort this out, I'll go down and re-lay the whole of Havelock Place with blue bricks in my spare time."

"Oh, it's surprising what Superintendents can do, Simon. Oh, and Inspectors."

The Super's voice was beginning to crack as his eyes crinkled up. Giggles could be heard from the corridor and I had now lost it all together. A wave of recognition coupled with relief swept across Simon's face as the truth dawned upon him.

"Sir!" Simon turned directly to face me. "Permission to call you a bastard?"

"Permission granted," I replied.

"*Bastard*!" Simon shouted out in a volume probably only ever heard before in the cell block.

The giggles outside had now turned to full laughter. Simon, who was also laughing for the first time that morning, turned to the Super and spoke in a quiet voice.

"Permission to call you a bastard as well, Sir?"

"Yes, go on, Simon! You deserve it, but not so loud this time."

"Bastard… Sir!" Simon whispered respectfully.

The photograph had been avenged!

It was around this time that, as an inspector, I was appointed investigating officer into an allegation of theft made by a member of the public against a police officer. The accusation had been made that five hundred pounds had been stolen during a house search. I successfully cracked the case discovering that a policewoman had indeed stolen the money from the man's wardrobe without the knowledge of the other officers engaged on the search. The policewoman's guilt came as a shock to her colleagues who had initially believed the man had made up the story. The case culminated in the woman being sentenced at Crown Court to eighteen months imprisonment and of course, quite rightly, to her being sacked.

This case was closely followed by another, which was concerned with corruption in another police force. I spent almost two years travelling between my home in Newcastle-under-Lyme to Stafford, Burton-on-Trent and other parts of the country. My travels included frequent train journeys down to Scotland Yard.

These two investigations were both distasteful. There was nothing memorable or enjoyable about them. It was during the last inquiry that I was appointed detective inspector in charge of Hanley CID. I would take up this post when the inquiry was finalised.

I'd completed almost twenty-seven years with the Staffordshire Police and I'd had the most amazing time. But the job was not the same, so many things had changed. Lots of different government enquiries into policing had been completed. The Edmund Davies Report back in the seventies had given us much better pay and conditions. Sweeping changes were brought in with the introduction of the 1984 Police and Criminal Evidence Act. Police powers and the ways we went about our everyday duties had changed time and again. The Crown Prosecution Service had been introduced, taking away the final decision by the police to prosecute offenders. The old police caution… *You are not obliged to say anything* had gone, only to be replaced by an even longer and more complex version. These were things which had been burned into my brain. A large and costly inquiry by Sir Patrick Sheehy had suggested a wealth of changes, but not much of it was used.

So much additional and unnecessary paperwork seemed to have crept into the job since I first started back in 1967. All those familiar forms, each one with its own identification number, were gone and had been replaced by reams and reams of multi-coloured, multi-paged documents.

All manner of squads, units and departments had started springing up. Everybody seemed to be specialising in some small aspect of the job rather than knowing how to deal with an incident from start to finish. Dozens of new desk jobs had been created to keep up with political correctness and appease minority groups. Some police stations were destined for closure and all were having their police clubs and bars closed. Worthwhile departments, such as Traffic were set to be phased out. It was of course all about budgets.

There were many good people still there doing the job, some of them had made it to the top. Geoff White (Chalky) eventually became Staffordshire's Detective Chief Superintendent and was awarded the ultimate police decoration of *The Queens Police Medal.* He retired in 2007.

My back problems had reoccurred. I was now looking at a further back operation and was not surprised when I was called to headquarters to be examined by the police surgeon. This was not a police surgeon like the one who visits police stations to take blood samples from breath test drivers. He was employed to examine officers whose health is suspect and to see if they are still fit to carry out their duties.

It was half past three on the afternoon of Friday, 29th September 1993, when I walked into the police surgeon's room at headquarters. He had all my medical history in front of him.

I wasn't surprised when after examining me, he said. "I'm going to have to retire you, inspector, how do you feel about that?"

I shrugged.

"That's life, thanks, Doc."

I shook his hand and gave a tight lipped smile as I left. He wouldn't have noticed a slight glisten in my eyes as I made my way back along the corridors of power over the marcasite vinyl floor tiles. They'd never had khaki-coloured lino here.

As I walked across the car park, I passed a couple of fresh faced young PCs each with a bundle of law notes. The overheard conversation was interesting.

"What you doing tonight, Reg?"

"Don't know yet, Reg," was the reply. "Perhaps go for a beer when I've done my homework."

I looked over at them and smiled to myself. They didn't even know who I was and they had even less idea why they were both calling each other Reg…

I climbed into my car and drove down towards the main road, passing by the white police dog training jumps and ladders which had been a feature of the front of Headquarters forever. I smiled as I remembered seeing them for the first time almost twenty-seven years before. The death knell for this landmark was approaching quickly with the removal of the regional dog training centre. In fact the entire police HQ was soon to be closed down and sold off in favour of cheaper and smaller accommodation.

I turned onto the A34 and headed for home, thoughts going back through the years – my three young friends who had lost their lives in that tragic road accident on a driving course came into my mind.

I drove slowly towards the city, passing through Stone – more memories. A hint of a tear dampened my cheek as I found it hard to come to terms with the fact that I was no longer 'in the job' and that I wouldn't be making it back to Hanley.

I jolted into concentration as a patrol car zoomed past me with lights blazing and klaxon blaring. Something was happening somewhere, but then again, it always was, it always would be.

As I neared home, my pager started to buzz in my pocket. I pulled onto a lay-by and read the message. It was Chalky.

REG… We've had a good result on a job… George & Dragon for a pint, if you can make it… REG!

Why not?

The End

Drinking coffee (now there's a novelty!) Picture taken in 2020.

Not really the end! I was seventy in 2020 and with four crime thriller novels behind me and other ongoing projects I spend most of my spare time writing.

I'm still in touch with many of my old pals from 'The Job' including, Geoff White, Ian Bruckshaw, John Bowers, Des Lewis, John Moss and Dixie Dean. Of course, they all retired a long time ago but our conversations (usually over a few beers and a curry) invariably drift back to some of those interesting, funny or tragic incidents that we were involved in and which undoubtedly turned us into the people we have become.

I still get to see quite a few members of the shift of youngsters I took over as inspector at Hanley, but of course they have now also all joined the ranks of the retired – more chances for a few laughs!

The next few pages contain:

A glossary of police terms which were in regular use in the police although several would have been particular to Staffordshire.

Details of my other books.

Additional information.

Glossary of Police Terms and Phrases.

Nightstick: The night duty Inspector.

Ticket: Search Warrant and Fixed penalty fine.

Form 12: Sudden Death Report.

OB: Occurrence Book – also known as The Number One.

Limbo dancer: Term for a creep as in 'going under the Boss's door'.

C.R.O.: A term for a person with a criminal record – Taken from the acronym *Criminal Records Office.*

Obs: Observations.

The Kremlin: Police Headquarters.

The Nick: A Police Station.

The Job: The Police Force.

Staff: Truncheon.

Cuffs, cuffing, cuffed: Handcuffs, handcuffing, handcuffed.

Cuff, cuffing, cuffed, a cuffer: in a different context meant 'to skive' or not carry out your duty properly – dealing with an incident improperly to get out of the paperwork or downgrading an incident to create less paperwork.

Mippy: An application to Magistrates' Court for a prisoner to be remanded in custody. Taken from the acronym M.I.P.Y.Ws 'May it please your Worships.'

Franked: Late for duty.

Snappin': Food taken at meal times.

A Tea Stop: Usually a shop or other business on your patch where you were welcome to call in for a brew. Often a good source of local knowledge and criminal information.

D & D: Drunk and Disorderly.

D & I: Drunk and Incapable.

Point: A 'point' was a pre-arranged location on constable's beat. He was expected to visit the location at an appointed time and could expect a supervisory visit.

R.T.A. Road Traffic Accident.

Domestic: A household argument.

Cough: An admission of guilt.
I.P. An Injured party or victim of crime.
M.O. Taken from a Latin term – 'Modus Operandi' or how a crime was committed.
S.O.C.O. Scene of Crime Officer.
Section 47, 20, 18: A quick reference to assaults of varying extremes of violence.
P.A.C.E. The Police and Criminal Evidence Act.
An I.D. (Identification). A term used variously – I.D. Parade, or an I.D. on a dead body or a personal I.D. as in a warrant card.
On his toes: Running off.
Action Man: The officer on a murder or major inquiry who is appointed to delegate 'Actions' (different enquiries).
P.M. A Post Mortem Examination.
Flasher: A person who indecently exposed himself.
Stooge: A volunteer who, along with several others agrees to stand in on an identification parade with the suspect in a crime.
Sally Army: Salvation Army.
The Box: The force computer system.
P.N.C. The Police National Computer.
A Weight: one pound of Cannabis resin.
A Break: A burglary.
Blowing in the bag: A request for a breath test.
Blown a green one: Blowing a positive breath test
Panda Cars Small area patrol cars. These were an integral part of the national 'Unit Beat Policing' system which became operational from the late sixties. At the very beginning the first forces using the system had the cars in a black and white livery, hence the name Panda. The colour scheme quickly changed to a light greenish blue and white.
Area Man As with Panda cars an area constable, often called 'Area Constable' was an integral part of the Unit Beat Policing system. The Policewomen's Department was a separate department and so Area Constable's were almost always male.

Other books available on Kindle and in paperback from Amazon by John Pye

Cathedral of Lies – the first book in the DI Doug Taylor series.

Field of Lies – the second book in the DI Doug Taylor series.

Guardian of Lies – the third book in the DI Doug Taylor series.

The Nick of Time – this book on also on Kindle

The Vampire of The Villas - a short story and the author's own true account of the death of a man who believed in vampires (only on kindle).

Where the Silent Screams are Loudest – A fictional crime/thriller novel set in 2019 Stoke-on-Trent (paperback and kindle). John Pye won the **Arnold Bennett International Book Prize 2022** with this book.

If you have enjoyed The Nick of Time or any of my books can I ask you to spare a little time by adding a review to Amazon (from where you purchased the book). Those good reviews are the lifeblood of the book and without them little known authors would fail. The positive feedback makes the months and sometimes years of research and writing worth the effort.

Printed in Great Britain
by Amazon

85490366R00169